The Chadwick House Publishing series on Health

We finish writing this book at a time when the BSc (Hons) Environmental Health Course at the University of Greenwich is closing after 28 years and one purpose in writing this book has been to consolidate our joint experience and knowledge, which we hope will play a role in bringing environmental health to the centre of public health in the future.

We would therefore like to dedicate this book to all the students who have studied Environmental Health at Thames Polytechnic and Greenwich University over the past years.

Jill Stewart
Fiona Bushell
Veronica Habgood

University of Greenwich, London, 2003

Jill Stewart

Fiona Bushell

Veronica

Chadwick House Publishing

Chadwick Court

15 Hatfields, London

SE1 8DJ, England

Publications

Tel: 0207 827 5830

Fax: 0207 827 9930

Email: Publications@chgl.com

Web: www.cieh.org

ISBN: 1-904306-27-6

Authors

Jill Stewart MSc BSc (Hons) MCIEH FRSH PGCE ACIH
Senior Lecturer in Environmental Health and Housing, School
of Health and Social Care, University of Greenwich

Fiona Bushell PhD MSc BSc (Hons) MCIEH FRSH
Senior Lecturer in, and Programme Director of MSc Health
Promotion and Public Health

Veronica Habgood MSc BSc (Hons) MCIEH
Director of Learning and Quality, School of Health and Social
Care, University of Greenwich

Contents

Foreword

Ian Gray, CIEH Policy Officer for Health Development

It is being increasingly recognised that improving health requires us to improve the well-being of individuals and communities as well as their environments, and to reduce the inequality and exclusion that so often confounds our efforts. The range of health determinants is vast and no one organisation or professional discipline can deliver public health. Therefore we must adopt a 'joined-up' approach to increasing the provision of better housing, accessible transport, enhanced community safety and economic opportunities and to developing healthier lifestyles and sustainable environments. To achieve this, public health policy and practice must avoid compartmentalisation and recognise the role of partnership working.

This book both sets the agenda and informs the practice of environmental health in modern public health and the case studies clearly demonstrate the important contributions that can be made. It has been written by respected academics engaged in teaching and training both our environmental health and public health colleagues. It is most appropriate that, at a time when we need to join up environmental health and public health, we have available reference material of this quality.

There is no doubt that our opportunity for a healthy life is linked to our environment and social circumstances and it has been said that it is a national scandal that our life expectancy is still determined by where we live, our educational opportunities, our employment or lack of it and the ethnic origins of our parents. These inequalities in health mean avoidable poorer health, reduced quality of life and early death for many people. The effects are felt not only by those who are exceptionally disadvantaged, but also among a large proportion of our population who are economically, environmentally and socially disadvantaged, and there are pockets of multiple deprivation even in the most affluent areas of our countries.

Successive governments have given increasing priority to tackling both the causes and consequences of health inequalities and to breaking the cycles of deprivation and resultant poor health. Most recently, the *Cross-Cutting*

Review on Health Inequalities (Department of Health, 2002) identified programmes, policies and resources across government that will have the greatest impact on inequalities in health pointing out environmental improvement as one of the key areas where interventions are likely to bring improvements in health.

The traditional role for environmental health has historically been concerned with addressing the wider determinants of health, including housing standards, health and safety, food, water, air quality, noise and environment issues generally. However, over recent years the mainstream practice of environmental health has become fixed on the delivery of a narrow agenda of regulatory and technical interventions in discrete areas, while neglecting its traditional role in addressing the wider determinants of health, the maintenance and improvement of public health and improving the population's quality of life and well-being.

A strategic vision of how environmental health can contribute to public health and well-being in the future is contained in the consultation report *Environmental Health 2012 – A key partner in delivering the public health agenda*, published by the Health Development Agency and produced in partnership with the Chartered Institute of Environmental Health (Burke *et al* 2002). The report recognises that environmental health practitioners have a unique contribution to make through their primary focus on maintaining health rather than curing illness, and many of those concerned with the delivery of environmental health are welcoming the shift in government policy towards local action aimed at improving public health and the well-being of communities and reducing health inequalities. To do so effectively, we must be familiar with modern public health practice and the structures through which it is to be delivered.

Modern public health

We now commonly use the term 'health and well-being' in our descriptions of public health to emphasise the broad meaning of health as set out by the World Health Organisation: *'Health is a state of complete physical, mental and social well-being not merely the absence of disease or infirmity'*.

The purpose of public health has been most recently defined through the work of The Tripartite Steering Group comprising the Faculty of Public

Health Medicine, the Multi-disciplinary Public Health Forum, and the Royal Institute of Public Health and Hygiene, together with the health departments of the four UK countries. The Tripartite Steering Group has produced standards for Specialist Practice in Public Health and has also commissioned a project group, Skills For Health, to develop National Occupational Standards (or competences) for public health practice in the NHS, local authorities, the independent sector and the voluntary sector.

The definition of public health that they recommend for use for all of public health, ie for the specialist practice standards and for public health practice standards, is shown below.

The purpose of public health is to:
- improve the health and well-being of the population;
- prevent disease and minimise its consequences;
- prolong valued life;
- reduce inequalities in health.

This is to be achieved through public health practice which:
- takes a population perspective;
- mobilises the organised efforts of society and acts as an advocate for the public's health;
- enables people and communities to increase control over their own health and well-being;
- acts on the social, economic, environmental and biological determinants of health and well-being;
- protects from and minimises the impact of health risks to the population;
- ensures that preventive treatment and care services are of high quality, based on evidence and are of best value.

Modern environmental health

The new model of environmental health contained in *Environmental Health 2012* recognises that it is concerned with all aspects of our living environment. It identifies that environmental health practice is about assessing, correcting and preventing the impact of the stressors on our environment, be they biological, chemical, physical, social or psychosocial, or any combination of these. We need to have a detailed understanding of our living environment and how these stressors act upon it in order for us to decide upon effective intervention strategies. We must also be prepared to evaluate our work and engage in research so that we can show that we are effective and thereby contribute to and increase the evidence base for future activities.

Only then can environmental health move forwards and meet the expectations of the modern public health agenda, good practice and evidence of what works. The report explores the projected development of environmental health practice in improving the public's health and reducing health inequalities over the next 10 years. Based on this, the strategic vision envisages that environmental health practitioners will:

- be key partners in protecting and improving the health and quality of life of individuals and communities and reducing health inequalities;
- tackle the wider determinants of population health by identifying, controlling and preventing current and future risks;
- play lead roles in community health and well-being strategies and actively contribute to the public health agenda of NHS public health structures.

As John Ashton, Regional Director of Public Health, North West, tells us: There are three kinds of people in the world:

- those who make things happen;
- those who watch things happen;
- and those who ask: 'What happened?'

The publication of this book *Environmental Health as Public Health* requires those of us involved in the delivery of either discipline to integrate our work and thereby maximise its effectiveness – a really worthwhile challenge. Many of us are already trying to achieve this – more of us must try.

References
Department of Health (2002) *Cross-Cutting Review on Health Inequalities*. London: DoH.
Burke, S. Gray, I., Paterson, K. and Meyrick J. (2002) *Environmental health 2012 – A key partner in delivering the public health agenda*. London: Health Development Agency.

Acknowledgements

We acknowledge that some material for this book was first published in the following journals:

- *Environmental Health Journal;*
- *Journal of the Royal Society for the Promotion of Health;*
- *Journal of Environmental Health Research.*

We are grateful to the editors of the respective journals for their permissions, support and assistance in the compilation of this book.

In particular, material drawn from the following papers is reproduced:

- Bushell, F. (2002) 'What on earth is going on?' *Environmental Health Journal,* 110 (3): 72 – 4.

- Stewart, J. (2001) 'Home safety', *Journal of the Royal Society for the Promotion of Health,* (1):16 – 22.

- Stewart, J. (2002) 'Housing health and safety rating – a new method of assessing housing standards reviewed', *Journal of Environmental Health Research,* 1 (2): 35 – 41.

- Stewart, J. (2002) 'A step in the right direction', in *Environmental Health Journal,* 110 (4): 104 – 207.

- Stewart, J. (2002) 'A small world', *Environmental Health Journal* 110 (3):68 – 70.

- Stewart, J. (2002) 'Housing Health and Safety Rating: a new method of assessing housing standards reviewed', *Journal of Environmental Health Research,* 1(2):35-41. Online. Available HTTP: http://www.jehr-online.org.volume1/issue2/5/index.asp

- Stewart, J. and Bushell, F. (2002) 'A question of need', *Environmental Health Journal,* 110 (12): 372 – 4.

- Stewart, J. and Nunn, G. (1999) 'A concrete future for concrete houses', *Environmental Health Journal*, 107 (7): 216 – 17.

- Stewart, J. and Rhoden, M. (2003) 'A review of social housing regeneration in the London Borough of Brent', *Journal of the Royal Society for the Promotion of Health*, 123 (1): 23 – 32.

We are also grateful to the Chartered Institute of Environmental Health for permission to use the illustration of Edwin Chadwick that appears in Chapter 2.

We are also greatly indebted to the following for providing the case studies that show the valuable and positive application of environmental health activity in practice.

• David Page	Newham Warm Zone
• Emma Lewis	Luton: strategy for fuel poverty in HMOs
• Lisa Harvey	Sussex Partnerships – working in practice
• Lucy Manzano	Globalisation and food: Bush meat in the UK
• Maureen Rhoden	Chalkhill: Regenerating social housing
• Nicola Wilson	Housing the homeless: Islington and the Bed and Breakfast Information Exchange
• Peter Sibley	An approach to dealing with domestic noise in the London Borough of Bromley
• Sarah Webb	Away from the coal face
• Steve Miller	Tackling tuberculosis in Newham: Partnership approaches
• Stuart Lines	An EHO in Public Health Specialist Training
• Tom Toumazou	Leeds City Council Landlord Accreditation Scheme

We are also grateful to Ian Gray, CIEH Policy Officer for Health Development, for his support in this book, and in particular for writing the Foreword.

List of abbreviations

A&E	Accident and Emergency
AST	Assured Shorthold Tenancy
B&B	Bed and Breakfast
BABIE	Bed and Breakfast Information Exchange
CBR	Campaign for Bedsit Rights
CHD	Coronary Heart Disease
CIEH	Chartered Institute of Environmental Health
CIH	Chartered Institute of Housing
CORGI	Certificate of Registered Gas Installers
DEFRA	Department of Environment, Food and Rural Affairs
DETR	Department of the Environment, Transport and the Regions
DFID	Department for International Development
DfEE	Department for Education and Employment
DHN	Democratic Health Network
DoE	Department of the Environment
DoH	Department of Health
DSS	Department of Social Security
DTLR	Department of Transport, Local Government and the Regions
DTI	Department of Trade and Industry
EA	Environment Agency
EAGA	Energy Action Grants Agency
EHCS	English House Condition Survey
EHO	Environmental Health Officer
EHP	Environmental Health Practitioner
EST	Energy Savings Trust
EU	European Union
FSA	Food Standards Agency
GIA	General Improvement Area
GIS	Geographical Information System
GLA	Greater London Authority
HA	Health Authority
HAA	Housing Action Area
HASS	Home Accident Surveillance System
HAT	Housing Action Trust
HDA	Health Development Agency
HECA	Home Energy Conservation Act

HEES	Home Energy Efficiency Scheme
HHSRS	Housing Health and Safety Rating System
HIA	Home Improvement Agency
HImP	Health Improvement Programme (then HIMP, now LDP)
HIMP	Health Improvement and Modernisation Plan (now LDP)
HIP	Housing Investment Programme
HMO	House in Multiple Occupation
HNA	Health Needs Assessment
HSE	Health and Safety Executive
IDEA	Improvement and Development Agency
IFST	Institute of Food Science and Technology
IHS	Institute of Home Safety
IMD	Index of Multiple Deprivation
JRF	Joseph Rowntree Foundation
LA	Local Authority
LDP	Local Delivery Plan (see HImP, HIMP)
LSP	Local Strategic Partnership
MOH	Medical Officer of Health
NASS	National Asylum Support Service
NEA	National Energy Action
NFHA	National Federation of Housing Associations
NHS	National Health Service
NHSS	National Home Safety Strategy
ODPM	Office of the Deputy Prime Minister
ONS	Office for National Statistics
PCG	Primary Care Group
PCT	Primary Care Trust
PHA	Public Health Association (USA)
PRS	Private Rented Sector
PSA	Public Service Agreement
PSE	Poverty and Social Exclusion
RoSPA	Royal Society for the Prevention of Accidents
RSL	Registered Social Landlord
SEU	Social Exclusion Unit
SRB	Single Regeneration Budget
StHA	Strategic Health Authority
WFT	Warm Front Team
WHO	World Health Organisation
WZ	Warm Zone

The authors

Jill Stewart worked as an environmental health officer specialising in private sector housing for several years before taking up her current position as senior lecturer at the University of Greenwich where she is currently involved in teaching housing and public health students at undergraduate and post graduate levels. She is a Corporate Member of the Chartered Institute of Environmental Health, a Fellow of both the Royal Society for the Promotion of Health and the Royal Geographical Society and an Associate Member of the Chartered Institute of Housing. Her research interests particularly include housing and community regeneration, and reintegrating health and housing through evidence-based practice. She has published and made various presentations in these areas.

After obtaining a degree in microbiology, Fiona Bushell trained as an environmental health officer and worked in three Kent local authorities for a period of around eight years. She became Senior Lecturer in Environmental Health at the University of Greenwich in 1990, specialising in food safety, and was programme leader for the BSc Environmental Health for four years. While at Greenwich University, she obtained an MSc and PhD and helped develop the BSc Public Health and MSc Food Safety programmes. In 2003, she joined the Centre for Health Education Research at Canterbury Christ Church University College and is teaching public health and health promotion students at undergraduate and postgraduate levels. She is a Corporate Member of the Chartered Institute of Environmental Health and Fellow of the Royal Society for the Promotion of Health and has presented papers at several conferences.

Following a degree in Environmental Science, Veronica Habgood worked for a number of years as an environmental health officer in Suffolk and London, concurrently undertaking further study in environmental protection. She has worked at the University of Greenwich since 1989, lecturing primarily in environmental protection, public health and the environment–health interface and is a contributor to a number of established publications. Veronica is currently the Director of Learning and Quality in the School of Health and Social Care at the University of Greenwich, and a Corporate member of the Chartered Institute of Environmental Health.

Chapter 1
Introduction

Introduction

Traditionally, public health has had a focus in environmental health including sanitation, safe water, pollution, housing and food hygiene. In the 21st century, public health has widened its perspectives to emphasise socio-economic issues affecting health. Many of the determinants of health are beyond the realm of medicine and action often lies outside the influence of the individual. Public health requires an approach that is inter- (and intra-)sectoral, collaborative, and scientific and which needs to address all the issues that interact to determine the health of the public.

The 'New Public Health' (largely named by Ashton and Seymour, 1988) recognises and places inequality at the root of poor health and encourages the development of innovative approaches to public health — a substantial move away from traditional hierarchical organisations delivering pre-defined and segregated services. The new approach seeks to engender a new dynamic relationship between professionals and communities, and new organisations that are able to respond to local need to bring sustainable health developments through appropriate strategy.

It has been estimated that over 70 per cent of what determines people's health is caused by demographic, socio-economic and environmental conditions (see table 1.1), and lies outside of the health services domain (US Office of Disease Prevention and Health Promotion, 1996). More recently, Health Development Agency (HDA) research showed that the public recognised factors such as low income, unemployment, poor housing and local environments, crime, low access to services, responsibilities to family, working conditions and racism both as barriers to decent health and factors influencing diet, smoking, exercise, drinking and drug taking (MORI Social Research, 2000).

Decent housing, good diet, adequate income and appropriate access to medical care are as important to maintaining and improving a person's health as the adoption of a healthier lifestyle. Rural issues such as isolation, lack of employment, the decline of local services and facilities as well as changing population structures need to be addressed and action taken to include those people belonging to ethnic minority communities who are socially excluded due to illness, disability, poverty, racism, and those seeking asylum in the UK.

Table 1.1
Factors affecting
health

Fixed	Social and economic	Environment	Lifestyle	Access to services
Genes	Poverty	Air quality	Diet	Education
Sex	Employment	Housing	Physical activity	NHS
Ageing	Social	Water quality	Smoking	Social services
	Exclusion	Social environment	Alcohol Sexual	Transport
		Food	Behaviour	Leisure
			Drugs	

Source: based on DoH (1999a)

The government drive toward improving public health is part of a wider agenda of inclusion, unfolding at a rapid rate of policy change through various government departments. Partnerships and joined-up government action through partnership working is seen as key to tackling and reducing health inequalities. The various pertinent initiatives have created a Minister for Public Health, set up the Social Exclusion Unit, established Health Action Zones, Health Improvement Programmes (HImPs, then HIMPs, now LDPs) and Healthy Living Centres and put new life into local regeneration programmes.

The role of environmental health practitioners lies at the heart of many of the changes. Environmental health is a key part of public health and practitioners are empowered to enable and enforce health improving changes in many aspects of people's lives, notably in respect of their living environments and the food they eat. The contribution of the environmental health profession to the wider public health agenda was most recently publicised through the 2002 CIEH Congress entitled 'Empowering Public Health' which received presentations from a variety of personnel involved in the discipline.

The CIEH and HDA jointly published 'Environmental Health 2012' (Burke et al, 2002) establishing a vision for the future contribution of environmental health practitioners as key partners in the public health agenda. This is seen as a move away from the narrow focus on regulatory performance management and toward addressing what really matters in combating inequality and improving health. Notably, the Chief Medical Officer was cited in the report as acknowledging that: ' (T)he EHO is the only local government professional considered to be a full time public health practitioner.' (Burke et al, 2002: 3). Such a view has also been supported by the Public Health Minister, Hazel Blears, who argued (Baker, 2002: 3) that: '(E)very environmental health officer ... can be a public health worker.' Additionally, Dr Ruth Hall, Chief Medical Officer for Wales, recently said: 'Environmental Health Officers are as important as doctors in delivering public health.' (cited in CIEH, 2003: 10).

Many have been concerned with the direction that environmental health – as a discipline – has been taking for some time and wish to see a revival of the profession as one which really addresses health inequalities, not just as a performance-managed, contract-based occupation that fails to truly deliver positive change in the required areas.

This book seeks to consolidate contemporary developments in the NHS, local authorities and allied health organisations and agencies whose mandate is to promote public health improvements and to place the environmental health profession at the centre of the debate. Clearly there is not scope in a book of this size to fully explore the environmental health practitioner's various functions. Therefore it focuses in particular on organisational change, and the relationship of food and housing to health in the context of what is currently being delivered and the actual and potential for strategic action.

The publication of this book coincides with the publication of the Public Health White Paper (DoH 2004b) and the Housing Act 2004 and the authors have made efforts to incorporate relevant issues where possible at such a late stage.

Synopsis of book
Chapter 2 explores the history of public health and how environmental health and public health are being reintegrated through individual drive and organisational and policy change.

Chapter 3 reviews current themes and priorities in environmental health and public health, including sustainability, the impact of globalisation, strategic approaches to public health, partnership working, social exclusion and inclusion, social capital, community development, health needs assessment and health impact assessment.

Chapter 4 focuses on food, nutrition and health and asks whether environmental health practitioners are really contributing to food security and how this might be done.

Chapter 5 considers some contemporary issues in housing and health, with particular reference to emotional health, temporary accommodation, fuel poverty, home safety and public health issues for Gypsies.

Chapter 6 consolidates issues from Chapter 5. It overviews local authority roles and new legislative approaches to reintegrate health and housing, including HMOs and current proposals for licensing and the forthcoming housing health and safety rating system. It then turns to strategic approaches to social and private sector housing regeneration, with a focus on current key issues such as the regeneration of tower block estates, expanding owners' responsibilities for housing conditions in the private housing sector and landlord accredation schemes.

Conclusions are then drawn in Chapter 7.

Chapter 2
Reintegrating environmental health and public health

Environmental Health and Public Health – the background

Health can be seen as a holistic concept with physical, mental, emotional, social, sexual, spiritual, environmental and societal dimensions. It is dynamic, as life involves adapting to change. For the individual, to be healthy means having the ability to think coherently, to express emotions, to express one's beliefs and sexuality, to cope with stress and anxiety, to make and maintain relationships, and to have peace of mind as well as physical health (Ewles and Simnett, 1999). It can be seen as the foundation for achieving a person's realistic potential. It empowers them to become all they are capable of becoming (Seedhouse, 1986). Health is a positive concept emphasising social and personal resources (WHO, 1984). There is a need to recognise the link between people and their environment and not to concentrate on changing people to fit the environment.

Health status is the outcome of the interaction of health services with social, environmental and lifestyle factors and genetics (Lalonde, 1974). Improvements in health can therefore be achieved by enabling people to adopt a healthy lifestyle, by improving living and working conditions and by providing a supportive economic, cultural, social and physical environment (Dahlgren and Whitehead, 1991). Non-communicable diseases such as coronary heart disease (CHD) and cancers, have replaced infectious diseases as the main causes of death and ill-health. People are also living longer, which accounts for the increase in degenerative diseases. However, health is not evenly distributed. There are inequalities linked to social class, gender, race and geography (Townsend and Davidson, Whitehead, 1988). The more affluent members of society live longer and enjoy better health than the lower income groups with income, housing and employment likely to be important factors. Low income can mean a lack of basic necessities (food, shelter, fuel), stress, lack of social support and health-damaging behaviours as coping mechanisms (Blackburn, 1991). Poverty also reduces choice. Work determines income levels, affects self-esteem and gives social support but can expose people to health risks and cause stress (Naidoo and Wills, 2000). Unemployment and associated poverty can also damage health, in particular mental health (Naidoo and Wills, 2000). (See Figure 2.1.)

Figure 2.1
The main determinants
of health

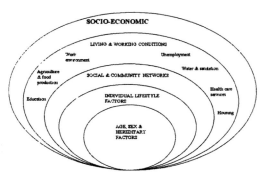

Source: Adapted from Dahlgren and Whitehead (1991)

Public health

In public health, there is a need to consider all the factors that have an impact on health. Medicine has for many years dominated the concept of public health despite research that it is poverty, poor housing and insanitary living conditions that have a major impact on health and disease (Cornell, 1996).

The Acheson Report in 1988 described public health as : 'the science and art of preventing disease, prolonging life and promoting health through organised efforts of society.' This was updated by Wanless (2004) to include a wider view of 'society' as: 'The science and art of preventing disease, prolonging life and promoting health through the organised efforts and informed choices of society, organisations, public and private, communities and individuals.'(Acheson 1988, Wanless, 2004).

It went on to say that lifestyle is as important as environmental hygiene in the prevention and promotion of health and that there should be closer cooperation between departments and no room for rivalry between preventive and curative medicine. Past health initiatives have failed because of rivalry between the professions and the separation of public and environmental health during local government reorganisation in 1974. The health service has concentrated on biological and lifestyle issues while local authorities (LAs) have been concerned with the environment and non-health lifestyle issues. There has been little attempt to develop a co-ordinated strategy for tackling health problems within the community (Cornell, 1996).

Williamson (1996) claimed that when public health medicine was removed from local government in 1974, many of the Area Medical Officers relinquished their involvement in housing, roads, leisure and even education with some relief. Many local authorities went on to set up health promotion units independent of those within the National Health Service (NHS) and usually without the involvement of public health medicine.

Environmental Health

The World Health Organisation's definition of environmental health in 1993 states:

> [Environmental health] 'comprises those aspects of human health, including quality of life, that are determined by physical, biological, social and psychosocial factors in the environment. It also refers to the theory and practice of assessing, correcting, controlling and preventing those factors in the environment that can potentially affect adversely the health of present and future generations.' (DoH/DoE UKNEHAP, 1996: 3)

Environmental health is a wide-ranging discipline which includes a diverse spectrum of professionals from Environmental Health Officers and public health physicians to engineers, planners, architects and surveyors. For EHOs, the integration of scientific, technological, social scientific, legal and associated practical skills forms the basis of a profession which has played a major role in securing improvements in public health since its inception in 1875 as inspectors of nuisances (Chambers, 1997).

Following the granting of a Royal Charter in 1984, the Working Party on Environmental Health Education produced a Consultative Document in April 1986 which set out a professional profile of an EHO and the document was approved by the General Council of the IEHO in January 1987. It states:

> 'The work of the EHO is concerned with the inter-relationship between human beings, their health and the natural and built environments including the impact of science, technology and socio-economic conditions. The primary role is to protect human health, ranging from the provision of solutions to specific problems to the development of strategies in furtherance of preventative health.' (Appendix 2)

The practice of environmental health has developed rapidly over the past twenty years. Today the tasks and responsibilities of environmental health professionals have only a little in common with those of the public health inspectors of two decades ago. In its response to the National Environmental Health Action Plan (NEHAP), the CIEH in 1995 stated that increasingly it is the social and psychosocial factors in the environment that are affecting health status. Environmental health must work to repair past damage, to control present risks and to prevent future problems. Initially sanitary inspectors had a medical base and dealt with infectious disease. The public health inspectors had an engineering base and the diseases became environment and lifestyle related. EHOs have more of a social and management basis at a time when the environment and lifestyle diseases are giving way to psychosocial diseases (MacArthur, 1995).

The nature of local government is also changing. Subtle shifts in emphasis are driving the changes in the structural, managerial and philosophical basis of local government (Goodwin and Painter, 1996). The local government system has been transformed in the last 15 years into one of local governance in which a multitude of unelected agencies have become involved. This change has implications for the environmental health profession which, having its roots in enforcement, needs to adapt to accommodate this climate of governance. Its role as stated in the National Environmental Health Action Plan (NEHAP) is the public arbiter of environmental health standards (1996 Annex 5 p122 para9). Chambers (1997) suggests that the role of advocate brings with it a need to consider its status as part of the wider environmental health community.

In order for EHOs to be effective, they must think beyond local government and work with other professionals to prevent and control the factors that have an adverse effect on the health of the public, such as inequalities and sustainable development. There needs to be a reintegration of public health and environmental health but not a return to the unequal partnership prior to 1974, the suggestion being that EHPs have been held back by the medical profession (Bickerdike, 1978).

Environmental health departments can enhance public health through health promotion and needs assessment, and through supporting environments conducive to health, strengthening community action, increasing knowledge and disseminating information, reorienting service provision, introducing healthy public policies, assessing health impact and targeting areas of greatest need and greatest scope for improvement.

The development of environmental and public health

There is a clear historical link between public health, environmental health and the structure and function of local government.

There was a dramatic expansion in the UK population from 9 million in 1800 to 36 million in 1900 and its distribution became increasingly urban. This placed intolerable stress on the natural and built environment. As towns expanded and the pace of industrialisation quickened, the need to house workers near the new and larger factories led to streets of small, ill-constructed houses. There was little provision for drainage or refuse disposal, water supplies were inadequate and grossly polluted, and there was considerable pollution from the factories. The bad environmental conditions were matched by the poor social conditions. Workers suffered from malnutrition as wages were low, hours were long, and health and safety provision at work was minimal. The social conditions left most of the population vulnerable to communicable diseases, especially tuberculosis, scarlet fever and smallpox. By the beginning of the 1830s there was a great deal of social unrest, especially over long working hours, the insanitary and dangerous conditions in workplaces, poverty and bad living conditions.

In the mid-19th century the social conditions demanded governmental intervention in a form which was to lay the foundation for contemporary environmental legislation and local government administrative structures and practices, and introduce the forerunner of the EHO, the Inspector of Nuisances. The key areas of legislative intervention that emerged were aimed at mitigating the worst excesses of urban living. There was an evangelical mood at that time and to most Victorians, epidemics were punishments. Sanitary reform, health care, visiting the poor, slum clearance and the education of the poor in matters of health and hygiene were all vital causes for people inspired by both the concept of duty and, increasingly, a concern for a well-ordered society (Wohl, 1984).

The belief was that physical well-being and a pure environment were the essential foundations for all other areas of social progress. Evidence was accumulating from data that health was linked intimately to environment, the key issues being living conditions, diet, workplace safety and pollution. There was little or no incentive for government action, however. What did prompt change was cholera. In response to continental epidemics, the government, acting in fear of the disease coming to Britain, created an advisory Central Board of Health in 1805. The disease did not enter the country and the Board had a limited life.

A second Board of Health was created in 1831 when again continental cholera was rife. It lasted until 1834 as cholera did strike with a significant number of deaths. There were other epidemics to follow. It was evident that mortality from cholera correlated closely with contaminated drinking water, poor hygiene and close living conditions. In response to the 1831 outbreak, the second board was able to bring in the rudiments of local sanitary control. Some 1,200 local boards were set up under the control of the central board and were responsible for securing improvements in hygienic practices. The fact that the 1831 epidemic died out naturally led to the second Board of Health and local boards fading away.

Running parallel with the two Boards of Health was the development of the Poor Law. The recommendations of a Royal Commission in 1832, whose remit was to review the provisions for the relief of the poor, resulted in the Poor Law Amendment Act 1834. The Secretary of the Commission of Inquiry was Edwin Chadwick, a barrister, who was to raise the profile of

EDWIN CHADWICK IN 1848
(From The Illustrated London News)

Figure 2.2
Edwin Chadwick in 1848
(From the Illustrated
London News)

public health. It established a rudimentary administrative structure via the Poor Law Unions and their Boards of Guardians, through which early public health measures could be introduced, eg the introduction of the Poor Law Medical Officers and the availability of access to vaccination. Chadwick (see figure 2.2) began to evaluate the living conditions of the poor, employing as his field researchers the Poor Law Medical Officers. His initial investigations from 1838 to 1839 culminated in his report on *The Sanitary Conditions of The Labouring Population of Great Britain* (1842). This led to the government instituting a Health of Towns Commission which brought together the medical and engineering professions. A Health of Towns Association and the Epidemiological Society were also formed.

A return of continental cholera spurred the government to pass the Public Health Act 1848 which created a third General Board of Health, which had a life span of five years. Chadwick was appointed as one of its three members. Public health was used to secure social change and the policies to emerge gave rise to local government, since by virtue of the 1848 Act it became possible for local boards of health to be established which would supervise issues relating to the water supply and sewerage, and the control of offensive trades and cemeteries. These boards also had the power to carry out surveys to evaluate public health conditions.

The Act also made it possible for a local board of health to appoint a Medical Officer of Health (MOH) who was to be responsible for overseeing the public health of the area, a borough engineer/surveyor and an inspector of nuisances. The 1848 Act was permissive but the General Board of Health could compel the establishment of a local board of health if the mortality rate exceeded 23 per 1,000 in seven successive years or if 10 per cent of the ratepayers petitioned for its introduction (Liverpool Corporation had made such appointments in 1847 under a Private Act).

It was a medic, John Snow, who showed that infectious disease was not a result of miasma. In 1854, he traced an outbreak of cholera in the parish of St James, Westminster to a water pump in Broad Street, Soho. The removal of the pump handle caused the outbreak to cease.

The MOH was medically qualified and charged with the responsibility of looking after the health of the local population. His preventive duties included inspection of and reporting on the sanitary conditions of the borough, a concern with disease epidemics and mortality, and the pointing out of any nuisances which may contribute to the development of illness. The inspectors of nuisances had no qualifications. Their job was to point out all breaches of the regulations and enforce the by-laws and rules of the council and health committee. The MOH was administratively responsible for the nuisance inspectors. Initially the MOH carried out inspections himself, but with increasing responsibilities coming with new legislation, this became more difficult.

> 'The medical officer of health wanted someone who would not be afraid to inspect any nuisance or go into any place where there was fever or other contagious disorders. It was necessary that he should be what was called a respectable man, and he had to be, to some extent, presentable in private houses. His duties were laborious, his salary contemptible.' (Sir Benjamin Ward Richardson, President of Sanitary Inspectors Association, 1892)

With the introduction of the Sanitary Institute of Great Britain in 1876 (later the Royal Society of Health) and specific training for the sanitary or nuisance inspectors, more of the inspection work was delegated. The change in the nuisance officer's role is reflected in the change of title to Sanitary Inspector, then Public Health Inspector and in 1974 to Environmental Health Officer. These changes mirrored increasing expertise. The public health inspectorate increasingly resented the MOH's position. The MOH came to have less involvement with housing, food hygiene, pollution, etc. but was still required to authorise actions of the public health inspectors in areas of slum clearance, dealing with verminous persons, etc. The initial disparity in status and education between the MOH and the nuisance officers sowed the seeds of rivalry and resentment. These attitudes hardened with increasing training of the inspectorate and changing responsibilities.

Although local government was born out of the 1848 legislation, it was the Public Health Act 1872 which introduced the predecessor to our present system of local government. It divided the country into Urban and Rural Sanitary Districts, with each acting as the enforcing authority for the emerging public health and sanitary legislation. In boroughs, the town council became the designated Sanitary Authority while in other areas, where there was a Local Board of Health, this assumed these legal responsibilities, or if no Board existed, the Improvement Commissioners became the competent authority. In the Rural Sanitary Authorities, the Board of Guardians became the enforcing authority. It was this 1872 legislation that made the appointment of inspectors of nuisances or sanitary inspectors obligatory.

The General Board of Health, the centralised body co-ordinating public health policy, survived from 1848 until 1858, by which time it had ensured that public health was firmly on the political agenda. The Privy Council with the Home Secretary took responsibility for its functions. The demise of the General Board of Health in 1858 created a gap which was filled in 1871 by the Local Government Board, which was invested with powers and duties to secure the objectives of protecting public health. The Public Health Act 1875 made the greatest impact. It provided a comprehensive range of environmental health powers to deal with sewage, drainage, water supply, nuisances, offensive trades, protection of food, infectious disease, highways, street markets, slaughterhouses the and making of by-laws. In 1919 the Ministry of Health was established to take over the functions of the Local Government Board and other duties.

In 1883 the Sanitary Inspectors Association was founded, now the Chartered Institute of Environmental Health. Its first President was Chadwick who was by then 85 years of age.

Throughout the 19th century, regulations caused improvements in workplace safety and conditions, while the construction of buildings and planning requirements, the availability of contraception and transport, communication and diet improved. By the late 19th century, sanitary reform was replaced by preventive measures such as immunisation and there was more understanding of the microbiology and the role of the individual in the spread of disease. At the outbreak of the First World War, vaccination programmes had halted infectious disease and houses were supplied with drinking water and drains.

Between the wars, housing was in crisis, with many forced to live in overcrowded, squalid conditions. The Local Government Board had been accused of being out of touch with public health and in 1919 a government department was created that would deal with health as a priority and a Chief Medical Officer appointed. Under the Housing Act of 1919, new homes were quickly built but a series of alternating cutbacks and subsidies caused a stop/start approach to house building. There was also a steady period of decline in industry in the 1920s and increasing national debt after the War. Public Health began to worsen in industrial areas due to insanitary housing and environmental decay. A policy of slum clearance was introduced and the Health Minister announced in 1934 plans to build thousands of new LA houses. The 1930s were years of depression, unemployment and poverty. Living accommodation was in poor repair and lacked facilities.

The Second World War brought food shortages and rationing which lasted until 1954. In 1947 the Ministry of Food set up the first food standards committee and comprehensive food hygiene regulations were introduced in 1955. The postwar years brought nationalisation and the Welfare State. In 1946, the government introduced national insurance, subsidised council houses were built, child allowances increased and a commitment was given to regeneration and full employment. However, the war had left thousands of houses in poor repair. There was also severe air pollution from industrial smoke which led to the Clean Air Act 1956.

By the 1960s, food was more plentiful, the birth rate had dropped and the standard of living had improved, but increased economic and social pressures and the devaluation of the pound in 1967 caused living standards to fall. In the 1970s, there were fewer jobs, more strikes, more involvement with Europe, a rise in the elderly population, a fall in the birth rate and a rise in immigration. In 1974, comprehensive health and safety at work legislation was introduced alongside the Control of Pollution Act, which dealt with air, soil, water and noise pollution. There was increasing interest in green issues at this time. Also, in 1974, public health medicine was removed from local government, which concentrated on the control of communicable diseases.

Table 2.1 Key public health policy developments

Date	Policy/initiative	Purpose
1974	NHS/LA split	
1980	*Inequalities in Health* – The Black Report	Assessed the achievements of the first 40 years of the NHS. Recognised the affects of poverty and deprivation on health.
1981	WHO Global Strategy *Health for All 2000*	In 1985 WHO issued targets, first of which was equity in health. Recognised the economic, environmental, social and personal factors that affected health status. Main determinants of health differences seen as living and working conditions. Poverty and social deprivation identified as key. Healthy Cities Project gave a focus for HFA in Europe.
1987	*The Health Divide*	Updated the Black Report. Use of more indicators and confirmed effects on health of material deprivation.
1992	*The Health of the Nation*	Selected five key areas for action – coronary hearth disease, cancers, mental illness, HIV/AIDS and sexual health and accidents. Strategy to add years to life and life to years. Pushed public health up the political agenda and recognised the role of health promotion.
1997	Minister for Public Health	New post of first ever Minister for Public Health established
1997	Social Exclusion Unit	Established to address deprivation (unemployment, poor housing, low skills, etc) to improve government action by producing joined-up solutions to joined-up problems.
1997	*Agendas for Change:* Environmental Health Commission	Reintegration of environment and health policies, sustainable development, community empowerment, health needs analysis, more of a public health role for local government
1997	*The New NHS: Modern, and Dependable*	Abolished GP fundholding; established Primary Care Groups (PCG)
1998	*Independent Inquiry into Inequalities in Health* – Acheson Report	39 recommendations addressing the wider socio-economic determinants of health, inequalities across lifecycle and related to gender and ethnicity. Report emphasised importance of social environment. Recommended health inequalities impact assessment.
1998	New Deal for Communities	To assist some of the most deprived communities and part of government's commitment to address social exclusion, to tackle worklessness, improving health, tackling crime and raising educational achievement.
1999	White Paper: *Saving Lives: Our Healthier Nation*	To improve health of the population as a whole and narrow the health gap. Priority areas – CHD, accidents, cancers and mental health. Partnership approach – Health Improvement Programmes, Healthy Living Centres, Health Action Zones.
1999	Health Act 1999	Legal framework introduced enabling PCGs to become PCTs – an independent statutory body (from 2000).

1999	Health Authority NHS Plan	Reinforced the need for HA and LAs to work together.
1999	Local Government Act 1999	Part of modernising local government to ensure improved quality of life for communities and individuals.
2000	Local Government Act 2000	As above, and a new duty to require preparation of community strategy to promote the economic, social and environmental well-being; also to contribute to UK sustainable development
2000	Best Value	New duty requiring local authorities to make continuous improvements in exercising their functions with regard to economy, efficiency and effectiveness.
2000	Health Development Agency established	Replaced the Health Education Authority; to raise standards of quality of public health in England.
2000	NHS Plan	Social services and NHS to pool resources
2001	Report of the CMO to strengthen the public health function	Called for better and more co-ordinated public health function and increased workforce
2001	Shifting the balance of power	Positioned PCTs as lead organisations to deliver public health at local level
2002	Wanless Report 'Securing our Future Health:taking a long-term view.'	Future health trends and resources required
2003	NHS Priorities and Planning Framework	Introduced LDPs
2003	Health Protection Agency set up	Co-ordinates responses to communicable diseases, environmental hazards and emergency planning
2003	Tackling Health Inequalities:A Programme for Action	Identified vital role for PCTs and LAs to work in partnership with communities. Fuel Poverty strategies, neighbourhood renewal and housing standards
2004	Wanless Report.'Securing Good Health for the whole population.'	Examined challenges and cost-effectiveness of action
2004	Choosing Health consultation document	Asked for views on how current health challenges could be addressed by working together
2004	Choosing Health White Paper	New initatives to enable healthier lifestyles

The 'New' Public Health

It was in 1974 that the then Canadian Minister of Health, Marc Lalonde, published a government report which focused attention on the fact that a great deal of premature death and disability in Canada was preventable. This new public health approach brought together environmental change and personal preventive measures with therapeutic interventions. It recognised the importance of the social aspects of health caused by lifestyles and the need for policies which focused on prevention and health promotion.

Medicine had dominated public health (see Table 2.1 and Figure 2.3) but McKeown (1976) recognised that the total contribution of medical

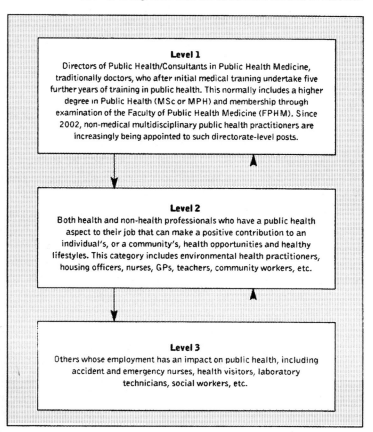

Figure 2.3
The tiers of public health in implementation: the NHS, local authorities and other partners

Level 1
Directors of Public Health/Consultants in Public Health Medicine, traditionally doctors, who after initial medical training undertake five further years of training in public health. This normally includes a higher degree in Public Health (MSc or MPH) and membership through examination of the Faculty of Public Health Medicine (FPHM). Since 2002, non-medical multidisciplinary public health practitioners are increasingly being appointed to such directorate-level posts.

Level 2
Both health and non-health professionals who have a public health aspect to their job that can make a positive contribution to an individual's, or a community's, health opportunities and healthy lifestyles. This category includes environmental health practitioners, housing officers, nurses, GPs, teachers, community workers, etc.

Level 3
Others whose employment has an impact on public health, including accident and emergency nurses, health visitors, laboratory technicians, social workers, etc.

Source: Lines (2003)

interventions had been small compared with the impact of environmental factors and political, economic and social measures. High death rates had been due to infectious disease with nutritional and environmental factors. He argued that the major contributions to improvements in health were from limitation of family size, an increase in food supply, a healthier physical environment and specific preventive and therapeutic measures. In the new public health, the environment is social and psychological as well as physical, and lifestyles, prevention, services and elimination of inequalities have to be taken into account (Naidoo and Wills, 2000).

The 1980s saw a revival in interest in public health as unemployment increased, inner cities fell into greater disrepair and the welfare state was held back. A series of reports were published which highlighted the social aspects of health, but this broader view was politically unpopular. Sir Douglas Black's group report in 1980 was commissioned to explain trends in health, to relate these to policies to promote health and to provide a comment on the achievements of 40 years of the National Health Service but it concluded that the most powerful explanation of the social class differences in health was that which related to material deprivation and poverty and therefore much of the problem lay outside the scope of the NHS. Those belonging to the manual classes made smaller use of the health care system, yet needed it more. People may be better off but still have too little for their basic physiological and social needs. Poverty, work conditions, deprivation in the home and environment, work, education, upbringing, family and social life indicate social policy is more important that lifestyle factors. The group recommended an anti-poverty strategy which included raising the level of child benefit, free school meals, improved standards at work and better co-ordination of housing policies. Few copies of the *Black Report* were made available, there was no press release or press conference and the Secretary of State dismissed the report as calling for unrealistic expenditure.

The Whitehead Report, *The Health Divide* (1987), gave an update on the Black Report and introduced new indicators – quality of life and psychosocial well-being. It was commissioned by the Health Education Council but in the months prior to publication plans were announced to disband the Health Education Council and reconstitute a Health Education Authority within the NHS. The report was considered 'political dynamite' in an election year (Townsend, Davidson and Whitehead, 1988). Members of the House of Lords could not obtain copies for a major debate on the NHS. A rush reprint was ordered amid accusations of a cover-up. In the House of Commons a debate on social and economic inequalities gave prominence to health inequalities. Twenty-six MPs put down a commons motion calling for a programme recognising the relationship between poverty and poor health. The important issue was that improvements in the health of the poor had failed to keep up with improvements enjoyed by the prosperous. A common response from Ministers was to suggest the differences were due to individual behaviour patterns. Differences in lifestyle are only part of the story. There is not always a choice.

The Archbishop of Canterbury's Commission in 1985 reported that a growing number of people were excluded by poverty or powerlessness from sharing in the common life of our nation. A substantial minority were forced to live on the margins of poverty or below the threshold of an acceptable standard of living. The critical issue to be faced was whether there was any serious political will to set in motion a process which would enable those who were then in poverty and powerlessness to rejoin the life of the nation (cited in Townsend, Davidson and Whitehead, 1988: 341).

The WHO – also in 1985 – reiterated and extended the argument for acceptable, inclusive living environments further, adding that 'without peace and social justice, without enough food and water, without education and decent housing, and without providing each and all with a useful role in society and adequate income, there can be no health for the people, no real growth and no social development' (cited in Townsend, Davidson and Whitehead, 1988: 339).

Tim Lang suggested that 'instead of exhorting people to eat better, smoke less and exercise more, Ministers should make it easier for them to improve their health – that meant tackling poverty by improving welfare benefits, improving the quality of food and making the industry tell people what it puts in their food' (Guardian, 22 April 1987, in Townsend, Davidson and Whitehead, 1988: 12).

Local authorities acting positively for health improvement

Some local authorities introduced an anti-poverty strategy, mapped concentrations of poverty, audited policies and services, strengthened the social support systems, improved the physical living conditions in disadvantaged areas and improved the income, skills and job opportunities.

The London Borough of Greenwich (Greenwich Poverty Profile, 1994) carried out a survey which revealed alarming levels of poverty. Many residents were going without heat, food and clothing, and poverty was on the increase. One in four adults suffered from depression, many had no hope for the future and over a third were in serious debt. The aims of the Greenwich strategy were: economic and social regeneration, accessible and high-quality services, more control to individuals and communities and influence over policies and practices of local agencies. All departments worked together with the residents and other agencies. The borough identified the need for jobs for local people, safe and affordable housing, affordable warmth, a reduction in domestic heat loss, an increase in disposal income and steps to tackle crime and violence. The intention was to encourage people to find their own solutions to their problems. Credit unions and local exchange trading schemes were introduced and developers were encouraged to employ local people to work in the borough as 35 per cent of the borough's unemployed had construction-related employment experience.

Over £7.7 million worth of benefits were going unclaimed in Greenwich every year, while 72 per cent of borough households included someone who suffered from a long-term illness or disability. There was a need to provide healthcare facilities, to promote healthy lifestyles, and to provide local health centres and more NHS dentists in the poorest wards. Crime was costing Greenwich £15 million in 1993 so there was a need to promote crime prevention, reduce the factors that contributed to crime and reduce the fear of crime. Also racism needed to be tackled. Activities for the young had to be provided like a portable gym and music equipment, and youth action projects were introduced in schools (Greenwich Poverty Profile, 1994).

Wider policy for health improvement

Early attempts to bridge the gap between health and environment were based on the WHO's Healthy Cities initiative, through which health and local authorities and many other bodies came together to improve their communities' health in line with the WHO Health for All by the Year 2000 programme. In this network, no one had precedence and the emphasis was on equal involvement and responsibility (Williamson, 1996).

The WHO Global Strategy Health for All (HFA) 2000 was accepted as policy in 1981 and had as a basis that all people in all countries should have at least such a level of health that they are capable of working productively and of participating actively in the social life of the community. The first of the targets was equity in health. HFA considered health to be a human right and a resource for individual and social development. The main determinants of health differences were seen as living and working conditions. Tackling poverty and social deprivation were regarded as essential elements of any policy for health.

In 1985, the WHO European Office developed a European Strategy for HFA with 38 targets (to which the UK has agreed) and established a Healthy City project to give a focus for HFA in Europe. Fundamental conditions were identified as: freedom from fear of war, equal opportunities, basic needs (food, education, water, sanitation, housing, work and a useful role) political will and public support.

The Healthy Cities project brought an ecological and holistic approach to health. The city was seen as the most suitable base on which to build a new public health movement. The city administration has access to a wide range of resources and networks and can act as a facilitator, mediator and advocate for improving its citizens' health (Ashton and Seymour, 1988). Liverpool was chosen as an unlikely healthy city – one of the most rapidly declining cities in Europe. A city is unhealthy if it cannot provide safe and adequate food, a safe water supply, shelter, sanitation and freedom from poverty and fear. Sheffield was the first to establish a focus for health policy across all council departments and compiled a health profile of wards.

Three core principles of public health emerged from HFA 2000 – participation, equity and collaboration (Naidoo and Wills, 2000). Participation can include community health profiles, feedback on service provision, support for self-help groups and liaisin with schools. Equity of material resources and power means provision of equal services for people with equal needs. It may involve ensuring clients have their benefit entitlement, giving help with forms or targeting areas of deprivation for more intensive interventions. Collaboration means partnership working as more fundamental changes are achieved with greater potential to promote health.

Out of the Rio Summit came Agenda 21, which encouraged government at every level to develop policies dedicated to sustainable development. Many LAs without the health authorities, joined the UK Local Agenda 21 Network and require a full environmental assessment of any new proposal. Their involvement in local environmental issues has meant the collapse of many Healthy City initiatives.

The government's 1992 Health of the Nation strategy was based on 'Health for All' but did not really cover environmental issues and avoided poverty and social inequality. It set targets for five key areas – coronary heart disease and stroke, cancers, mental illness, HIV/AIDS and sexual health, and accidents. The programme was mandatory and led by the health authorities, with little acknowledgement of local authorities. Later government advice on how LAs should participate in healthy alliances did little to mitigate the resentment (Williamson, 1996).

The 1998 *Acheson Report* came 18 years after the Black Report, which had first highlighted the link between poverty and ill health. The preface to the report claims that it addresses social justice and, although the last 20 years have brought a marked increase in prosperity and substantial reductions in mortality to people in England as a whole, the gap in health between those at the top and bottom of the social scale has widened. Acheson acknowledged that the range of factors influencing inequalities in health extends far beyond the remit of the Department of Health and that a response by the government as a whole will be needed. He made 39 recommendations addressing the wider socio-economic determinants of health and inequalities. High priority was given to the health of families with children and steps were recommended to reduce income inequalities and improve living standards. The report emphasised the importance of the social environment and good social networks. Recommendations included: a health inequalities impact assessment, an expansion of employment opportunities, better quality housing, an integrated affordable public transport system, access to healthy food, a reduction of the suicide rate and the promotion of healthy behaviour. He argued for the distribution of resources according to need and partnerships between HAs and LAs.

The UK National Environmental Health Action Plan (UKNEHAP, 1996) straddles Health of the Nation and Local Agenda 21 and acknowledges that the local authorities will need some input from the health authorities. The definition of environmental health in UKNEHAP has lost the implicit distinction between health and non-health behaviour and the primacy of the Health Service in lifestyle adjustment (Williamson, 1996). The success of policies to enhance health and the environment are said to depend on a harmonious and effective interdisciplinary collaboration. One of the basic principles of environmental health is the concept of dealing with problems at source.

Environmental Health at a crossroads

The Environmental Health Commission's Report *Agendas for Change* (1997) concluded that environmental health was at a crossroads. Most of the initiatives on environment and health have tended to perpetuate a 'top-down' and compartmentalised approach to specific problems. Improvements, it suggests, require reintegration of environment and health policies and organisations, and the integration of environmental health objectives into a broader strategy for sustainable development. Inequities in health and environmental quality associated with the widening gap between rich and poor must be addressed. The most deprived communities should be active participants in helping to improve their environment, health and quality of life.

The Commission recognised that the traditional environmental health approach to dealing with specific problems has its value and should not be abandoned or weakened, but piecemeal interventions which fail to address the fundamental problems should be avoided. Also, the traditional approach is reactive and more concerned with control than prevention and does not comprehensively address concerns of quality of life. There needs to be a coherent overview of the balance of priorities, a needs assessment and an assessment of the contribution each function of environmental health makes to the health of the community. Areas of environmental health could be simplified, reduced or integrated into a broader function.

Agendas for Change also placed environmental health within a wider public health context and a renewed focus on addressing inequalities. It furthered the proposition that environmental and public health should be effectively resourced and reintegrated, with an emphasis on partnership working to constantly question and tackle health inequalities. The report cited the eight areas or agendas for change as concerning quality of life, inequality, lifestyle, sustainability, globalisation, democracy, information and integration, each of which has now found its place in contemporary policy and is discussed in this book.

In 1999, the White Paper, *Saving Lives: Our Healthier Nation* (DoH, 1999a), was introduced. It was a more comprehensive programme of action, tackling the complex causes of ill-health, ie personal, social, economic and environmental. It referred to a three-way partnership between individuals, communities and government. More attention and government action was to be placed on the things that damage people's health which are beyond the control of the individual. More attention was also to be given to areas most affected by air pollution, poverty, low wages, unemployment, poor housing and crime, as well as to major killer diseases, local action and lifestyles, social and economic issues, the environment and services. The aims were to improve the health of the population and reduce inequalities. Priorities included reducing deaths from CHD, stroke, accidents, cancer and mental health by 2010.

Initiatives have included:
- Health Improvement Programmes (HImP) (then Health Improvement and Modernisation Plans (HIMP), now Local Delivery Planning (LDP)) which seek to identify local needs and translate national contracts into local action. These focus on schools, workplaces and neighbourhoods and place particular emphasis on health inequality. The aim is to tackle poverty, poor housing, pollution, low educational standards, joblessness and low pay;
- Healthy Living Centres (see box 2.1) – local flagships for health, reaching people who have been excluded. These focus on deprived and rural areas, raising awareness on diet, smoking, drink, drugs and activity;
- Health Action Zones (due to be disbanded at the time of writing) – where priority is given to areas of greatest need. There is a locally agreed strategy to improve health with measurable and sustainable improvements in health and better integrated treatment and care.

Box 2.1 Project Sunlight – A healthy living network for Medway

In 2002, an old laundry in Gillingham was demolished to make way for a central Healthy Living and Family Centre based on the concept of a multi-use community centre. It aims to improve the health and well-being of all communities in Medway by improving the environment, increasing community safety and reducing social exclusion. Its core principles include: addressing inequalities in health, supporting local health aims, involving the community, working in partnership and ensuring sustainability. The centre is multi-disciplinary and multi-agency, which facilitates partnership working between voluntary and statutory agencies and community empowerment. It addresses health issues in a holistic way, bringing preventive health, community education and medical expertise together and providing access to services and activities that will improve health, well-being and quality of life. Funding has been provided by the New Opportunities Fund of the National Lottery, Medway Council, Medway PCT and North Kent Gateway Partnership.

The facilities and services being developed include:
* Social well-being – community café; youth, adult and community groups; art, music and dance; food cooperative, Local Exchange Trading System (LETS); computing facilities; spiritual well-being activities; credit union; financial counselling; crime prevention initiatives; stress management; counselling services.
* Childcare – day nursery; breakfast clubs/homework clubs; toy library; parenting skills training; parent and toddler groups; crèche; summer clubs.
* Education – careers guidance; employment service outreach; computing facilities; adult education; basic skills support/skills training; after-school learning; parenting classes; cooking skills; community development training; recording studio.
* Health – GP practice and health services; community pharmacy; complementary therapies; smoking cessation clinics; family planning advice; health support groups; physiotherapy clinic; health promotion; drug and alcohol advice.

The choice of services introduced was based on a needs assessment and consultations with a wide variety of local people. Community outreach workers make sure hard-to-reach groups are not excluded.

The project recognises the key role that the diverse voluntary sector has to play in improving and complementing public sector care and in promoting health. There are approximately 350 voluntary and community groups in Medway providing services for addiction, carers support, community centres, counselling, older people, domestic violence, health and disability. Health workers in this sector go into homes and recognise early warning signs. They also tackle issues in priority areas and the harder to reach groups. A model for joint working between the voluntary and statutory agencies, or Compact, is being developed to be in place by April 2004.

Community development interventions are complex and difficult to evaluate. The University of Greenwich, School of Health and Social Care Research Centre and the Council for Voluntary Services (Medway) are undertaking research into the ways in which the voluntary sector currently and could potentially contribute to the public health strategy, with particular reference to coronary heart disease. Research is also planned to facilitate evaluation of the services provided at the Sunlight Centre through the development of innovative participatory techniques. The aims and objectives of a sample of service providers will be determined and suitable evaluation methods and data collection tools devised that are relevant and applicable. Participatory techniques for collecting data include videos, role play, art, questionnaires, collage development, bubble dialogue, focus groups, diaries and interviews. A sample of clients with multiple health and social care needs will be tracked for a period of six months to determine how professionals work together to meet the needs of the client, the way the services support the individual to improve their health and the client's perceptions of which aspects of the service have been of the most benefit.

Future challenges to public health could come from globalisation and widening inequalities. Ashton (1998: 25) goes so far as to suggest that, sustainable, equitable world development is the prerequisite for public health and environmental health in the 21st century.' Additionally, the major factors affecting health and the environment in cities in developed countries are 'those associated with technological changes, increased consumption of energy and other resources, changing residential and transportation patterns, and the declining capacity of the environment to absorb wastes' (MacArthur, 1998: 36). These issues present environmental health practitioners with a rapidly changing, increasingly challenging agenda.

The NHS and LA's from 1997: leading partners in health improvement

There has been a recognition of the need to reconnect local authorities and the NHS at the organisational level and also calls for a redistribution of power and local flexibility with local communities. This renewed focus on health inequalities and poverty, with social inclusion seen as key, is part of the challenge to traditional bureaucratic, hierarchical organisational structures and seeks to empower communities.

Much of the literature relating to health improvement has been administered by the Department of Health (DoH) rather than the (now) Office of the Deputy Prime Minister (ODPM). Under the auspices of the DoH, the NHS is fundamentally about medical health care, not a broader perspective of socio-economic health as defined earlier in this chapter. It is therefore ironic that the government's commitment to address health inequality rests fundamentally within the remit of the NHS, which does not hold responsibility for many of the determinants of health such as poor living environments and access to decent food – which remain functions of local authorities and other organisations.

The New NHS: Modern, Dependable (DoH, 1997) was part of the Labour government's drive toward modernisation, to become increasingly important in the wider public service health agenda. It established mechanisms to meet health care need. Crucially, the White Paper included proposals and milestones to introduce:

- Health Action Zones (HAZ) – to target resource via health authorities bidding for additional funding for geographically deprived areas experiencing poor health status, with an emphasis on partnership and innovation to explore new, flexible, local ways of delivering health and healthcare to tackle inequalities with measureable targets (at the time of writing, these are soon to be superseded);

• To introduce new approach to partnership, notably through the introduction of Health Improvement Programmes (HImP) for the period beginning 1999 – 2000; and

• consolidate activity of the Primary Care Groups (PCG) to drive the new focus on quality.

While the new approach was to be welcomed, some aspects of performance management – just as in local authorities – tended to contradict the drive toward a broader perspective on health.

Health Service Circular (HSC) 1998/167 – which has a similar status in the NHS to DoE/DETR/ODPM Circulars in local authorities – required health authorities' actions in respect of HImPs to be in place by 2002 (DoH, 1998b). While it encouraged a partnership approach, the advice was circulated to local authorities and others for information only, not for action. It encouraged local needs and inequality assessment as a basis for improving service delivery through jointly resourced arrangements, although many local authorities found it difficult to engage with the PCGs at this stage through the lack of an explicit legal basis to develop policy and practice. More recent HSCs (DoH, 1999b; DoH, 1999c) confirmed that HimPs were to be strategically led by the NHS through PCGs and emerging Primary Care Trusts (PCTs), although the circulars used both the terms health and health care, with renewed emphasis on additional funding for successful initiatives to stimulate HImP progress.

The NHS Plan: A Plan for Investment, A Plan for Reform (DoH, 2000a) largely focused on health care. However, the paper represented the first stage in taking a broader look at NHS and social service partnerships to pool resources and encourage service integration, with the (new) PCTs being able to commission health and social care services, supported by an implementation plan (DoH, 2000b). A subsequent Guidance Note followed (DoH, 2001a), repositioning HImPs as Health Improvement and

Modernisation Plans (HIMPs). This reinforced the importance of partnership working – particularly through Health Authorities, the new strategic health authorities (StHA), PCG/T's NHS Trusts, local authorities and local communities – reflecting a coherent, integrated approach to strategic health improvement planning, to include well-being, health care and treatment (DoH, 2001a; DoH, 2001b; DoH, 2000a; Ham, 1999). Priority areas are cancer, heart disease, mental health and services for older people.

Shifting the Balance of Power: The Next Steps (DoH, 2002a) was concerned with patients and staff at the centre of the NHS, but also in changing the culture, notably in giving PCTs new powers and control over resources. Such organisational change was seen to provide a new opportunity to review delivery of significant functions and to develop more appropriate arrangements for public health, with a strengthening of relationships with local authorities and across government, designed around health and social care pathways, at the heart of the modernisation process. The PCT's roles and responsibilities from October 2002 – placing public health firmly with PCTs, – were reiterated as being:
- to improve the health of the community;
- to secure the provision of high quality services; and
- to integrate health and social care locally. (DoH, 2002a; DOH, 2002b).

The NHS has undergone reorganisation to provide regional directorates of health and social care, each having a regional director of public health. The existing health authorities are being replaced by a lesser number of strategic health authorities (StHA), with a director of public health to develop a partnership approach to tackle health issues. These teams manage the new PCTs whose role is to include public health, with devolved – and therefore increased – budgetary opportunities and responsibilities at this level. It is at this level that local authorities and the NHS can forge partnerships to improve the health of local communities and deliver wider objectives for socio-economic regeneration – a complex and time-consuming task if real results are to be delivered (MacArthur, 2001; Wright, 2001).

PCTs are the main focus for partnership working in delivering public health improvements. PCTs now lead the development of the Local Delivery Plans (LDP) focused on tackling deprivation through partnership working. Local partnership working should acknowledge links between social exclusion and health inequalities and initiate partnership action that supports the inclusion of vulnerable groups such as the young, older people, ethnic minorities and people with disabilities. This should be within the framework of the concept of 'the twin pillars of health improvement' through confronting the causes of ill health and health inequality and helping the most vulnerable members of the population by modernising the NHS and social care services and creating closer integration across the health and social care system.

Partnerships have been well established across the PCTs. They set priorities, agree action and develop fresh solutions best suited to local needs in order to improve local people's health. Their work will include linking into existing regeneration and social inclusion initiatives. Membership of the partnerships comprises of PCTs, local authorities and their education, housing and social services departments, voluntary sector organisations and local commercial businesses. However, while such an approach is laudable, there remain calls for clarity, reassurance and a comprehensive system enabling the sharing of good practice in respect of partnership arrangements.

Additionally, strategies driven by the PCTs should be aligned with local authority Community Strategies and inform a health perspective through Local Strategic Partnerships (see Figure 2.4), both of which will now be defined and discussed.

Local Delivery Plans

Local Delivery Plans (LDP) replaced HIMPs as part of the DoH's Priorities and Planning Framework for 2003 – 2006 (DoH, 2003a). It is a new system for planning and performance management, which builds on the earlier changes introduced under Shifting the Balance of Power. LDPs are different from previous plans and need to identify the expected progress of milestones for each priority area over the three-year period and be supported by a financial strategy and plan. The LDP will cover the whole strategic health authority area but be based on PCT-level plans. The LDP is a live DoH document which, through a PSA, aims to transform the health and social care systems so that it produces faster, fairer services that deliver better health and tackle health inequalities (DoH, 2003). The DoH website has a link at *www.doh.gov.uk/himp/index*.htm which outlines the future of the (then) HIMP process.

Figure 2.4 – Partnership basis of PCTs and local authorities

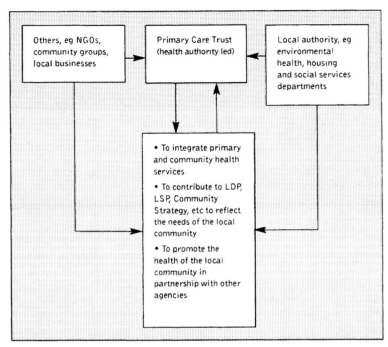

In response to the Priorities and Planning Framework, the HDA published a Draft Paper (HDA, 2003) exploring how the targets could be achieved through public health interventions based around the HDA Evidence Base Briefing and guideline documents and focuses on issues such as what the evidence is saying about effective ways of tackling health inequalities

Local Strategic Partnerships

The DETR (2001a) summarised an LSP as being a single body at local level that:

- brings together different parts of the public, private, business, community and voluntary sectors to enable different initiatives and services to support each other and to work together;
- is a non-statutory, non-executive organisation;
- operates at the right level for strategic decisions to be taken that are close enough to individual neighbourhoods for community-based decisions to be made; and
- should be aligned with local authority boundaries.

The key principles that LSPs and other partnerships should follow include strong community involvement, effective private sector involvement, a clear vision for the future, clear objectives and a commitment to working in partnership. All areas should have a LSP and its partnership approach is emphasised to help sustainable growth and social, physical and economic regeneration in deprived areas to meet local need, to give local communities more influence over decision-making in their neighbourhoods and to encourage non-governmental sectors to take a more active role. They are seen as pivotal to finding a joined-up approach to help tackle key priority areas for local people, notably crime, jobs, health and housing. Government guidance (DETR, 2001a) states that local authorities are best placed to get LSPs started, but that they need not retain a leadership position.

LSPs are seen – alongside other initiatives – as an important part of the drive toward neighbourhood renewal strategies in priority areas to help bridge the gap between the most deprived areas and the rest of the country in the key areas of education, employment, health, crime and social housing (DETR, 2001a, 2001b). LSPs are important in the context of neighbourhood renewal strategies to ensure that an agreed vision and commitment to positive change are in place for those with a stake in the neighbourhood. These should be set within wider plans for the area, ensuring that those involved have the necessary skills and knowledge. One model for such strategic action is neighbourhood management, which many local authorities already support through NDC partnerships (see Box 2.2) and the government is set to support other pathfinder initiatives.

Box 2.2 The New Deal for Communities: regeneration at South Kilburn

The New Deal for Communities (NDC) is a key programme in the Labour government's policy to assist some of the nation's most deprived communities, which was launched in 1998 as part of its commitment to addressing social exclusion. NDC seeks to bridge the gap between some of the poorest members of society and the rest of Britain in combination with other local initiatives and funding regimes. NDC seeks to address the four key interrelated areas of tackling worklessness, improving health, tackling crime and raising educational achievement. It seeks to deliver through a range of partnerships between local people, community and voluntary organisations, public agencies, local authorities and business which in combination are able to sustainably tackle some causes and effects of social exclusion. The values and vision are about joined-up solutions to joined-up problems. Its commitment to partnership is summarised in its principles, whereby the wider community appoints representatives who form a board which appoints staff to do the work who report to the board which feeds back to the representatives who feed back to the wider community (London Borough of Brent, 2001: 5).

The London Borough of Brent, one of 22 areas identified by the government, was invited to bid for NDC funding in 1999 in an attempt to transform a deprived neighbourhood in its area. South Kilburn was selected (see table 2.2), and the area has already received substantial resource from the Single Regeneration Budget (£28 million over six years) and the Urban Programme (part of the European Regional Development Fund) (£1.8 million), and is seeking funding from Sure Start. Each of these programmes was interrelated to some extent with the NDC opportunity. South Kilburn is an area in long-term decline, with the majority of the high-rise public housing dating back to the 1950s and 1960s and resulting from slum clearance and major socio-economic problems, despite being conveniently located. Unemployment is four times the national average (16.3 per cent) and more than a third of households have an income of less that £10,000 pa. South Kilburn is within the top 3 per cent of the most deprived wards in the UK as measured by the 2000 Index of Multiple Deprivation; for example, the housing stock and local environment is poor; children tend to underachieve in school compared to neighbouring areas; unemployment for those under 20 is 21 per cent – three times the borough average; residents' health is generally poor; many crime statistics remain higher than the borough average, and residents have been disappointed in response to crime.

Turning this around requires commitment, resources and a long-term vision. Initial households survey work and community participation events have shown that resident's priorities include addressing whole-scale housing renewal, unemployment, crime, the environment and the accessibility and standards of community facilities. To be successful the NDC funding needs to be combined with the £41 million per annum already spent in South Kilburn; that is not seen as another government initiative, but as a long-term change in the way of life. Regeneration schemes are still being considered as housing is seen as core to the whole process, particularly because local people need to be able to see their views and aspirations coming to very visible fruition, and the financial cost of new housing is likely to be in the region of £466 million.

The NDC is a new policy initiative which has the community at the heart of the process and expects partnerships to base their plans and activities on evidence, learning from management and delivery programmes that actually work elsewhere, and ensuring continued monitoring and evaluation that helps maintain sustainable, long term change. Since the focus is very much about learning from others, there is now a NDC unit within the ODPM comprised of a Regional Panel of Advisers from whom NDC partnerships can draw advice an issues such as crime, health and other initiatives that have been found to work elsewhere and are part of its mutual learning and good practice networking remit to share information on what works and discourage what does not. A website has also been set up (http://www.regen.net), which serves as an information network for regeneration partnerships and which contains the NDC exchange forum.

The move away from other regeneration initiatives is also clear in what NDC programmes are expected to deliver by measuring project outcomes rather than specifics, as outcomes are seen to be more likely to deliver longer-term, sustainable change (DETR, 2001). Its sets a new regeneration agenda, where 'baseline information' (a defined problem) is identified, 'outcomes' (clear, measurable targets) determined, and 'milestones' (relevant benchmarks of progress) are recorded.

Activity continues to transform the 61-acre patch into a desirable place to live and work. However, there has been some controversy surrounding the position and role of the independent tenants' advisers, the Tenant Participation

Table 2.2 Examples of data for South Kilburn's NDC submission

Baseline data for South Kilburn	Outcomes	Milestones
Average age of death of females is 6% lower than Brent average; average of males is 55, lower than Brent average; only 42.7% men and 59.3% women reach 75 years, respectively, 37% and 10% lower than Brent average.	**Broad health improvement** Increase life expectancy to the borough average by 2011.	Increase average age of death for men and women to borough average by 2001, reducing gaps by 2004, 50% by 2007 and 75% by 2009; increase the number of people reaching 75 years to the borough average by 2001; reducing the gaps by 20% by 2004, 50% by 2007 and 75% by 2009.
Proportion of households with someone with a long-term illness is 91% above the London level; death rate by circulatory conditions is twice as high than the rest of UK.	**Long-term illness** To reduce the number of households with someone with a long-term illness to the London level by 2001	Reduce gaps between the proportion of households with long-term illnesses in South Kilburn and London levels by 20% by 2005, 50% by 2007 and 75% by 2009.
Infant mortality rate (IMR) is 12.2%, more than double the London and national average; teenage pregnancies are 46% higher than the London average and twice the Brent rate.	**Families and young mothers** Reduce infant mortality to London average by 2001; reduce teenage pregnancy to at least London average by 2011.	Reduce IMR year on year, decreasing the gap with London and national averages by 20% by 2005, 50% by 2007 and 75% by 2009; reduce the gaps between teenage pregnancy levels and the London rate by 70% by 2004 and 90% by 2007.
Mental health related hospital admission rates are 53% above the Brent average.	**Emotional health** Reduce the number of people admitted to hospital or consulting primary care about emotional and mental health problems to the borough average by 2011.	Reduce the mental health admission rates year on year from 2004, decreasing the gap with the borough average by 25% by 2006, 50% by 2008 and 80% by 2010.

Source: Based on London Borough of Brent (2001)

Advisory Service, which is now set to be superseded (Gibson, 2003: 18). Decisions have yet to be taken – with tenants' consent – about the main options for the estate that have been developed by Mace. One is to refurbish the 2,100 properties at a cost of £360 million, the other to rebuild new homes, costing £600 million. At the time of writing, regeneration remains in its early stages. The NDC has identified £28 million for housing regeneration, so further decisions remain to be made such as whether to build homes for private sale to regenerate income, although the NDC has requested £50 million additional

funding to rebuild at a density of 558 homes per hectare. At the time of writing, regeneration activity at South Kilburn remains ongoing.

Acknowledgement: This is part of a paper that was first published in Stewart, J. and Rhoden, M. (2003) 'A review of social housing regeneration in the London Borough of Brent', Journal of the Royal Society for the Promotion of Health, 123 (1) pp: 23 – 32.

Local Authorities and Community Strategies

The changing role of local authorities is embodied in the Local Government Acts 1999 and 2000 which aim to modernise local authorities to ensure an improvement in quality of life of communities and individuals. Services should be responsive to local needs, improve continuously, be co-ordinated to avoid duplication, maximise effectiveness and give a comprehensive response to complex problems such as social exclusion and neighbourhood renewal.

The Local Government Act 2000 requires local authorities to prepare a community strategy for promoting or improving the economic, social and environmental well-being of their area and contributing to sustainable development in the UK. The Act also enables them to do anything they think will achieve this end. The duty to prepare a strategy does not necessarily mean that every authority must prepare a separate strategy. There needs to be effective interaction between different tiers of local authorities and between neighbouring authorities to ensure strategies are developed in ways which best suit the needs of the communities they serve rather than the service providers. In preparing or modifying their community strategy, a local authority must involve appropriate persons and have regard to guidance issued by the Secretary of State following consultation (DETR, 2000i).

A community strategy should aim to enhance the quality of life of local communities and must allow communities to articulate their aspirations, needs and priorities, co-ordinate and focus the actions of all the organisations involved and contribute to sustainable development with local action. The strategy must have a long-term vision focusing on outcomes, an action plan identifying shorter-term priorities and activities, a shared commitment to implement the action plan and proposals for doing so, and arrangements for monitoring, reviewing and reporting progress. The strategy should be prepared and implemented by a broad LSP and based on needs assessment and availability of resources. National and global concerns should be addressed through local action. Where deprivation, social exclusion, a poor quality environment and health inequalities are significant factors, the community strategy will need to address how these are to be tackled and how the quality of life can be improved. There will be priorities based on specific needs of communities and there should be joined-up services to tackle the issues in an integrated

Box 2.3 Sussex Partnerships – Working in practice

Local authorities are required by the Local Government Act 2000 to produce a Community Strategy following consultation for promoting or improving the economic, social and environmental well-being of their area. The power given to them under this Act allows for the implementation of the strategy for the whole or part of the area or all or any persons resident in the area.

Local authorities in East and West Sussex are participating in activities identified in their Community Strategies, usually targeting specific groups of residents. These activities involve partnership working with other agencies, voluntary groups, businesses and individuals. One popular scheme in Sussex is the Junior Citizen or Safety in Action week where school children participate in a range of activities designed to educate them about safety. Sussex Police, the Fire Brigade, the Ambulance Service, Environmental Health, Trading Standards, Animal Welfare Officers, Seeboard, Transco, the Health and Safety Executive, Rail Track and the Primary Care Trust are just some of the agencies involved. They work together by providing a varied and exciting set of scenarios to promote safety inside and outside the home. A competitive element between the participating schools can be introduced with questionnaires for the children to complete as they go, testing whether the safety messages are getting across. The events have proved popular and educative over the years, and were recognised in 1992 with the Domestos Health Education Award.

Another award winning scheme has been the 6th Form Seminars organised and co-ordinated by Wealden District Council for the last ten years. Each year, around 80 students from local schools/colleges are invited to attend a one-day event on a particular issue. Topics covered have included AIDS and HIV, mental health and mental well-being, food, substance misuse, and law and order. Depending on the focus of the day, the council works in partnership with relevant agencies. For example, the recent mental health and well-being day brought together the local Primary Care Trusts, the charity Rethink and the NHS Acute Trust to provide presentations, workshop groups and a question session. Evaluation of the seminars has shown a high success for increasing the knowledge of students on a specific topic. In 1997 the Department of Health awarded a Commendation under the Health Alliance Awards for these seminars.

A smaller partnership scheme also exists between Wealden District Council Environmental Health and two Primary Care Trusts, Sussex Downs and Weald, and Eastbourne

Downs. Many years ago it was noted that a significant number of children under five attending accident and emergency at the local hospital had injuries due to accidents in the home. The three agencies got together to provide the Wealden Child Safety Equipment Scheme, where various safety items are provided to families with under fives who are on income support or in special circumstances. The scheme is funded by the Primary Care Trusts and co-ordinated by Environmental Health, including the purchase and storage of the equipment. The range of equipment includes stair gates, fireguards, non-slip bath mats, socket covers, coiled kettle flexes, window locks, pram reflectors etc. The Primary Care Trust Health Visitors assess a client's needs to identify the appropriate equipment, and inform the Environmental Health Officer who co-ordinates the scheme and completes the administration. Clients collect and return the equipment from the Health Visitors' base. In 1998 this scheme received the Health Alliance Award and the NHS South Thames Region Award for partnership working.

At the other end of the age spectrum, an example of promoting and improving the social well-being of people over 60 included the Life Is For Living day (1 October 2002) organised by Horsham District Council and the Horsham and Chanctonbury Primary Care Trust. The focus of the day was to help people over 60 get the most out their life through new activities; access to services; information on grants, safety, housing, energy efficiency and carer support etc. The day was also to celebrate the International Day of Older People and the 15th anniversary of the Community Link personal alarm service and to directly consult individuals on the Council's Older Persons Strategy. More than 50 organisations provided a combination of sponsorship; exhibition stands; try-out sessions such as yoga, Internet use and shop mobility test drives; and safety checks like electric blanket testing and changing rubber stoppers on walking sticks. As well as being a free informative and fun day for over 500 local residents, the agencies, businesses and voluntary groups involved gained invaluable insight into each other's contributions. An evaluation of the day through a short questionnaire revealed the issues that concerned older residents included public transport, household maintenance and cleaning to help them remain independent and in their own homes, safer communities, local medical and long-term residential care services, and information on benefits. These concerns are helping to shape the Community Strategy for Older People.

Case study provided by Lisa Harvey.

way. Preparation of the strategy should be a bottom-up approach to ensure local ownership. The key to success is partnership working and community involvement. Only by working across organisational boundaries will the broad range of outcomes be delivered (see Box 2.3).

Many local partnerships have already been set up to contribute to HIMPs (and more recently LDPs), Neighbourhood Renewal, Agenda 21, the Healthy Citizen initiative, Healthy Living Centres and Health Action Zones and so on. It is essential that existing partnership initiatives are integrated to avoid duplication and unnecessary bureaucracy. For example, the National Strategy for Neighbourhood Renewal depends on partnership working but local strategic partnerships could take on this role, producing deprivation-focused renewal strategies as part of the community strategies. Regional government offices have a good knowledge of existing partnerships and can facilitate the sharing of good practice and identify activities at local, regional and central levels to avoid duplication. The Regional Development Agencies take an integrated and sustainable approach to economic issues, which include tackling unemployment, skills shortages, inequalities, social exclusion and physical decay. They can help bring businesses into the partnerships. However, it is the voluntary and community sectors that are often best placed to reach and involve the sections of the community that the public sector finds hard to reach.

Public Service Agreements

Local Public Service Agreements (PSAs) offer local authorities the opportunity to commit themselves to delivering key national and local priorities in return for operational flexibilities and grants. Authorities that meet the more stretching performance targets agreed in local PSAs will also gain access to a Performance Reward Fund. Each local PSA will focus on about 12 key outcomes which reflect a mix of national and local priorities, including where appropriate targets to improve outcomes for areas or groups most at risk of social exclusion. Key PSA targets include improving education, housing and employment and reducing crime and health inequalities. Local authorities will need to demonstrate that the local priorities they are proposing are important to, and supported by, local people and partners. Partners will need to develop means to work with and consult local people, build commitment, develop and publicise aims and priorities, value all contributions, share information and good practice, support local initiatives, develop a common performance management system and provide a forum for debate and common decision-making (DETR, 2001a).

Local authorities and Best Value

The development of a comprehensive community strategy is inextricably linked to the delivery of a local authority's duty of Best Value. The strategic priorities should be reflected in the setting of the authority's objectives and performance measures. Without a clear understanding of local needs and the value of a partnership approach, a local authority will be unlikely to achieve best value in the provision of its services. Best Value service reviews will need to examine the extent to which existing services are meeting community priorities. In some cases community priorities will cut across traditional service boundaries, for example community safety, neighbourhood renewal and social exclusion, and Best Value reviews should reflect this.

An authority's annual Best Value Performance Plan should provide an important means of monitoring and informing the public of the effectiveness of the authority's contribution to tackling the priorities identified in the community strategy. The well-being power should be used to develop innovative approaches to service delivery. The well-being power provides a strong basis on which to deliver many of the priorities identified by local communities and included in community strategies. Local authorities can fund activities, take on functions currently undertaken by other service providers, provide staff, goods, services and accommodation, and form or participate in companies, trusts or charities. In order to achieve the duty of best value, authorities need a wide range of means of service delivery.

Local authorities, environmental health and the PCTs

Local authorities are best placed to take a comprehensive overview of the needs and priorities in their local areas and communities, as community leadership is at their core (DETR, 1998d; 2000i). It is essential that local authorities play a major role in tackling health inequalities. Plans to reduce health inequalities could fail unless local authorities are given a more formal role in the new health structures. The Democratic Health Network (DHN) argues that local authorities are better placed than the NHS to take the lead on tackling health inequality because of their involvement with people through housing, social services, employment and environmental health functions (cited in Spear, 2002).

However, many in local authorities are expressing increasing concern about the direction public health delivery is taking (Wright, 2001), suggesting that local authorities may take a secondary role to the NHS in delivering key developmental objectives, possibly because the environmental health agenda has become enforcement driven in recent years rather that based on wider public health outputs (MacArthur, 2001). Core areas of environmental health work have got left behind the public health agenda by failing to address either inequality or overall health improvement, possibly due to increasing performance monitoring requirements. There is a need for a more progressive and outcome-focused agenda that does not stifle innovation and real progress.

As a result, environmental health departments in particular need to raise their profile as their contribution is essential. PCTs will be responsible for up to 75 per cent of NHS spending by 2004, but local authorities have no statutory right to be represented on their boards. Although a PCT executive is required to have a social services representative, it has to be an officer not a councillor, so there is little democratic representation. The DHN also raises concerns about the way the partnership trusts have been set up. They fear that health inequality issues will be dropped down the agenda in preference to sickness-led health services. The NHS is restricted by central government and aims to standardise performance and quality, which restricts flexibility to respond to local issues (Spear, 2002).

Although the Health Development Agency (HDA) has called for closer collaboration and integration between the NHS and local authorities, the extent to which this is happening in reality is unclear. As new organisations vie for funding and status – and made more inevitable in a climate of constant change – there are invariably some organisational and professional boundaries being drawn up which are not helpful when all are essentially working toward the goal of reducing health inequality. For local authorities, this is of little surprise as much public health literature originates in the Department of Health – where the Minister for Public Health sits – rather than a department more closely allied to environmental health issues, such as regeneration and inclusion – notably the ODPM.

Local authorities have a fundamental role to play in delivering health improvements (MacArthur, 2001) but are frequently having to fight their way into newly emerging partnerships. There is a need for local authorities to re-engage with – and to promote – traditional public health issues with the public health agenda as a springboard, promoting their existing strategies through partnership arrangements. Local authorities risk playing a secondary role to medical public health if they do not grasp the initiative now.

Environmental health as public health: An integrated approach to complex issues

Many in environmental health believe their work to be absolutely fundamental to the public health agenda (see, for example Burke et al, 2002), since it continually recognises, challenges and addresses key public health issues and inequality. In order to engage closely with the public health agenda, environmental health practitioners need to promote their role and find a new status and function in new organisational structures. Many have been extremely successful in taking up new posts both in and outside of their traditional location in local authorities (see Boxes 2.4 and 2.5), but there still remains some way to go.

Box 2.4 Away From the Coal-Face

In 1998 Lincolnshire Health Authority employed me as a Principal EHO. At the time it was very unusual for an EHO to be employed directly by the NHS. During my employment with the health authority I was involved in many areas of work including communicable disease control, emergency planning, accident prevention, housing and a wide range of transport issues. Primarily this was a strategic role, making the links between the health authority and those agencies that deliver the operational side of many public services.

Support to do a Masters Degree in Public Health and a major NHS reorganisation in 2002 has led to another role: Public Health Specialist for East Lincolnshire Primary Care Trust. The focus for public health in primary care is somewhat different. An important part of my work recently has involved analysis and presentation of health data to help inform the planning processes of a very new organisation. It has provided me with the opportunity to extend my skills and also helped to influence the way services are delivered at a local level. There is a strong emphasis in this work on reducing inequalities and narrowing the health gap.

During my career in the NHS my environmental health skills and experience have been invaluable, as has a working knowledge of local government. The view of some colleagues when I first moved to the NHS was that the job would make me remote from the profession. My experience is that the opposite is true. I feel my work in the last few years has brought me closer to the core values of the profession than my time in local government. An ability to take a holistic approach to health has been a big advantage. In some ways I have become a generalist EHO again.

There is increasing evidence that the key determinants of health are things like poverty, transport and access to services, education, employment opportunities and social capital. These factors relate directly or indirectly to the environment and communities in which people live. These things will be dear to the hearts of many EHOs particularly those of us old enough to have done an old fashioned district job where and EHO had a defined geographical area and did a bit of everything. Greater complexity in the technical aspects of environmental health and associated legislation made greater specialisation inevitable. It is perhaps unfortunate that at around the same time as the public health agenda was taking off, the same government that had published *Saving Lives: Our Healthier Nation* (Department of Health, 1999) was setting performance indicators that did not generally have health improvement as their goal. Not only have these become the main benchmark of performance for environmental health services; they have also effectively narrowed the public health role of EHOs in local government. A consequence of this has been that EHOs have found themselves working and thinking in silos, for example just doing food safety for most if not all of their career to date. This is not what we are trained for and probably results in lower job satisfaction for many.

The NHS in recent years has been subject to enormous organisational upheaval. April 2002 has seen the abolition of health authorities and the devolution of many functions including public health to primary care trusts. There has been a shift in political emphasis towards health improvement through a reduction in inequalities. This has led to significant changes in public health delivery particularly within the NHS. PCTs, as they are known, have many responsibilities such as the management of budgets, commissioning of services in the acute sector and delivery of primary health care. However, one of the main objectives is to improve the health of their local populations. To do this they must work in partnership with other agencies and organisations in their area. Local Strategic Partnerships will be very influential in this process. Local Authorities have now got responsibilities for well-being and to produce community strategies. The Second Report of the Select Committee on Health in 2001 noted the importance of the role that local government had to play in health improvement. Public health skills will be a key tool to help ensure that communities derive the maximum health gain from the wide range of activities and services that local authorities undertake. EHOs should be undertaking an important role in this regardless of where they work in the public sector but particularly taking a public health lead within local government. In some authorities this is happening but in others, especially where the function has become fragmented, it is not.

In the future, environmental health practitioners should be seen as the key players in local regulation for health protection, strategy development for health improvement and as advocates for local communities. A multi-agency approach involving local authorities, primary care teams, local businesses, the voluntary sector should become commonplace.

Another consequence of the changes in Public Health is likely to be an opening up of new opportunities to environmental health officers. Appointments and secondments of EHOs to NHS organisations have become more common over the last couple of years. There is currently a shortage of well-qualified public health specialists from both medical and non-medical background. While there is potentially a big pool of public health practitioners such as health visitors to draw on, well-rounded EHOs have a unique view of public health having worked at the coalface for so long. Stepping back from that into PCTs can offer EHOs opportunities for professional development and new career prospects such as that of public health specialist. The Faculty of Public Health Medicine now offers other public health professionals the opportunity to become accredited through the same route as public health doctors. It may not be long before we could see a dual registered EHO becoming Director of Public Health.

Sarah Webb MCIEH, MPH, Public Health Specialist, East Lincolnshire Primary Care Trust

Box 2.5 An EHO in Public Health Specialist Training

Background
Formal training in Public Health in England has traditionally only been available to qualified medical practitioners. The Faculty of Public Health Medicine (FPHM) has ensured that doctor wishing to specialise in this area meet the required standards. This has been achieved through undertaking a five-year training scheme during which the Specialist Registrar (SpR) sits the Part I and Part II membership examinations and receives regular competency-based in-training assessments.

Through this route doctors become members of the FPHM and can enter a career as a Consultant in Public Health Medicine (CPHM). This route has, however, been closed to the many other disciplines, which contribute to the practice of improving the health of the population. These groups possess a wide range of academic and professional qualifications and experience but have enjoyed little formal status, lacked structured career pathways and have had limited opportunities for further education and professional development.

Change

By the mid-1990s pressure for change was mounting. Public health practice in the NHS became increasingly multi-disciplinary and there was rising concern about this inequitable situation both in terms of the limited opportunities available to non-medical public health professionals and in ensuring effective public health practice. As a result the Multi-Disciplinary Public Health Forum (MDPHF) was established to take forward the development of training opportunities, career structures, accreditation and continual professional development (CPD) for this group. The demands for change reflected the Government's commitment to the development of multi-disciplinary public health and *Saving Lives: Our Healthier Nation*¹ was a key document in this process. One of its stated aims was to unlock the potential of the entire public health workforce in order to deliver on the government's health improvement agenda. The FPHM responded to these emerging changes, and recognising the contribution of wider public health practice. It started moves towards creating all-embracing faculty for public health.

Developments

Since 1998 the MDPHF, the FPHM and the Royal Institute of Public Health (RIPH) have worked together as the Tripartite Steering Group to ensure that high standards of practice for public health specialists are developed and maintained.

Faculty Membership

In 1998 the FPHM allowed diplomate membership to all professional groups that undertook a common examination. It was agreed that entry to Part I be extended to all those from a non-medical background with sufficient academic qualifications and professional experience. In 2000 it was agreed that honorary members of the faculty be allowed to be nominated for

Table 2.2 Key events leading to the establishment of the UK voluntary register for public health specialists :

	Voluntary register and public health competences
1998	FPHM (now FPH), MPHF and RIPH – agreement to work together for accreditation system for trained and competent PH professionals. Representation from broad range of disciplines, including EH, nursing, HDA, NHS executive, DoH, etc
1999 onwards	Proposal strengthened in Saving Lives White Paper, post of specialist PH established; Healthwork UK commissioned to develop national standards; mapping PH functions and implications for **competencies** and **national standards** considered covering: • Surveillance and assessment of population's health and well-being • Promoting and protecting the population's health and well-being • Developing quality and risk management within evaluative culture • Collaborative working for health and well-being • Developing health programmes and services for reducing inequalities • Policy and strategy development and implementation • Working with and for communities • Strategic leadership for health and well-being • Research and development • Ethically managing self, people and resources Tripartite Group then began work on developing Register
2001	Minister of Health indicated government support for establishing Register
2003	DoH across UK supported the development of PH Register ensuring high standards of practice; PHM announced launch of register

Useful websites:
- UK voluntary register http://www.publichealthregister.org.uk
- PH specialist competence self-assessment framework http://www.education-brokering.org.uk
- Tripartite Group (Faculty of Public Health Medicine) http://www.fphm.org.uk
- Multidisciplinary Public Health Forum http://www.riph.org.uk

fellowship in the same way as those that are medically qualified and in 2002 Part II was also opened up.

Voluntary Register
As part of this work the group have identified the need for a professional register for public health specialists. This Voluntary Register, with funding from the Department of Health, is now underway – see table 2.3. Registration will be opened up to senior public health professionals with demonstrable experience and competency, assessed through a portfolio.

A recent study commissioned by the MDPHF and the FPHM Honorary Members Committee was carried out to examine how existing training schemes are responding to the changes. It found that, since the opening up of Part I, there has been a group of non-medical specialists, not on a training scheme, who have taken the route independently. The Public Health Resource Unit (PHRU) has led support for these professionals. Other regions are now going through the process of identifying such individuals and offering them support.

NHS Training schemes
Several NHS regions in England responded to these developments by providing the funding necessary to develop public health capacity and capability, and so started recruitment of non-medical trainees onto their specialist training schemes. The backgrounds of those joining such schemes are varied, but the majority tend to come from a nursing, statistical, economic or geographical background. Multi-disciplinary public health training has also been developed in Wales.

Forging a new path
I joined the NHS Eastern Region in April 2001 and became the first EHO to enter such a training scheme. I have since taken the MSc in Public Health at St George's Hospital Medical School and have sat Part I of the Faculty membership examinations in January 2003. During my time on the scheme I have so far had placements in a Health Authority and a Primary Care Trust (PCT). Other potential placement include the regional Government Office, the Chemical Incident Response Service (CIRS) and the Centre for Communicable Disease Control (CDSC). I have also been able to become involved in a variety of events and initiatives, from emergency planning to flu immunisation for the elderly.
Coming from a local authority background meant that I could offer different experiences, knowledge and views on public health. I had previously worked in most environmental health areas, including housing,

nuisance, food safety and health & safety. I was therefore in a position to help develop links between public health and environmental health, a split that had occurred almost 30 years earlier.
However, being a 'guinea pig' from outside the NHS has presented me with challenges. The NHS is a gargantuan organisation and its workings, funding, hierarchy and processes take time to understand and get to grips with. This was particularly the case during one of the most dramatic overhauls of NHS organisation in its history initiated by *Shifting the Balance of Power'*.
The SpR trainees in the Region have welcomed me and offered support. They are therefore to be congratulated for this, as there is still a small, but persistent, resistance from some doctors to this change. I have also found support through the Association of Public Health Specialist Trainees (APHST). This is a national group founded by multi-disciplinary trainees and which has recently amalgamated with the Trainee Members Committee of the FPHM, traditionally a doctor-only committee. This has helped forge better links and demonstrates the gradual convergence between medical and non-medical training schemes.

The SpR scheme is well established and has national terms and conditions, which have been negotiated through the BMA. For Specialist Trainees, however, there are still several issues that need to be addressed. Parity in terms and conditions with medically trained colleagues is a concern, as are on-call arrangements and variations in the length of training contract nationally. At present there is no national agreement on terms and conditions and accreditation for Specialist Trainees and so more work is needed in these areas. The likely outcome may therefore be the full integration of the medical and non-medical schemes and the elimination of these discrepancies.

Future trends
Entry onto specialist training schemes has become highly competitive. There is an increasing demand for specialist public health input from both PCTs and local authorities. *Shifting the Balance of Power* has enhanced opportunities for public health specialists. Every PCT is now expected to have a Director of Public Health (DPH) to lead on their local health improvement agenda and many of those being appointed nationally are now from non-medical backgrounds. These changes are part of the wider move to the development of a multi-disciplinary public health workforce, incorporating all those able to contribute to the improvement of the population's health. Environmental health has a key role to play in this process.

Source: Stuart Lines, Public Health Specialist, NHS Eastern Region

Notes
1. *Saving Lives: Our Healthier Nation*, Department of Health (1999).

2. Specialists in Public Health: proceeding to Part II FPHM membership (June 2002) Yvonne Cornish and Teri Knight.
3. *Shifting the Balance of Power*, Department of Health

The recent report, Environmental Health 2012: *A Key Partner in Delivering the Public Health Agenda* (Burke et al, 2002; Gray, 2002) reaffirmed the crucial role of environmental health practitioners. It acknowledged their unique contribution in maintaining health rather than curing illness and commended the shift in government policy to addressing inequality and improving public health and community well-being. However, it also recorded a narrow, enforcement-led, sometimes fragmented agenda and called for this to be addressed so that wider determinants of health can be properly addressed with adequate resource, organisational arrangements and skills in strategic planning, partnership working and community development. It recorded the need for an evidence base and effective procedures to evaluate and research environmental health initiatives and progress. The report also pointed to the importance of recognising the environmental health potential in encouraging practitioner motivation in a revival of the profession in its widest sense.

Therefore the vision for the contribution of environmental health to public health by 2012 is for environmental health practitioners:

 • to support key local and national partners in efforts to protect and improve health and quality of life of individuals and communities by reducing health inequalities;
 • to maintain a direct relationship with the public, applying expertise as appropriate for individuals while also tackling wider health determinants by identifying, controlling and preventing current and future risks; and
 • to play a lead role in local authority development, co-ordination and implementation of community strategies through local strategic partnerships (LSP) and contributing to the public health agenda, as well as tackling relevant issues at regional, national and international levels (Burke at al, 2002; Gray, 2002).

The public health agenda: where are we now?

Sustainable health promoting activities should lie at the heart of the public health agenda. The Ottawa Charter (1986) suggested that the themes of health promotion included building a healthy public policy; creating supportive environments; developing personal skills; strengthening community action; and reorienting health services towards prevention and health promotion. Building on this foundation, the Jakarta Declaration (1997) sought to promote social responsibility for health, increase investment for health development, expand partnerships for health promotion, increase community capacity to help empower the individual and to secure an infrastructure for health promotion.

The current New Labour Third Way approach to health promotion through the public health agenda, which combines European social democracy, U.S. style communitarianism under a governmental policy agenda for public health. This is packaged as a Social Contract for health, with (new) rights and responsibilities for all in health improvement (ie, stemming from the Green Paper, DoH, 1998a). For further discussion see Thomas and Stewart (2005).

While it may be tempting to assume that all involved in the public health agenda are moving in the same direction, recent research suggests that this is not necessarily so. Although partnership frameworks are now well established, there remain concerns over the extent to which they are really aligning and sharing values, focus, vision, direction and objectives (Hunter and Sengupta, 2004; Wills and Woodhead, 2004), as well as retaining some uncertainty about public health roles (Evans, 2004). The 'fully engaged' public health scenario (HM Treasury and DoH, 2002), still seems to be some way away.

The Chief Medical Officer (DoH, 2001c) in *Strengthening Public Health* called for a wider understanding of health, better and more co-ordinated public health function, partnership working, community development and public involvement, more capable and increased public health workforce and increased health protection. Grey and Sarangi (2003) suggest that contemporary health threats include:
- An acute major incident (radioactive leak)
- Major food poisoning outbreak or food contamination

- Public accident (major rail crash)
- Longer term and chronic health threats (air pollution)
- Uncertain hazards of new technologies
- New and re-emerging infectious diseases and antibiotic resistance

The risks to health are increasingly global and include bioterrorism, communicable diseases and food implicated health threats. The Chief Medical Officer's report *Getting ahead of the curve* (DoH, 2002c) and *Creating a Health Protection Agency* (DoH, 2002d) addressed the need for more effective risk assessment, risk management and risk communication procedures.

As a result, the Health Protection Agency was set up in April 2003 to coordinate responses to communicable disease, environmental hazards and emergency planning. It is a national expert advice centre which supports coordination of surveillance and response. It includes the Centre of Applied Microbiological Research, National Focus for Chemical Incidents and Public Health Laboratory Service including Communicable Disease Surveillance Centre and National Radiological Protection Board. At regional level, there are laboratories and emergency planning advisors. At local level there is liaison with the Directors of Public Health, health protection units and EHPs.

Tackling Health Inequalities: A Programme for Action (DoH, 2003b) was concerned with action to address inequalities. The report identified a vital role for PCTs and local government to work together in partnership with local communities to tackle causes and consequences of health inequalities. It included fuel poverty strategies, housing standards and neighbourhood renewal.

The consultation document *Choosing Health?* (DoH 2004a) proposed a focus on improving health, preventing illness and public engagement by working together to make a real difference, with a priority to ensure improved and faster access to high quality health services in key defined areas. In particular, it explored the possibilities to:

- Work together more effectively to promote the health of all
- Ensure our children are given the best start in life
- Ensure people have a healthy retirement

• Ensure people have the local environments, services, facilities and information they need to choose healthy lifestyles
• Overcome barriers that have hindered progress

A summary of current health challenges still prevalent is shown in table 2.3: Choosing Health.

Table 2.3

• 1 in 5 children does not eat any fruit in a week
• Incidence of obesity has trebled in 20 yrs
• 1 in 10 sexually active young women are infected with Chlamydia,
• In 2001/02, 33 million working days were lost due to work-related ill health
• Men in Manchester are likely to die on average 8.5 yrs earlier than men in Rutland
• People in most deprived areas are twice as likely to suffer from lung cancer as those living in most affluent areas, and
• nearly 3 times as likely to be out of work and on sickness/disability benefits if you live in the NE than in SE
• 2.5m homes are cold enough to cause ill health during any winter in England
• Suicide is the most common cause of death in men under 35
• Volatile substance abuse is responsible for more deaths in young people aged 10-16 in E&W than illegal drugs use
• Since 1991/93 the proportion of primary aged children walking to school has declined from 60 to 51% with an increase from 29 to 41% in the numbers being driven to school
• Smoking kills more than 13 people an hour, every hour, every day.
• Over 1.4 m people say they have missed, turned down or chosen not to seek medical help over the 12 months to Feb.2003 because of transport problems
• Between 15,000 and 22,000 deaths each year are associated with alcohol misuse
• Injury is the leading cause of child death in E&W

DoH (2004a)

The subsequent White Paper, *Choosing Health* (DoH, 2004b) was published on 16 November 2004. It set out new initiatives on enabling healthier lifestyles, notably in the areas of smoking, obesity and sexual health, but also to encourage more sensible drinking and to improve mental well-being. The emphasis was on increased information, advice and support to enable healthier decisions based on informed choices for individuals, communities and across public and private sectors. The White Paper sought to consolidate the tension between public wants and effective evidence based practice. In particular, new measures included action to increase numbers of smoke-freee workplaces; promotion of healthier food through helping improve healthier foods to children and better nutritional food labelling; NHS Health Trainers guide individuals in healthier lifestlyes; and measures to tackle social and geographical health inequalities.

Securing Good Health for the Whole Population (Wanless 2004) set out the challenges and looks at the cost-effectiveness of action. It pointed out that there is so much written about public health but rigorous implementation of solutions is often lacking and there is limited assessment of the long-term impact on population health and inequalities of key policies. Wanless also reported the widespread systematic failures that influence individuals' decisions, including lack of information, engrained social attitudes, addictions, inequalities, etc. He also referred to the very poor information base for public health and lack of funding for research, and the continuing low evidence base about the cost-effectiveness of public health and preventative policies or their implementation. While a wide range of initiatives has been introduced, these often lack clear objectives, and have little quantification of outcomes, so it is difficult to sustain support for them.

Recent policy and activity has been directed at strengthening the public health role of the NHS and local government and facilitating partnership working, but difficulties include capacity problems, impact of organisational changes and lack of alignment of performance management mechanisms between partners.

The Wanless report cited several other concerns about the direction of public health which square closely with EH 2012 (Burke et al, 2002) as follows:

- Lack of comprehensive health data
- Health Policy has not been rebalanced away from health care
- Narrow use of targeting
- Government does not have a comprehensive set of objectives for key lifestyle risk factors at national and local level and there is often little evidence on how to reduce their burden.
- There is little evidence about what works among disadvantaged groups to tackle some of the determinants of health inequalities or differential impact of interventions across the socio-economic gradient.

EHPs have much to offer to the current public health agenda. There has been recognition of their skills and attributes, but also where there are currently gaps in being able to participate fully, such as in community development roles, etc. This, however, has been acknowledged and training opportunities remain under development.

In addition, the Health Development Agency (HDA) website increasingly offers evidence-based documentation. There is scope for EHPs to both contribute to, and learn from, good practice in their public health work. See http://www.hda-online.org.uk/evidence

Local authorities are already delivering a range of successful public health initiatives (see, for example, Hamer and Easton, 2002). Most local authorities have grasped the public health nettle in reintroducing health activities into core tasks in innovative ways (Brown, 2002). High-profile examples include Coventry's environmental health department – working in close partnership with allied health organisations – whose health development unit tackles health inequality in areas as diverse as home safety, sexual health and food poverty. Sheffield City Council was recently awarded Healthy City Status by the World Health Organisation, providing the impetus for new health-centred partnerships. Activities include health and environment audits in deprived areas, one result being improved local public transport (Brown, 2002). The New Deal for Communities programme (see Box 2.2) has been pivotal for many deprived social housing estates, such as South Kilburn in Brent, where the local authority is addressing the multiple levels of socio-economic deprivation – including worklessness, poor housing and local capacity – through many partnership strategies, but most notably with residents (London Borough of Brent, 2001). The list goes on, and on as EHPs seek to develop more innovative, partnership-based strategies to promote health.

Chapter 3
Themes and priorities in environmental health and public health

Environmental Health: Back to Basics

Public health – and addressing deprivation and inequalities – has become key to improving the nation's health and remains a rapidly moving multi-organisational policy area. Some aspects of environmental health fall clearly within the remit of public health – notably housing and environmental controls – yet other functions have moved away from addressing inequalities toward enforcement-based regimes and this needs to be addressed for environmental health to take its place in health improvement. The environmental health as public health role needs to be able to fully address and incorporate several issues if it is to take a pioneering role in the future. It is largely down to environmental health departments to be able to publicise and promote their functions and potentials to take their rightful and proactive place in the future of public health.

This chapter reviews some contemporary issues that environmental health departments need to be able to recognise and fully incorporate into their routine operations in linking policy to addressing inequality under the following general headings:

- Sustainability
- The impact of globalisation
- Strategic approaches to public health
- Partnership working in public health: statutory organisations and local communities
- Social exclusion: assessing inequality and moving forwards
- Social capital
- Community development
- Health needs assessment
- Health impact assessment.

Sustainability

Sustainable development was first defined in 1987 as 'development that meets the needs of the present without compromising the ability of future generations to meet their own needs' (World Commission on Environment and Development, 1987). This notion was taken forward at the Rio Earth Summit in 1992. Sustainable development is an attempt to reconcile the tensions between two basic aspirations of society:

- the need to achieve economic development to secure rising standards of living both now and for future generations; and
- the need to protect and enhance the environment now and for the future.

The outcome of the Rio Earth Summit was an agreement on 27 principles supporting sustainable development, a wide-ranging Plan of Action (known as Agenda 21) and the establishment of the United Nations Commission on Sustainable Development.

The first principle that arose out of the Rio Declaration on Environment and Development was that 'Human beings are at the centre of concerns for sustainable development. They are entitled to a healthy and productive life in harmony with nature' (United Nations, 1992a). Agenda 21 recognises that health is dependent on the management of the physical, biological, spiritual, economic and social environments and acknowledges that a majority of development activities impact on the environment which in turn influences health. Within the Plan of Action agreed at the time, Chapter 6 is concerned specifically with protecting and promoting health and establishes five global priority actions:

- meeting primary health care need, particularly in rural areas
- controlling communicable diseases
- protecting vulnerable groups
- meeting the urban health challenge
- reducing health risks from environmental pollution and hazards (United Nations, 1992b).

Within Chapter 6, three key vulnerable groups were identified: women, children and indigenous people, although the special health needs of the aged, the disabled and the displaced were acknowledged. There was also the recognition that the eradication of poverty is a fundamental prerequisite for providing health for all. The WHO was charged as the Task Manager for Chapter 6 of Agenda 21.

Reviews of progress have taken place in 1997 and again in 2002, and address Chapter 6 from a global perspective. The review in 2002 identified steady gains in global health but also highlighted emerging concerns for health, most notably: the impact of the globalisation of trade, travel and culture; food safety; the health threats to ageing populations; and global threats to health such as climate change, depletion of the ozone layer and the spread of persistent organic pollutants (WHO, 2001).

The WHO acknowledges that many of the key determinants of health lie outside the control of the health sector in such areas as environment, education, employment, trade and housing (WHO, 2001). It is further acknowledged that tackling the wider determinants of health is important in ensuring ecologically sustainable development and sustained improvements in health over time (WHO, 2001). Much emphasis is placed on the need for the health sector to work in partnership with others, particularly at a local level.

Local Agenda 21

Although Agenda 21 has a global focus, it identifies that there is a need for action at a local level and, as a consequence, the phrase 'think globally, act locally' came to epitomise the focus for local, sub-national initiatives. The prompt for this 'local' approach to sustainable development can be found in Chapter 28 of Agenda 21, which calls upon local authorities to produce their own Local Agenda 21, in consultation with their community (United Nations, 1992b).

The Council of European Municipalities and Regions (1997) identifies the characteristics of a sustainable community as including:

- good environmental quality that protects health;
- a health service that is both preventative and curative;
- a level of pollution that can be assimilated through natural processes without giving rise to degradation;
- access for all to water, food, shelter and fuel at reasonable cost;
- effective use of resources and minimisation of waste;
- community empowerment.

The aim of a Local Agenda 21 strategy is thus to promote an economic, social and environmental agenda that encourages better and more efficient ways of doing things.

Sustainable Development in the UK

The UK government was among the first to produce a national sustainable development strategy – *Sustainable Development: The UK Strategy* in 1994. It was superseded, however, in 1999 when the Labour government produced a new strategy – *A Better Quality of Life – a Strategy for Sustainable Development in the UK* (DEFRA, 1999). This strategy is likely to be succeeded following consultation on a new sustainable development strategy during 2004. The current Strategy sets out four broad objectives:

1. The maintenance of high and stable levels of economic growth and development;
2. Social progress which recognises the needs of everyone;
3. Effective protection of the environment;
4. Prudent use of natural resources;

It also incorporates ten overarching principles:

- putting people at the centre;
- taking a long-term perspective;
- taking account of costs and benefits;
- creating an open and supportive economic system;
- combating poverty and social exclusion;
- the application of the precautionary principle;
- using scientific knowledge;
- transparency, information, participation and access to justice;
- making the polluter pay;
- respecting the environmental limits.

The Strategy also identified 150 indicators of sustainable development, of which 14 were selected as 'headline indicators' and published as a benchmark against which progress can be assessed (see Table 3.1). A significant number of these headline indicators are closely coupled with health and with the direct function of local authority environmental health intervention activity.

To move sustainable development forward from a paper exercise towards implementation, the government established the Sustainable Development Commission in 2000. Its role is to advocate sustainable development

• Economic output	• Climate change
• Investment	• Air quality
• Employment	• Road traffic
• Education	• River water quality
• Health	• Land use
• Poverty and social exclusion	• Waste
• Housing	• Wildlife, farmland and birds

Table 3.1
Sustainability:
Headline indicators
of sustainable
development

across all sectors, to review progress and to encourage further progress. Sustainable Development Regional Frameworks have now been established in all English regions in accordance with the statutory requirement under the Local Government Act 2000 and over 90 per cent of local authorities have a Local Agenda 21 strategy (DEFRA, 2003).

Arguably, the UK sustainable development strategy is the epitome of the government's joined-up approach. It acts as a hub, with themes linking it to other Government policies and strategies such as those for health, air quality, housing, food, climate change, ambient noise, energy, waste, regeneration and transport.

Sustainable development and promoting better health

The government's objective for the headline indicator 'Health' is to improve the health of the population overall, but especially the health of the worst off in society. This accords with the twin goals of the Health White Paper *Saving Lives: Our Healthier Nation* (DoH, 1999a) to improve health and reduce health inequalities. Although much of this work is focused in the NHS, particularly in primary care, it is acknowledged that working in partnership with local government, the community and other local organisations will support achievement of the objectives. Some local authorities have successfully integrated the health agenda into their Local Agenda 21 strategies. For example, in the London Borough of Bexley, although the main focus for their Local Agenda 21 strategy is towards environmental issues, it also identifies the development and promotion of healthy lifestyles and health delivery through partnership as important. Other local authorities have participated in (the former) Health Improvement Programmes as an integral part of their Local Agenda 21 strategy and many Health Action Zones had links with Local Agenda 21 on issues connecting health and the environment. The London Borough of Hammersmith and Fulham has worked with local health professionals to agree a series of local health indicators of sustainable development. Other local authorities have close links with Healthy Living Centres as part of their Local Agenda 21 strategy. Further commentary on these health initiatives and the role of the environmental health professional can be found elsewhere in the book.

Sustainable development, environmental quality and health

The WHO recognises environmental quality as a fundamental determinant of health (WHO, 1997). Degradation of the environment is a major contributory factor to poor health and compromises sustainable development. Those living in deprived areas are far more likely to be at risk from poor environmental quality. The UK government recognises that environment is important but concedes that some decisions will *'require trade-offs between economic, social and environmental objectives'* and highlighting the importance of a consideration of the *'cumulative impact of decisions on overall environmental capital'* (DEFRA, 2003). Congruent with the aspirations of sustainable development, the government's aim in respect of environmental matters, is to prevent further deterioration and seek to *'secure enhancements which contribute to an overall improvement in quality of life'* (DEFRA, 2003). One of the key national initiatives is the joint DEFRA/DTLR (now ODPM) campaign *Are you doing your bit?* This is about involving people in individual actions to secure improvements for the environment (DEFRA, 1999).

Of the five target areas in Agenda 21, the reduction of risks from environmental pollution has been most actively taken up by local authorities. It is not difficult to see why. A long-standing function of local authority environmental health professionals has been the protection of the environment and the quality of the air, land and water are important determinants of health. In many local authorities, policies and programmes of work focusing on, for example, home energy conservation, waste minimisation and recycling, and noise reduction are emerging. All are closely allied to the environment/health interface.

Many improvements in environmental quality have occurred over the past 25 years, but new challenges emerge (for example, the fate and potential long-term impact of man-made oestrogenic substances in water), and old ones present themselves in a different guise (for example, the refocusing away from traditional UK air pollutants of smoke and sulphur dioxide towards those of mobile origin, notably NO_x and O_3). Air quality in particular has received much attention and it is worthy of more detailed consideration.

Air quality is an established health determinant and has a known influence on the development of diseases such as chronic respiratory disease, coronary vascular disease and cancers, as well as impacting adversely on the quality of life. The inhalation of air pollutants can give rise to adverse health impacts on the respiratory system and may bring about more systemic effects if taken up in the blood and transported around the body. Ingestion of pollutants may occur where food and water are contaminated by deposition on soil, plants and water bodies. In the UK, air pollution is estimated to bring forward the death of 12,000 – 24,000 people each year (DEFRA, 2003). For many local authorities, tackling poor air quality is an important element of their Local Agenda 21 strategy. The *Air Quality Strategy for England, Scotland, Wales and Northern Ireland: Working Together for Clean Air* (DEFRA, 2000) and its Addendum (DEFRA, 2003): *The air quality strategy for England, Scotland, Wales and Northern Ireland: Addendum* introduces health-based air quality standards and sets out a framework for the action at national and local levels. The thrust of action is at the local level, where local authorities are charged with assessing the quality of air in their area and taking all necessary action to manage influences on air quality to ensure that pollution levels are reduced to meet national objectives. Such measures will frequently involve consultation with stakeholders and working in partnership across different sectors including the community and local businesses to agree an Air Quality Management Action Plan. A broad range of measures is being introduced, such as low emission zones, traffic management and regulation schemes, home zones, and walking and cycling strategies.

Some measures that are being introduced to improve air quality have an impact on health in more than one way. For example, the 'walking bus' to encourage children to walk to school reduces emissions from motor vehicles, reduces the potential for injury caused by motor vehicle accidents and promotes physical activity in school children.

Local authorities are also responsible for the regulation of emissions to the atmosphere from certain industrial and commercial operations. The emission limits set are essentially to protect the environment but ultimately health is protected too. This is reinforced by guidance issued by the Committee on the Medical Effects of Air Pollution (COMEAP) on behalf of the Chief Medical Officer, which sets out a five-stage process for investigating the health impact of local air pollution from industrial sources. The guidance is aimed at public health professionals in health authorities to facilitate the gathering and dissemination of good quality information relevant to the regulation of industrial emissions (DoH, 2000c).

Sustainable development and public health – the future

It is very easy to be upbeat about the progress in achieving the objectives of sustainable development in respect of health in the UK. There is much evidence in the form of written policies and strategies but much less evidence of real action. The benchmark indicator for 'health' is the expected years of healthy life. This has shown no significant change between 1990 and 1999, and there remains inequity in the life expectancy of those in unskilled occupations compared to others (DEFRA, 2002). The establishment of the Sustainable Development Commission is, in part, designed to help progress work but progress may be strengthened from another direction – the statutory requirement for local authorities to prepare community strategies. The aim of a community strategy is to promote or improve social, economic and environmental well-being in an area and contribute towards the achievement of sustainable development (DETR, 2000g). It is envisaged that local authorities will prepare community strategies through their Local Strategic Partnership. Where deprivation, social exclusion, poor environmental quality and health inequalities are evident in an area, community strategies will need to address these issues. It is the government's view, that sustainable, socially inclusive communities are central to the aim of enhancing local quality of life (see, for example, Boxes 2.1, 2.2, 2.3, 3.3 and 5.5) (DETR, 2000i) and that community strategies provide the focus for an approach that advocates joined-up thinking and a coherent, integrated way of working. Arguably, the work that has been done in developing Local Agenda 21 strategies in many local authorities has laid a robust foundation for the partnership working and long-term vision necessary for developing and implementing a community strategy and working towards the objectives of sustainable development.

The impact of globalisation

Globalisation – as it is currently understood – really emerged as a result of increasingly neoliberal policies since the 1980s, pioneered and hastened by a rapid increase in technological development. Globalisation can be seen as an increasingly single global economy, resulting from either extended neoliberal policies, growing interdependence and interconnectedness or the growing power base of transnational companies. It is able to adapt as the world changes to secure new markets, such as with the breakdown of communism and state governance across Eastern Europe. The globalisation process enables those with an already powerful market advantage to escalate their powerful positions by spreading into new locations, largely using their own rules of engagement.

The Department for International Development (DFID) sees globalisation as a positive concept that, if carefully managed, can drive world change to benefit all. DFID (2000a) define globalisation as meaning:

'the growing interdependence and interconnectedness of the modern world through increased flow of goods, services, capital, people and information. The process is driven by technological advances and reductions in the costs of international transactions, which spread technology and ideas, raise the share of trade in world production and increase the mobility of capital.'

They argue that globalisation is illustrated by a diffusion of global norms, values, spreading democracy and the proliferation of global agreements and treaties – notably international environmental human rights agreements. DFID suggest that globalisation can help find solutions to meet the needs of the world's poor through appropriate international effort (DFID, 2000a; 2000b).

Others (for example, Stephens, 2001) are more inclined to focus on some of the issues of power and powerlessness inherent in the globalisation process:

'Technically [globalisation] describes the integration of economic systems, capital movements and opportunities for different peoples through improved information and communication technologies. But locally it has come to mean the increased insecurity and powerlessness that people (particularly poor people) feel in the face of global processes.'

Table 3.2
Structural changes
and public health shifts
arising from
globalisation

Economic changes	Political and cultural changes	Public health changes
Affects employment inequality and resource control	Affects control over policy decisions	Direct health impacts of globalisation, eg shifting disease patterns, behavioural changes, changes in trade union laws affecting workers' health, as well as the effects of global trade in agriculture and food security

Source: Stephens (2001)

Stephens is concerned with structural changes brought about by the globalisation process – including who is making and influencing policy decisions – and how this forges shifts in public health, notably in respect of employment, inequality, power and health impacts. This is summarised in table 3.2.

Chomsky (1993) views the globalisation process more fundamentally as an evolving form of capitalism which has a direct impact on the poor in the developed and developing world, suggesting that:

> 'A corollary of the globalisation of the economy is the entrenchment of third world features at home; the steady drift toward a two-tiered society in which large sectors are superfluous for wealth enhancement for the privileged. Even more than ever, the rabble must be ideologically and physically controlled, deprived of organisation and interchange, the prerequisite for constructive thinking and social action'.

Regardless of one's perspective on the nature of globalisation, there are some serious concerns to be raised about the changing power balance of accountability of transnational companies and nation-states. The globalisation process has been legitimated by trading agreements between powerful nations which are able to expand their markets by creating favourable trading conditions throughout the world, raising serious questions about the impacts and accountability of transnational companies on national governments.

Globalisation affects livelihoods, employment opportunities, security, lifestyles and consequently public health in both the developed and developing world. The poor face increasing risks to health. They are the most likely to live in deprived environments with low quality public health and health promotion services which comprise the primary influence on health and development – and have the least power to be able to do anything about it. As globalisation makes the world's poor – in both the developed and developing world – increasingly vulnerable and dependent, they are frequently also those who suffer its negative consequences.

Globalisation brings new wealth, technology and knowledge, but it is not evenly distributed and its sustainability is sometimes questionable. It has aggravated inequality within and between countries, and also dependency. Globalisation has brought some benefits and there has been enormous developmental progress in many areas (see Table 3.3). However, increasing poverty in the developing world (Watkins, 2000) is partly responsible for population migrations, represented for example by rapid urbanisation extra-legal behaviour activity becoming the norm due to the absence of formal property rights in the developing world as populations attempt to participate in capitalist economies (de Soto, 2001), and the rise in numbers seeking asylum or otherwise migrating elsewhere.

Positives	Negatives
Increased wealth	Growing conflict
Technology	Poverty
Research	Marginalisation
Knowledge	Environmental degradation
Potential for sustainable development	Decreased opportunities for education and health

Table 3.3
Effects of globalisation

Globalisation means that capital is – and can be – very mobile, with people able to move to sources of employment and higher wages. This is contributing the increasing pressure on environmental conditions as well as housing and food availability. Such a mobile – an often impoverished – population, has detrimental health affects, including increased vulnerability to disease due to reduced immunity to malaria, tuberculosis (see Box 3.1) and diarrhoea, and also an increase in sexually transmitted diseases, especially HIV/AIDS (DFID, 2000b). The world's poor disproportionately suffer poor health and malnutrition, which further diminishes the economic cycle in developing countries, creating pressure there and elsewhere.

Globalisation: the issues for environmental health practitioners

Globalisation is becoming one of the major challenges now facing the environmental health profession (Environmental Health Commission, 1997) and impacts daily work at local, national and international levels in explicit and more discrete ways. French (2002: 99) argues that 'the potential impacts of an increasingly global world – inequalities between rich and poor, climate change, loss of bio-diversity, urbanisation, mass migration, re-emergence of disease, etc – are the biggest threats to human health this century will face.' Environmental impacts and the issue of sustainability are discussed elsewhere.

Poverty, inequality and exclusion are invariable side effects of globalisation in the developed and developing world. Among other government public health policy documents, DFID (2000a; 2000b) sees globalisation policies as consistent with domestic policy to tackle UK poverty and social exclusion, and recognising sustainability and poverty as international issues, not just a concern of the developing world. This is part of the current inclusion and empowerment agenda, with inequality as a pivotal concept in the public health agenda.

The globalisation of food also holds important implications for environmental health practitioners. Through globalisation food production becomes more complex and provides greater opportunities for contamination, which can take on global dimensions (WHO, 2000). Although some have the choice of internationally available foodstuffs at and economic price (Lang, 1996), there are concerns about quality, safety and food-borne disease. With increasing food imports, there is an increased risk of disease being imported such as the recent outbreak of foot and mouth in the UK due to infested imported meat, the movement of animals across long distances and intensive farming methods (Hatchett, 2001). Additionally, there are concerns about the impact of genetically modified foodstuffs on potential technological, environmental and socio-economic status (IFST, 1999).

Box 3.1 Tackling tuberculosis in Newham: A partnership approach

The London Borough of Newham has one of the most diverse populations in the United Kingdom with over 50% non-white indigenous people. However, it has one of the highest rates of tuberculosis in the UK, peaking at around 123 per 100,000 in 2000.

Working together with the local Primary Care Trust (Newham PCT), Newham's Environmental Health set out to tackle the problem of TB in Newham with the assistance of funding from Government by use of a Public Service Agreement (PSA).

The PSA sets out stretch targets around :-

1. reducing medium treatment time for TB ie reducing delay in diagnosis/onset of treatments;
2. increasing the number of patients completing treatment for TB.

However ultimately, reduction in the incidence of TB in Newham is the aim.

The project is a good example of a Public Health Initiative being carried out between Local Authority and the NHS and, in this case, Council led.

The driving force for the project has been a taskforce made up of representatives from:

* Environmental Health
* Housing Department
* Policy Section of Chief Executive's Department
* Social Services Department
* TB nurses
* CCDC
* Local pharmacists

Which meets once per month.

The project receives £100k per annum from the Public Service Agreement (PSA) and a bidding process is undertaken to decide distribution of the money. The taskforce decides upon the successful bids. The PSA runs from April 2001 – March 2004.

Project element
Front-line Training
Many myths and stigma exist in respect of TB and many people are unaware that the disease is treatable upon medication and is unlikely to be caught by fellow workers or by sitting next to someone on a bus. All keyworkers,

e.g. Social Workers, Housing staff, Environmental Health Officers, Care Assistants, etc. have undergone basic training to understand about the disease and how it is spread. This training is around half day in duration and is now being spread out to NHS staff and other agencies such as the Police.

Health Promotion Material
The project has had to deal with getting the messages around TB out to very many people often with English not as their main language. A Newham-based video has been produced which has been dubbed into eight different languages. In addition, audiocassettes have been produced in ethnic languages as well as a range of leaflets and posters.

Health Promotion material is available not only at main Council outlets but at many community events, fetes and events for voluntary organisations.

TB Screening
The funding has paid for 1.5 full time equivalent extra TB nurses to work at a centre, screening New Entrants and Asylum Seekers. The approach has been holistic in that people newly arrived are not only screened for TB but advised to register with a GP in the area and given a health check. Although only small numbers of TB positive people have been discovered, the sufferers picked up would have escaped the net in the past prior to the extra nurse's appointment.

Outreach Work
The TB Health Promotion workers have taken the video and promotional material out to a variety of audiences in the borough. The Bed and Breakfast Hostels and Hotels have been addressed on TB. This has included not only the residents but also the Proprietors of the properties. This has raised the profile of TB and the availability of treatment at the chest clinics in the borough.

Due to the ethnic make-up there are a large number of ethnic groups particularly from the African and Asian subcontinents. Often TB is found to be a taboo subject or at the very least a stigma attached to it. Education and information is given to these groups in the format most appropriate to the audience. In the same way Mosques, Temples and other faith groups are also addressed.

Vitamin D Deficiency Research
There appears to be a link between lack of Vitamin D and the susceptibility to the TB germ. Many entrants into

Newham from other countries have dark skin and Vitamin D is produced with the assistance of sunlight. The UK has far less sunlight than either Africa or Asia and often new entrants suffer from a lack of Vitamin D. A research project, funded by the PSA looking at the effect of Vitamin D injections on close family contacts of TB sufferers as a protection from contracting TB, is being undertaken.

Statistical Research and Informing the Solution to TB
In order to deal with the problem of TB in Newham the reasons or possible reasons for its prevalence and its increase need to be understood. Traditionally, poverty, poor diet, poor housing conditions, overcrowding and lack of ventilation are the reasons given. The taskforce felt that it needs to know more about the people suffering from TB and their socio-economic factors as well as information on their housing conditions. As much information as possible is therefore being gathered to enable geographical mapping of data and statistics that help pinpoint some of the areas of work, particularly for Environmental Health, that will enable reduction in TB cases.

Joint Working
The project finished in March 2004. The Borough's Scrutiny Commission have examined how TB in Newham is tackled and have made recommendations that the project should be made sustainable and continue into the future.

All works around the project have been carried out jointly between NHS and Local Authority. Teams on projects have consisted of staff from both employers and a lot of enthusiasm has been put into the campaign. Although not quite there, the targets are well on the way and many other Local Authorities and NHS Regions are keen to replicate the work.

The project overall has shown that with the breaking down of percieved professional barriers between health care workers and environmental health practitioners and the potential differences between employing authoruthy level. PCTs and local authorities in many areas have conterminous boundaries and the coupling of the joint skills and competencies of primary care and council employess working together as health professionals through joint working and tasking gives such a project the synergy so often looked for in solving local health problems.

Source: Steve Miller, Head of Environmental Health & Trading Standards, London Borough of Newham

Food security is under threat as the developed world makes increasing demands for common standards (Lang, 1996; James, 2000) at a time when the world's population is rapidly growing and environmental and socio-economic conditions risk being undermined (DFID, 2000b). There needs to be a renewed focus on food production, sustainability and poverty reduction (James, 2000; DFID, 2000b) so access to decent food is not based solely on ability to pay (IFST, 2000).

One issue of growing concern in the UK has been the increase in illegally imported bush meat (see Box 3.2). The trade in bush meat also presents humanitarian and conservation issues in the countries where bush meat is being harvested to destruction. The trade is simply not sustainable, creating greater food deserts for the indigenous rural communities of Central and Western Africa, where bush meat is an important source of protein, and without which many communities would cease to exist (Bush Meat Task Force, 2000).

Many species of wildlife found within the bush are and have been legally hunted, providing indigenous rural communities with a secure protein source. However, it is illegal to hunt endangered species for bush meat, and subsequent importation into the UK is also illegal. Non-endangered species defined as 'bush meat' can be legally imported into the UK, as long as they comply with food safety importation legislation, and Her Majesty's Customs and Excise Controls. Nevertheless, legal imports of bush meat are extremely rare (UK Bush Meat Campaign, 2000).

Strategic approaches to public health

Government is setting the policy framework nationally so that conditions are right for improving public health – including combating social exclusion, supporting families and tackling housing, education and welfare. Changes at government level include the appointment of a Minister for Public Health, the establishment of the Social Exclusion Unit and Health Development Agency, the introduction of the New Deal for Communities programmes and the consolidation of several government departments into the Office of the Deputy Prime Minister (ODPM) contributing to the public health agenda (see table 2.1).

Emerging organisational and community partnerships are seen as a fundamental shift in defining and delivering services, through an alliance of health promotion, equality, empowerment and enhanced organisational, management and service regimes. Tackling the root causes of poor health and inequalities is vital to underpin local public health action, taking account of national priorities (DoH, 2002a). Such continuing changes are creating the basis for cross-departmental, partnership-based solutions to complex public health issues with professionals and communities working closely together. The nature and culture of local authorities and NHS organisations and the extent to which the new organisations are willing and able to work jointly are seen as key to how successful public health delivery – in all its forms – will be in the future.

Box 3.2 Globalisation and food: Bush meat in the UK

Bush meat is the term used to refer to species of wildlife found predominantly within the forests ('bush') of Africa. Bush meat can include such animals as gorilla, chimpanzee, forest antelope, porcupine, bush pig, cane rat, pangolin, monitor lizard, guinea fowl, land snails, crocodile, bat and various birds (Bush Meat Task Force, 2000).

Access to bush meat in the UK is facilitated through globalisation. Unfortunately, bush meat has the potential to spread disease on a global scale. Scientific evidence concludes that virulent animal-borne diseases can jump between species from non-humans to humans. Therefore the handling, killing and consumption of bush meat exposes individuals and the public at large to such diseases as Ebola, Monkeypox, HIV-1 and many other emerging animal-borne diseases, all of which have the potential to have an impact on global health (Bush Meat Crisis Task Force, 2000). Concerns regarding the illicit trade were further fuelled by the Foot and Mouth epidemic of 2001, which saw strains of the virus type O, Pan-Asia devastate farming communities across the UK. The Origins of the 2001 Foot and Mouth Disease Epidemic report, confirmed that the epidemic was most probably caused by contaminated meat, illegally imported into the UK (DEFRA, 2002a).

The issue of illegal imports of bush meat into the UK is one that has significant ramifications for public health. As a result, a study reviewing the effectiveness and relevance of the Government's Illegal Imports 2002-2003 Action Plan (GAP), and the Food Standards Agency's (10 point) Action Plan (FSAAP), to prevent and prohibit illicit meat imports was conducted, looking specifically at the illegal importation of bush meat into the UK (Manzano, 2003).

Partnership working for food safety
Existing import controls are insufficient, confusing and complex. Co-operation and liaison between agencies remains a significant barrier to effective joined-up action to counter smuggling activities. Consumer demand and the lucrative street value of bush meat, has resulted in a flood of illegal meat imports, engulfing the system, which is enforced by a complex network of agencies including Port Health (PH), Customs and Excise (C&E), Department for Environment, Food and Rural Affairs (DEFRA). Weakness in communication and poor insight into the roles and responsibilities of fellow colleagues from supporting agencies is a major obstacle to effective partnerships. In addition, poor perception of the risks posed by bush meat is evident among the key agencies outlined. Baseline evidence is needed to assess the risks posed by the illicit trade so that

appropriate and effective resources can be targeted and their impact reviewed (Manzano, 2003).
The Origins of the 2001 Foot and Mouth Disease Epidemic report, highlighted significant weaknesses within the imported food control system, one of which was the omission that up until 2001 seizures of illegally imported meat were not recorded, so no evidence existed to notify officials to the extent of the illicit trade; in fact the degrees of public health risk remains contested between organisations such as the Food Standards Agency (FSA), Chartered Institute of Environmental Health, Association of Port Health Authorities and the National Farmers Union. Without risk assessments it remains unclear as to how effective current or future action to prohibit the illicit trade will be in terms of public health.

A fundamental aim of GAP and FSAAP is to improve liaison; co-operation and co-ordination between agencies. Issues surrounding multi-agency work are significant and of particular importance within the imported food control system, due to its complex nature of enforcement and distribution of responsibilities. Collaboration between agencies is therefore essential, improvements have been noted but progress is slow, although agencies are increasingly encouraged to share information and co-ordinate action to target suspected illegal meat consignments both within the port and trans-boundary (where illegal meat imports are commonly destined). Such action is in its infancy and infrequent.

Moving forward: skills and education
Training is an essential element of a progressive system and is undoubtedly lacking within the imported food control system. Training is needed to clarify roles and responsibilities across the enforcement spectrum. It is also imperative that guidance issued, is consistent and integrated with the work of other agencies and that appropriate time is allocated to keep staff at all levels, fully informed.

Accurate identification of seized meat is essential if an evidence base is to be established to facilitate horizontal action across government departments, to tackle the trade from numerous angles. Knowing the type of species commonly imported, and monitoring patterns and changes, will be an invaluable tool aiding any future risk assessments. However, a skills gap is apparent, as identification is multifaceted; products are commonly subjected to unfamiliar killing and preservation methods, and presented in sections, which all further complicate identification.

Port Health Officers (PHOs) have little documentary support to consult to assist in identification and risk assessment, and there is argument for increased resource to enable more proactive sampling and monitoring to aid detection and build on the currently limited evidence base. The FSA have responded to this skills gap to some extent by introducing a series of training sessions, referred to as 'step change' to address training issues in regards to exotic meats.

Figure 3.1 (a) Cane rat; (b) whelly rat.

These animals are clearly unusual in comparison to common meat species. Palpation is not possible as carcesses are commonly very hard due to preservation methods and time since death. This further prohibots the use of smell in the identification process. Without obvious characteristics many items of bush meat remain unidentifiable.

A further issue is that of public awareness. Clearly, poor risk perception is crucial, as those buying bush meat may not be aware of, or understand the implications of their actions; such as potential health risks both to themselves and others. Publicity and education is paramount. To date, DEFRA have issued campaign videos which outline the risks posed by illegally imported meat. The videos are hard hitting, but are having little impact as they have been poorly advertised, had few screenings and are still not available in-flight.

Summary of issues arising from the Research Study

The study by Manzano (2003) highlighted several factors that are restricting the success of both action plans and hampering progression and change within the imported food control system. These are:

- Poor perception of risks posed by bush meat
- Cooperation and liaison between agencies
- Weaknesses in communication.
- Poor professional confidence in work conducted by the FSA
- Skills gap

- Confusion over guidance and delays in dissemination
- Scepticism surrounding ILAPS database, relevance and use of data gathered
- Lack of public awareness of the risks posed by bush meat
- Ineffective powers of search
- Use of detector dogs
- Lack of restriction of point of entry for products of non animal origin

This study suggests that major deficiencies exist within the current imported food control system, which in effect facilitates the illicit bush meat trade. Both GAP and the FSAAP have failed to address the wider socio-economic factors that influence the trade. Such factors are complex and immense, yet overlooked by policy makers and therefore blighting efforts to prohibit the trade (Bowen-Jones, 2002; DEFRA, 2002b). This study concludes that GAP and the FSAAP have not been effective and their impact to date on the illicit trade is debatable. The government has a long way to go to secure border controls and in effect close the door on emerging animal borne diseases which have the potential to impact on global health (Manzano, 2003).

References

Bowen-Jones, E. Brown, D & Robinson, E. (2002) Assessment of the Solution-orientated Research needed to Promote a more Sustainable Bush meat trade in Central and West Africa. DEFRA, Wildlife and Countryside Directorate

Bush Meat Task Force (2000) Eco-Economics & Health & Disease
Available Online from: http://www.bushmeat.org

DEFRA (2002a) Origin of the 2001 Foot and Mouth Disease Epidemic.
Available Online from:
http://www.defra.gov.uk/corporate/inquiries/lessons/fmdorigins.pdf (Accessed on 10/10/02)

DEFRA (2002b) Illegal Imports: Government Action Plan 2002 – 2003. Available Online from:
http://www.defra.gov.uk/news/2002/020328b.htm (Accessed on 10/10/02)

Manzano L. A. (2003) A Review of the Effectiveness and Relevance of the Government's Illegal Imports 2002 – 2003 Action Plan, and the Food Standards Agency's (10 point) Action Plan, in preventing and prohibiting the illicit importation of bush meat into the UK, Undergraduate dissertation submitted as part of the BSc (Hons) Environmental Health at Greenwich University, May 2003. Unpublished

A Corporate strategic approach – the developmental phase

Well-designed strategies have become increasingly important in responding to rapid organisational change in the public sector – notably in forging proactive partnerships and commissioning services – as well as to make greater use of available resource. A good strategic approach can help attract additional resource to an area in an increasingly competitive funding environment and help ensure a co-ordinated approach across like organisations, which are all essentially delivering health improvements. Local authorities have tended to become enablers rather than providers of service, seen to deliver 'customer-focused' services through flatter, less bureaucratic structures. The emphasis is increasingly on the public health agenda of addressing inequalities and exclusion through a client-centred approach, rather than delivering historic, prescribed services driven from the top down.

Local authorities already have many resources necessary for developing and implementing strategies including financial resources, assets, capabilities, knowledge and skills. They are also well placed to nurture and oversee partnerships – which have become paramount in delivering the new public health agenda. Because public health is so complex and multi-faceted, an integrated, partnership approach is essential.

The link between corporate, partnership-based strategy (eg.social inclusion) and issue specific strategies (eg. improving housing conditions in multiply occupied housing) should be a two-way street. Strategic plans need to be integrated in a matrix across the inter- and intra-organisational boundaries. If they are not, they risk being bolted on and probably being not very effective. There are explicit and implicit overlaps and similarities and possible duplication of resources in organisational strategies such as Agenda 21, special care needs, homelessness, area regeneration and equal opportunities. Early joint consultations – in appropriate forums for their different purposes – with parties relevant to different stages of the strategic process are required to assess and maximise everyone's current and future role(s), and collate this into a proper workable strategy identifying where all of the resources will be coming from.

One initial problem can be deciding how to get started. It can be easy to compile too much information, making it difficult to decide the best way forward. Local authorities already have a mass of information that can be pooled from key players and partners in developing and implementing a corporate, workable strategy. This may include both quantitative and qualitative – even impressionistic – data that can help inform choices at regional, sub-regional and local level. There needs to be thorough assessment and analysis of local problems and issues: a health needs assessment. Objectives should be consistent across the organisation and its priorities to help set direction and make clear that changes are needed and why, allowing for different ways of achieving them.

It is essential to consider all options and identify the best approach for tackling those options identified as responding to the to the values, corporate agenda and strategic vision of the organisation(s) involved (for further information see Goss and Blackaby, 1998). This helps establish aims, objectives, targets and output measures and permits prioritisation against available resources. Goss and Blackaby, (1998) suggest that considerations could include:

- costs – both to public and private sector and the knock-on effects;
- impact – both positive and detrimental. Are the benefits sustainable?
- equity – does the option treat people in similar circumstance equally?
- strategic fit – how does it fit into the corporate strategy?
- risk – what are the chances of the option failing, eg unforeseen events?
- acceptability – to politicians, the public and other stakeholders
- ease of implementation – is there over-reliance on others who may not be cooperative? Are additional resources required?
- partnerships – are they viable, realistic and addressing what is needed? Can their presence help attract additional funding?

Whichever way forward is agreed, the initial strategic objectives need to be clear, unambiguous, precise and realistic. (see Table 3.4 and figure 3.2).

• Leadership, teamworking and qualified, dedicated staff
• Corporate and partnership approaches to develop and implement strategy
• Identify problems to be tackled through health needs assessment
• Identify who should be genuinely involved and consulted and how
• Consider and evaluate all options and identify the best approach for tackling problems
• Agree aims, clear objectives, realistic targets and output measures and prioritise against available resource
• Draw up a clear implementation plan
• Develop effective monitoring procedures and ensure regular review
• Regularly review performance against targets and priorities
• Consider publication and promotion of the strategy

Table 3.4
Key points in developing strategies

Based on DoE (1996c), Goss and Blackaby (1998), Stewart (2001)

Figure 3.2
The four fundamental
stages of strategic
development

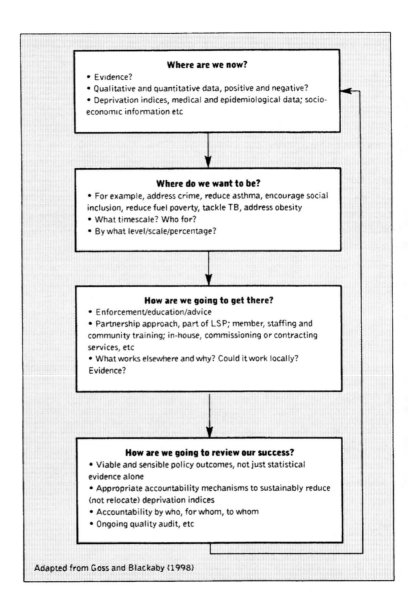

Where are we now?
• Evidence?
• Qualitative and quantitative data, positive and negative?
• Deprivation indices, medical and epidemiological data; socio-economic information etc

Where do we want to be?
• For example, address crime, reduce asthma, encourage social inclusion, reduce fuel poverty, tackle TB, address obesity
• What timescale? Who for?
• By what level/scale/percentage?

How are we going to get there?
• Enforcement/education/advice
• Partnership approach, part of LSP; member, staffing and community training; in-house, commissioning or contracting services, etc
• What works elsewhere and why? Could it work locally? Evidence?

How are we going to review our success?
• Viable and sensible policy outcomes, not just statistical evidence alone
• Appropriate accountability mechanisms to sustainably reduce (not relocate) deprivation indices
• Accountability by who, for whom, to whom
• Ongoing quality audit, etc

Adapted from Goss and Blackaby (1998)

The implementation phase – who and how, with what funding?

Adequate resourcing is fundamental to the whole process. Funding may be cross-organisational or cross-boundary. Resources may need to be collated with other organisations and their budget obligations in partnership arrangements – including, for example, the police, other local authorities, PCTs, voluntary organisations and other agencies. It is important to consider whether the actual decision made is the right one, as there may be other preferable options. For example, can funding come from alternative sources such as the New Deal for Communities (NDC) or the Private Finance Initiative (PFI)? Some options may be mutually exclusive according to the funding possibilities available – for example, it may be preferable to go ahead with housing stock transfer due to accessing funding, although a local authority may ideologically oppose such a course of action.

Different options need to be appraised through discussions and meetings, which rely on quality information being properly presented. Have better solutions been missed? The process should be transparent with the relevant parties properly consulted. The degree of formality in decision-making and subsequent option appraisal depends in many factors, but probably the resources required are the most crucial in determining the preferred option. It is important to consider the preferencess of local people and to evaluate the current provision and the demands that will be placed on local services both now and in the future.

Monitoring and evaluation phase – did it really work?

In any strategy, there needs to be tangible results. There is no point in developing a strategy that looks good on paper, but which does not actually deliver the goods at the coalface. Leadership, consultation, teamworking and qualified, dedicated staff with the right skills are key to a successful strategy. Monitoring success is a continuous process to see if the strategy is proceeding as planned provides and an opportunity to identify the need for remedial action. It may include summaries of customer surveys, demographic data, needs assessments and house condition surveys. This forms a basis of strategic choices and offers supporting analysis for internal and external evaluation. The strategic process must be emphasised. Monitoring is concerned with inputs, processes and outputs and is mainly quantitative.

Monitoring procedures must be effective and tailored to the process. Performance should be regularly reviewed against targets and priorities based on established evidence. Elements of an agreed strategy may have different timescales. For example, a longer-term move toward social inclusion (a process-based strategy) may take a decade – and be driven by government funding and timescales – while other issues such as an aspect of service delivery may change frequently. Close monitoring and review is fundamental so progress can be assessed and adapted if appropriate and any new needs identified catered for. Monitoring of service performance may be annual, bi-annual, quarterly or even monthly.

Evaluation needs to be periodical and carried out at interim and final stages of the programme. It is backward looking and finds out what happened and why. It is concerned with the impact, outcomes and achievement and is both qualitative and quantitative. Evaluation is about asking whether a strategy is really working and this needs to be built in at the objective-setting stage.

Reviews need to be honest. Good strategy is also about learning lessons from past strategies: what worked well and what did not and how this can inform further strategies. The process should be one of exploration and diagnosis rather than simply just checking figures, because reasons behind a strategy are complex. There is no point is driving through a strategy that has failed to understand a changing environment, or has been granted the wrong resource, or that has misdiagnosed a problem in the first place. Money used should be well spent. Reporting of performance against objectives is vital and should be open to public scrutiny. For further information see Goss and Blackaby (1998).

Partnership working in public health: statutory organisations and local communities

Hutchinson and Campbell (1998: 2) suggest that partnerships are valuable to:
- bring together a range of interests from more than one sector;
- seek to develop common aims and a strategy to achieve them;
- share risks, resources and skills;
- seek to achieve mutual benefit and synergy.

In addition, good management and sustained resourcing is necessary for partnerships to be successful and able to perform to their full potential.

The partnership process has become pivotal to strategic development in the government's modernisation agenda, its implementation and accountability in recent years to address a wide range of social and economic issues. Organisations increasingly have to show that they are offering comprehensive, partnership-based strategies to attract government funding. The DETR (2000i) described local authority partnership as a 'process in which a local authority works together with partners to achieve better outcomes for the local community, as measured by the needs of the local stakeholders, and involves bringing together or making better use of resources [requiring] the development of a commitment to a shared agenda, effective leadership, a respect for the needs of the partners, and a plan for the contributions and benefits of all the partners.' The process requires specific goals to be identified and performance to be evaluated and a reassessment of the link between activities and needs or priorities.

By its nature, environmental health is multi-disciplinary. Informal and formal partnerships have existed for many years, although the momentum has recently shifted as a result of reports such as *Agendas for Change* (Environmental Health Commission, 1997) which called for new co-operative, partnership-based activity to nurture sustainable change by recognising the many existing positive aspects of environmental health work and the need to reintegrate public and environmental health with clearer local accountability. This new approach took a holistic perspective to encourage interdependence and inter-collectiveness to help broaden concerns and perceptions of new links through a revision of traditional professionalisms able to respond to rapidly evolving public and organisational expectations. Such an approach was seen as flexible, inclusive and task orientated – to help find sensible solutions to overlapping problems. (see Table 3.5).

• Problems tackled are common ones in which all participants have a stake • Not only government agencies but all organisations with an interest are involved • Policy-makers, technical and service staff and volunteers at national and local level have functions to perform • Various participants play leading or peripheral roles • Co-operation in defining proposals, issues, prioritising need, information, considering alternatives, building capabilities for implementation • Stable co-operative mechanisms are established, nurtured and revised

Table 3.5
Issues in partnership working

(Source: MacArthur 1999: 5)

Partners come in many shapes and forms and consultation arrangements need to address the timing and purpose of joint working to maximise partnership potential. Partnerships may operate within or outside of organisations, and be on a statutory or non-statutory footing. Those involved include:

- councillors – eg by workshops or seminars;
- corporate board or management team – for consensus and support for action, replanning of resources;
- strategy, commissioning and service staff across various departments – eg may incorporate social services officers for joint commissioning purposes, planning and housing staff in respect of using of brownfield sites, land release and transport policies, tenure diversification, economic development, rural area etc;
- other neighbouring local authorities or county councils where not a unitary authority;
- PCTs;
- potential partners in other statutory, non-governmental, voluntary and private sectors as well as community-based organisations;
- community representatives, residents, etc – eg consult via post, focus groups, special meetings, exhibitions, village appraisals, community profiling, listening surveys, etc.

How successful can partnerships be expected to be?

Establishing and maintaining partnerships is not always as straightforward as it might seem and outcomes are not automatic (Hutchinson and Campbell, 1998). Professions and organisations have different roots, objectives and priorities and may see intersectoral collaboration as a threat to their own roles and funding regimes. There may be discrepancies in priorities, legislative requirements and joint assessments, as well as in the ideologies and values of different organisations. There may be difficulties in deciding who holds – or who thinks that they hold – the ultimate responsibility, rather than finding viable joint solutions to joined-up problems or even none (Cowan, 1999). There may be increasing bureaucratic hierarchies, leading to confusion and duplication of functions as individual organisations risk becoming less certain of their evolving role, particularly with so many short term public health projects seeming to take precedence over longer-term strategies. Crucially, will they really be able to achieve what more traditional organisations could not apparently achieve? There can be no guarantee that they will actually work, timescales may be limited and constant appraisal is required to ensure that resources invested are used wisely.

Effective partnerships need to operate on a variety of levels to 'add value' to what is already there (Hutchinson and Campbell, 1998). The organisational level – such as the local authority or PCT – is only one stage of the process. What is really important is how professionals work together in overcoming barriers and delivering change. There are invariably power struggles and tensions involved (Hudson, 2002; Hutchinson and Campbell, 1998; University of the West of England, Bristol and the Office for Public Management, 1999) as different professions vie for their own status and boundaries, particularly at a time of such change and where so many are involved in delivering public health objectives. Allied to this is the extent to which professionals – particularly at the local authority level – are willing to dynamically share power with local communities, crucial to establishing democratic and accountable policy processes. (see Table 3.6).

Table 3.6
Establishing partnerships: overcoming barriers

Barriers to partnerships
- Existing government legislation (focus on national initiatives may divert resources from local priorities)
- Financial constraints
- Cultural factors (resistance to change, lack of willingness or clarity)
- Insufficient resources – including time and staffing for co-ordination,
- Difficulties in selecting measures that could be attributed to the partnership alone
- Lack of clear criteria that are appropriate and quantifiable against which to measure success
- Lack of recognition of the importance of evaluation

Overcoming barriers to partnership
- Shared vision and commitment (supported by shared data, agreed priorities, joint service planning and review)
- Good leadership
- Clear objectives, roles and responsibilities (clear purpose and evaluation, benefits for all, identification of each partners aims)
- Using member resources more effectively
- Changing organisational structure
- Commitment, honesty and trust, understanding limitations and culture of partners, willingness to share advantages and disadvantages
- Skills of partner representative (decision-makers, enthusiastic, professional, efficient, innovative and open-minded)
- Well trained and motivated staff to deliver high-quality services

Based on Goss and Blackaby (1998), DETR (2000j)

Despite some emerging concerns about partnership working, the drive for partnerships is legislatively and resource based as the government has sought to maintain momentum as part of the modernisation agenda. Currently, the key issues within environmental health departments – working in partnership with other organisations – need to be able to address are inequality and sustainability, paramount to the government's health and inclusion agendas. Partnership working includes working with other allied health and social care organisations to help ensure long-term, sustainable change.

IDeA has developed 'Beacon Scheme' status for the operation of local health strategies, together with the key features and critical success factors required. These are summarised in Tables 3.7 and 3.8.

Table 3.7
IDeA's 'Beacon Scheme' for local health strategies

- Excellent grasp of health and commitment to the health agenda
- Addressing health inequalities (including health poverty profiling) and improving health by creatively targeting disadvantage
- demonstration of strong and wide-ranging consultation, esp. hard to reach groups
- Clear vision, aims, targets, processes and outcomes for health improvement strategy, approach clearly documented and presented, active monitoring of outcomes and ability to demonstrate where change has occurred
- Good partnership working across cross-agency planning and pooled budgets; strong links to other strategies (eg HIMPs (now LDPs), community regeneration)

Tables 3.8
Key features and success criteria of 'Beacon' councils' local health strategies

Key features
- Recognition of wider determinants of health and the role of mainstream council services in tackling them
- Effective interagency partnerships focusing on heath, leading the development and implementation of plans and strategies
- Effective officer implementation group in place to deliver the health agenda and the use of jointly funded posts and units to support implementation
- Effective analysis of health issues; specific programmes, initiatives and targets set for reducing health inequalities
- Well developed integrated planning and services delivery across health and social care services
- Training and development support to members engaging in the health agenda

Critical success factors
- Using relevant policy documents in modernisation, health inequalities and social exclusion
- Development of a shared vision and clear strategy
- Member commitment
- Recognition of the importance of the public health function
- Willingness to take risks and learn
- An effective process for developing and supporting partnerships through and commitment to inclusiveness and resourcing partnership development

Source: IDeA (2000), in Hamer and Easton (2002)

Partnerships with communities

Local authorities and PCTs exist to serve communities, though until recently communities have had few opportunities to be able to participate in decisions being made about them and for them. The emphasis has tended to be about the local authority or PCT determining its community's health and need and making remote decisions about making improvements. It may be that an organisation's understanding of the concepts of health and need are quite removed from the community's, a key issue in seeking to develop sensitive and appropriate policy. The community voice has become increasingly important to policy-making, implementation and accountability in recent years, but neglect of participation in the past means that much work will be needed to start to engender new forms of local participation where communities lie at the heart of decision-making processes.

Community empowerment is crucial to establishing democratic and accountable policy processes. Empowering communities requires developing new participatory frameworks to take a wide overview of activities undertaken on behalf of that community, resulting in better decisions being made, enabling influence – or even control – over decision making (Arnstein, cited in Gaster and Taylor, 1993; Taylor et al, 1992; Taylor, 1995). This is figuratively represented by the 'Ladder of Participation' where at the bottom

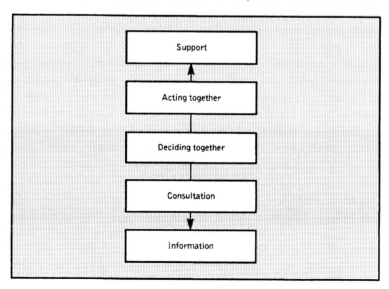

Figure 3.3
Communities at the heart of decision-making: the Ladder of Participation – based on Arnstein, cited in Taylor (1995)

stage, state organisations simply provide information about what they are doing, to the top stage of participation where communities and the state share power, with local authority and PCTs supporting self-identified community development initiatives. (see Figure 3.3).

Communities and professionals need to learn from each other as both have much to offer policy development. Communities have the grassroots knowledge of how they operate and which direction they might like to take. Professionals have knowledge of policy processes. Professionals may need to develop skills to facilitate citizen empowerment and question their own (perhaps unknown) prejudices and judgements about people's lives. This may not be popular, and may be seen as a challenge to 'professional' status. In this way policies can be developed that are relevant to the very people they seek to serve, and are able to tackle each situation uniquely without imposing a standardised solution. Government organisations need this 'expert knowledge' from communities.

Community partnerships are fundamental to social inclusion and finding joined-up solutions to joined-up problems. Community partnership processes can help yield more accountable, democratically based services that respond to local needs, especially where the voluntary sector and existing social capital can realistically operate to fill in gaps in state provision where appropriate. Forging community partnerships is part of bottom-up, rather than top-down, policy-making to increase local confidence and capacity in delivering sustainable, sensitive and appropriate services. This is a fundamental part of moving toward a process of social inclusion rather than a defined end product. Developing community capacity and capital in this way is key to a long-term strategy to address exclusion and finding what support communities need to instigate their own solutions. State organisations needs to support local capacity, not assume they know best what the community needs.

Involving the community is not always straightforward. The community may have preconceptions about local authorities that relate to earlier negative experiences, or have their own agenda – and the early stages of developing a relationship and mutual trust are crucial. It is important to consider at what stage, why, who should be consulted and how – and indeed about what. Many communities are exhausted with constant consultation that seems to lead nowhere. Such attitudes may need to be turned around which can be done – and with dramatic effect. Methods include surveys, telephone surveys, focus groups, citizens juries and community conferences. What is the balance of different needs in the community? There needs to be negotiation and consensus building. It is important to consider and to be prepared for a realistic amount of feedback in relation to the groups(s) selected and how they are asked for their views – there may be a better way of doing it. Such an approach must be ongoing.

Communities are increasingly seen as crucial to informing the policy process to redress inequalities at a very local level (Naidoo and Wills, 2000) and to driving change where its need is really felt. This is because those in greatest need of health services often have least access to them. Poor physical and mental health, age and ethnic groups can prevent social and economic participation. This must be recognised and taken on board in the policy process.

Current health improvement policy favours community participation as a pivotal force in bringing positive change for the following reasons (cited in Campbell and Mclean, 2002):

- The participation of grassroots community representatives in decisions regarding designs and delivery of health services is vital to address differential access, cultural differences, racism, language, etc as barriers to socially excluded groups.
- Local people should participate in health promotion projects designed to promote healthy behaviour – people are more likely to change if they see their peers changing their behaviour.
- There is growing recognition of the influence of neighbourhood conditions on health and that participation in local community networks has a positive impact on health.

Social exclusion and inclusion: Assessing inequality and moving forwards
In his speech at Stockwell Park School, Lambeth, Prime Minister Tony Blair (1997), recognising and responding to multiple disadvantage and deprivation as part of a wider programme of social reform, said:

'Social exclusion is about income but it's about much more. It's about prospects and networks and life chances. It's a very modern problem, and one that's more harmful to the individual, more damaging to self-esteem, more corrosive for society as a whole, more likely to be passed down from generation to generation than material poverty.'

Social exclusion comprises a form of static, stagnant lifestyle and experience that is difficult to escape by individual action alone. Clapham et al (1990) argue that markets and institutions continually reinforce disadvantage: because social exclusion is caused by and results from interconnected issues these must be identified and addressed to bring real, sustainable change.

The London Voluntary Service Council (1998) see social exclusion as a matter of 'barriers' preventing full access to society, consisting of discrimination (including disability), poverty, employment, fear of crime, and a lack of access to decent transport, education, health provision, childcare and housing. A combination of these barriers – together with a constant struggle on a low-income – results in an undermining of citizenship rights and relationships leading to feelings of powerlessness. It is difficult for individuals to overcome these barriers alone: social mobility is limited as poverty and barriers to inclusion tend to repeat across generations. Additionally, Balchin and Rhoden (2002) suggest that self-exclusion may occur in black and Asian communities which may have different lifestyles, values and beliefs to the rest of society leading to racial harassment in some neighbourhoods.

However, establishing agreement on what constitutes poverty and social exclusion among academics and policy-makers remains elusive. Social exclusion can happen when individuals or areas suffer from a combination of linked problems – poverty, poor housing, low educational standards, unemployment/low pay, fear of crime and isolation. People lack the means to participate effectively in social, political and cultural life. The environment needs to be safe, secure and sustainable.

Inequality and deprivation grew during the 1980s: there was a rise in low-income households; more children lived in poverty; there were higher rates of unemployment among young adults and an inability to find employment;

there were more pensioners on low incomes/benefits; and disadvantage was increasingly concentrated in certain communities (Balchin, 1995; Howarth et al, 1999; JRF, 1999). However, the then government did not acknowledge 'social exclusion', a term that by then had found wider recognition in much of Europe (Spicker, 2002), and the related concept of an 'underclass' was also gaining momentum (cited in Payne et al, 1996). Social exclusion is not just about poverty but the degree to which groups of people are excluded from lack of access to mainstream society – such as through access to employment and services.

It was not until the Labour government was elected that the Social Exclusion Unit was established in 1997 as a fundamental policy area to address the root causes of inequality and deprivation in order to nurture sustainable living environments and relationships and thereby encourage social inclusion. Policy needs to be able to respond to the complex interrelationships between barriers to enable social inclusion. The government has since instigated many policy initiatives across departments and organisations to address socio-economic exclusion. Traditional one-dimensional strategies are no longer seen as appropriate: joined-up solutions are required to respond to the joined-up causes and impacts of social exclusion and this could be best addressed by a bottom-up approach. Progress of a range of policies such as the New Deal for Communities (See box 2.2) can be monitored by a system of baseline indicators and outcomes, rather than fixed statistics. A sustainable, dynamic response – rather than short-term, high-profile projects – is required to tackle social exclusion as this is the best way for government and communities to jointly address integrated issues including social policy, employment opportunities, area-based poverty and lifestyle. It is useful to explore how inclusive societies and communities operate and learn lessons from this.

Measuring the excluded: poverty, inequality and deprivation indices

Poverty is a politically contested term, and may refer to absolute or relative poverty. The United Nation's (UN) Mary Robinson – in its decade for the eradication of poverty – sees poverty as a denial of fundamental human rights. The European Union (EU) defines poverty in terms of excluding individuals and families from a minimally acceptable way of life in each member state. UK incomes have become increasingly polarised since the Thatcher administrations, and the UK now has the highest rate of child poverty in the EU in terms of crude income, worsened by the complexities of the benefit system and the poverty trap and expressed as health inequality, putting a major burden on the NHS (cited in Gordon, 2002).

Tony Blair has stated his commitment to eradicate poverty in 20 years as a key part of reducing health inequality, enabling people to participate fully in society. Combating poverty and social exclusion is a government priority, but one for which is difficult to quantify, monitor and evaluate progress, particularly when issues are so interrelated and often qualitative rather than quantitative. Such a policy therefore requires rigorous, scientifically valid measures of success (Gordon, 2002; Bradshaw, 2002).

The first difficulty is finding concensus in definitions of both poverty and social exclusion, which vary according to socio-political (class and cultural) systems in different countries. In the UK, social exclusion is currently defined in terms of multiple deprivation and what happens to individuals or communities who suffer linked problems including unemployment, poor skills, low income, poor housing, a high crime environment, bad health and family breakdown. For this reason, the inclusion agenda relates to topics such as school exclusion, teenage pregnancy and deprived urban areas (Spicker, 2002). It is likely that indices of deprivation – representing differential opportunities for access to consumption – are to assume greater importance in the research agenda than more conventional or theoretical class analysis of inequality in the future (Payne et al, 1996).

There is little doubt that exclusion manifests as poor health, but how can this be accurately reported? Previous indicators of social deprivation have included the DoE Local Conditions Indices, Townsend, Jarman and Breadline Britain, each of which include some different indicators for different purposes. The New Policy Institute initially set up indicators to help monitor social exclusion through a series of baseline statistics covering 1996 – 7, grouped according to lifestyle rather than types of problem (such as employment difficulties) and commenting on whether the situation was steady, improving or worsening (Howarth et al, 1999).

The government has recently introduced the Index of Multiple Deprivation (IMD) to provide a measure of deprivation for every ward and local authority area in England. It combines several indicators covering a range of domains – income, employment, health deprivation and disability, education skills and training, housing and geographical access to services – into a single deprivation score for each area, which is designed to be comparable by area, as well as over time (DETR, 2000g; 2000h). However, this approach is geographically biased and some individuals living in poverty elsewhere may miss out (Gordon, 2002). Additionally, there are few overlaps between such poverty measures in government poverty indicators, which may reinforce anxieties about income as the only measure of poverty, and a broader base measure of poverty and well-being would have the capacity to incorporate overlaps and opportunity for all (Bradshaw, 2002).

Additionally – and at the time of writing – other information sources are under development to support *Saving Lives: Our Healthier Nation* (DoH, 1999a) and *the NHS Plan* (DoH, 2000a). The HDA Evidence Base (HDA, 2002a) aims to provide the best available information on what works to improve health and reduce inequality. This includes circulating policy and practice information – including reviews, research reports and journal articles, Internet sites, expert opinion, government guidance and research databases that help promote public health and reduce health inequalities. Work remains ongoing to provide systematic research and reviews of effectiveness. The ODPM is also seeking to make better use of data by ensuring that ONS Housing Census presentation is 'joined up' and that projects are increasingly consolidated as part of wider reporting.

The Joseph Rowntree Foundation Poverty and Social Exclusion Survey

The Joseph Rowntree Foundation (JRF), in September 2000, published a report on *Poverty and Social Exclusion (PSE) in Britain* and used income, lack of necessities and subjective measures of poverty (Gordon et al, 2000). It was the first national study to attempt to measure social exclusion. It confirmed that poverty rates had risen sharply. In 1983, 14 per cent of households lacked three or more necessities because they could not afford them. This rose to 21 per cent in 1990 and 24 per cent in 1999. By the end of 1999, 26 per cent of the British population were living in poverty, 9.5 million people in Britain could not afford adequate housing, 7.5 million people were too poor to engage in common social activities, 2 million British children went without at least two things they needed, 6.5 million adults went without essential clothing, 4 million were not properly fed,

10.5 million suffered from financial insecurity and 1 in 6 considered themselves to be living in absolute poverty.

Gordon et al (2002) established a set of deprivation indices and linked this to a standard of living scale using reliable objective and subjective measures. This sought to test the validity of each method in scientifically determining how poverty is perceived by personal and political opinion as seen in terms of an enforced lack of socially perceived necessities. This was felt necesssary in an attempt to realistically depict the lived and felt experience of poverty (Gordon et al, 2000; Gordon, 2002). They distinguished four dimensions of social exclusion as:

- impoverishment (exclusion from adequate income or resource; eg low income expressed as receipt of income support);
- labour market exclusion;
- service exclusion (eg no access to transport, doctor); and
- Exclusion from social relationships (eg common social activities such as ability to visit sick people in hospital or to give children birthday presents – a more subjective poverty).

These interrelated factors need to be taken into account in policy leading to a socially inclusive society.

The PSE sought to ask: *how poor is poor?* as well as to take a complexity of factors into account in order to provide a more comprehensive basis for policy-making. Measuring income alone is not particularly scientifically valid or comparable in itself and there are variables between households and their expenditure – notably in London where household expenditure has a substantial impact on income – as well as within households where parents may be defined as poor, but their children not as their parents protect them from its consequences (Bradshaw, 2002). Additionally, poverty is not just about low income, but is also about a *low income which causes a low standard of living* (Gordon, 2002). It is dynamic, not static, and people move both into and out of poverty.

The PSE survey results showed that – at the dawn of the 21st century and as perceived by the majority of the population – 25 per cent of Britains were living in poverty and 9.5 million could not afford adequate housing conditions or have access to decent food. Poverty was found to have become more widespread, but not necessarily more extreme since the 1990s. Their research challenged many current theories of social exclusion, particularly the relative weightings of government resource allocation biased toward areas of high deprivation indices rather than individuals, but also aggravated by wider fiscal policy of indirect taxation, etc.

The PSE research found that poverty can be measured in a scientifically valid way but that a complex measurement is needed. Exclusion can be measured in relation to poverty, other responsibilities, the ability to participate, access to services, relationship to the labour market and the quality and quantity of social networks. Fuller findings of the research are due to be published by the Joseph Rowntree Foundation, but cannot be incorporated into this book.

Housing and social exclusion
Although social exclusion has been particularly identified with certain social housing estates, this approach may result in further stigmatisation and labelling of social housing itself as an excluding agent, rather than simply a location of poverty and deprivation (Joseph Rowntree Foundation, 1999). It is relatively easy to map geographically deprived communities and point to excluding features such as the Index of Multiple Deprivation (IMD) and 'estate culture' such as drug-taking, anti-social behaviour and norms different to the rest of society (cited in Balchin and Rhoden, 2002). Equally deprived households are located elsewhere – such as in bed and breakfast temporary accommodation – and may miss out on necessary support (Joseph Rowntree Foundation, 1999).

Many see housing as fundamental as it is the living environment that can be key to health and life chances and should no longer just represent a 'bricks and mortar' approach (see, for example, Boxes 2.2, 3.3 and 5.5). There is a relationship between poor housing environment, motivation and the willingness to work (Balchin and Rhoden, 2002) which needs to be addressed by government policy if socio-economic attributes are to be improved and communities empowered (CIH, 1998; Power, 1993 and 1999). Speakers at Homeless International's (1998) conference argued that housing should lie at the heart of inclusion and pointed to the importance of a dynamic policy response, which recognises the need for the following:

Box 3.3 Exclusion to Inclusion: Stonebridge Park, London Borough of Brent

Stonebridge Park was conceived in the 1950s and constructed in the late 1960s as an innovative multi-storey design to house large numbers and provide new local amenities, seen as an ultra-modern, ideal environment replacing drab Victorian houses in narrow street layouts (Brent Civic Review, 1967; Cameron, 1967). However, even by the early 1970s, Stonebridge Park had become stigmatised, as new residents protested against architecture and design faults, nuisance from children, vandalism and urination in common parts, noise, dampness and flooding of landings and walkways and by the 1990s, some saw the area as a housing disaster with high levels of crime and drugs.

Even by 1978, Brent Council had set up pilot projects to respond to increasing concerns about tenants' difficulties in living in high-rise, high-density areas and concerns about allocation policies. Resident profile was skewed by both age and ethnicity, with around two thirds of residents either under 16 years, or over retirement age. Unemployment was around four times the national average, incomes generally were low and most residents claimed income-related benefit (London Borough of Brent, 1982; Inside Housing, 1994; Sherrington, 2000; Stonebridge HAT, 2000). See table 3.9

Table 3.9 Facts and figures on the Stonebridge estate around the commencement of the Housing Action Trust

- Mixed race population with a very high level of social, economic and environmental problems
- Highest unemployment rate in Brent – 29% according to the 1991 census; the average being 13.2%
- Rent arrears at 48%, twice the rate of the rest of the borough
- Void level at 1.6% compared to 1% borough average
- Average time to re-let properties of 97 days, compared to 83 days elsewhere
- Homeless families refusing homes on the estate due to its poor reputation
- More recorded crime than any other estate in Brent – 142 allegations per 1,000 people, 1/3 being burglary between 1992 –3
- Third highest level of single parent households in the borough at 16%
- In January 1994, 63% residents on housing benefit
- Only 3% residents owner occupiers

(Source: Inside Housing, 1994)

It was clear that the estate needed major regeneration investment but local authority capital and revenue budgets were simply inadequate to address not only the poor housing, but also wider socio-economic decline.

Regeneration was made possible in the mid 1990s as part of the Housing Action Trust policy (which has now been superceded) and Stonebridge fulfilled the HAT criteria of having high levels of social, economic and environmental problems. There was more recorded crime there than for any other estate in Brent in 1992-3, with 142 allegations per 1,000 people, 17 per cent of residents were unemployed and 70 per cent had an income of less than £200 per week. Over 15 per cent of households were headed by lone parents and 57 per cent of residents claimed housing benefit (Sherrington, 2000; Stonebridge HAT, 2000). The estate was ethnically diverse, the 6,000 strong population made up of 25 per cent Caribbean, 25 per cent black British, 21 per cent African, 24 per cent white and 4 per cent Asian. The age of the population is skewed, with around two thirds of residents either under 16 years, or over retirement age. Tenants were requesting transfer at around twice the rate of non-similar council housing stock in other parts of the Borough.

A shadow HAT was established to develop a relationship with tenants, but the actual HAT was not declared until 1994. With some £165 million funding from rental income and the then Department of the Environment over 10 years, and a possible additional £50 million from the Private Finance Initiative to bridge the funding gap, Stonebridge HAT now had a varied team of staff to regenerate the estate and provide new opportunities. Following a survey and consultation with tenants, works completed on the first phase of redevelopment by 2000 to provide low-rise mixed tenure units to replace the 1,775 1960s and 1970s built concrete panel tower blocks (Sherrington, 2000). The regeneration is primarily very visual, but tenants are also fundamental in bringing long term regeneration to the area and recent surveys continue to show that the fear of crime has dropped and that people increasingly want to remain on the estate.

Tenants have a regular chance to participate in the regeneration, including through the Stonebridge Tenants Advisory Committee (STAC) and other structures such as boards, sub-committees and block-based Tenants Associations as well as Youth and Older People's Forums. The HAT has found that giving tenants real choice encourages active engagement. For example, the new homes were deliberately built so that tenants could design the interior – choosing small internal rooms, or one larger room, and having a choice of amenities and decoration and even agreeing road names. Such involvement also enabled a new relationship to emerge between HAT, developer and tenants, through a mutual learning process.

The HAT is committed to supporting individuals as part of a wider process of inclusion. It is increasing employment opportunities by offering basic skills training, contractually supporting, training (through partnership with local colleges and training providers) and using local labour to help provide longer term opportunities, offering self-employment services and Stonebridge Training Employment Project (STEP) offers IT training, childcare, a learning centre and so on. The Residents Resource Centre has helped 1,100 people find work or vocational training through setting up a local labour register, links with local employment agencies and running training programmes. The Resident Participation Team supports people on the estate and other initiatives such as include community organisations, young people producing their own magazine, funding for health workers and drug advice centres as well as initiatives to cut crime (Stonebridge HAT, 1997; Sherrington, 2000).

Being within Brent Council, Stonebridge HAT is able to access wider regeneration opportunities, notably the Harlesden Health Action Zone, part of the Social Regeneration Scheme to improve both health and the environment. Through local links, such as with Community Health Action Stonebridge, community groups are able to engage in mutual learning and share skills to promote holistic health such as through growing vegetables, healthy eating, local arts events and attending courses. This is to be funded by the Department for Education and Employment's (DFEE) Sure Start budget and bidding to the Healthy Living Centres Lottery Project for £1 million. The new health centre and community centre in Stonebridge is to be funded by partnership with the HAT and the local PCT.

Acknowledgement:
This is part of a paper that was first published in Stewart J and Rhoden M (2003) 'A review of social housing regeneration in the London Borough of Brent' in Journal of the Royal Society for the Promotion of Health March 2003, 123 (1) pp. 23 – 32.

References
Brent Civic Review (1967). The Changing Face of Stonebridge. *Brent Civic Review* 1965 – 75; January 1967 No. 7. Unpublished.
Cameron B (1967). Stonebridge '72 – An £8m. Space-age project for 2,000 new homes. *Wembley Mercury*; 13 January 1967.
Inside Housing (1991) Tenants on Brent estate throw HAT in the ring. *Inside Housing*; 4 October 1991, 1.
Inside Housing (1994) Facts and Figures on the Stonebridge estate. *Inside Housing*; 15 April 1994, 11.
London Borough of Brent (1982). *Who Lives Where? A survey of tenancies on Chalkhill, South Kilburn and Stonebridge Estates.* London Borough of Brent, May 1982. Unpublished.
Sherrington M (2000). As you like it. *Inside Housing*; 18 February 2000, 34 – 35.
Stonebridge Housing Action Trust (1997). *Working together for a better Stonebridge.* London: Stonebridge HAT.
Stonebridge HAT (2000) *Transforming Stonebridge. A partnership with residents for lasting change.* London:

• Housing to be looked at as an ongoing process in people's lives, not just a series of ever-changing projects since housing and the elimination of poverty are clearly interlinked in a way that many other social policy areas are not;

• professionals to support the people, not vice versa, to help restore a sense of dignity, pride and ownership;

• recognition of the importance of the direction and mindset of the government and professionals as part of a process, not just as a solution – support is not the same as intervention, and professionals can easily take over the people's process without even realising;

- ensuring that policy response rewards productive dynamism, not passivity;
- community resources need to be mobilised and energised to establish a foothold in the policy-making agenda as a central point of tackling poverty; and
- once housing regeneration is underway, other issues of community can be taken on board and may follow naturally without having to be forced, because change is already positive.

The role of housing in tackling exclusion requires a bottom-up approach whereby policy to support community initiatives through long-term sustainable, holistic solutions is required, not just high profile examples. The emphasis needs to be on prevention and it requires huge resource investment. As the CIH (1998: 2) points out:

'The creation of mixed, inclusive communities, in the right location and within easy reach of a range of facilities and services [that communities] need is essential to avoid creating new areas of exclusion.'

Meanwhile, policy needs to encourage and support bottom-up, community-driven solutions and nurture existing social capital, as well as to encourage further community development to yield sustainable change. Housing is one key policy area where such change can be delivered, but perhaps more easily through social than through private sector housing as housing management is already established.

Social Capital
Why social capital?
The *Saving Lives* White Paper (DoH, 1999a) recognised the complex nature of health solutions, including broader social, cultural, economic, political and physical environments in respect of health and well-being. It was argued that a social approach to health organisation and delivery may have considerable potential for health improvement, especially in deprived communities. Social capital is one 'construct' which could allow the social approach to health to be improved – but it is only one part of the process of strengthening marginal communities and reducing health inequalities, and must be accompanied by wider fiscal and regeneration policies to have the optimum chance of improving health (Campbell and McLean, 2002; Cattrell and Herring, 2002;

Swann and Morgan, 2002). Any action needs to be taken with caution and sensitivity, as poverty can undermine community networks and relationships.

What is social capital?

Social capital includes social relations, resources and networks in civil society that help formulate and maintain collective community action. Social capital is a community attribute, where grassroot community networks – rather than state organisations – yield mutual benefit, local identity and shared norms, a sense of belonging and membership, trust, reciprocal help and support, capacity and assets, civic engagement as well as formal and informal networks. The resources which arise benefit individuals as well as communities in achieving positive outcomes in health and well-being (Health Development Agency, 2002b; Morrow, 2002; Sirianni and Friedland, undated; Swann and Morgan, 2002; Social Capital Formation, 2001; Putnam, 1993, 2000).

Social capital has become increasingly important in the inclusion agenda and key to public health as communities at a very low level can be innovative, productive and positive, which can have a snowballing effect. However, policies must be able to take into account differences in communities (particularly deprived communities) in creating, sustaining and accessing social capital as well as how social capital relates differently to different age groups, gender and ethnic groups, so as not to culturally favour middle classes over marginal communities which are discussed later (Blaxter and Poland, 2002; Campbell and McLean, 2002; Swann and Morgan, 2002).

Building a thriving participatory community takes time, opportunities, facilities, motivation and effective empowerment – there are no guarantees that people will wish to engage, although policy is increasingly directed here (eg the enabling state, third way, joined-up thinking, etc). There are limits to, and complexity of, the extent to which poor people can be expected to cooperate with reciprocal aid and so on (Cattrell and Boneham, 2002; Blaxter and Poland, 2002). Such differences in social capital in different contexts must be sensitively responded to and the government role may nurture and create or even erode what is there (Blaxter and Poland, 2002).

Assumptions must not be made that all deprived communities have depleted social capital, or that it operates similarly in different areas, or that communities would be willing or able to participate more actively. Social capital must not be relied upon for everything. The role of sustained state services is also important in health-related fiscal and regeneration policy – living conditions (built environments, area reputation, low-income, etc) are stronger predictors of health than measures of social capital and support (Cattrell and Boneham, 2002; Swann and Morgan, 2002).

Putnam (1993, 2000), a key influence in the social capital debate, suggests that social capital consists of informal networks (family and friends), spatial networks (people known in the neighbourhood), voluntary networks (eg sports clubs, religious activities) and formal community networks (linked to local government). These networks, norms and trust embodied in social relations facilitate co-ordination and co-operation for mutual benefit to pursue shared objectives.

Putnam identifies different forms of social capital as bonding, binding and bridging, and Morrow (2002) additionally identifies linking social capital. For Putnam, social capital can be investigated by exploring several indicators including levels of membership in clubs/societies, time spent socialising, time spent in reciprocal activities, beliefs/norms about the intentions of others, and the extent of friendship and networks. Factors eroding social capital include a lack of time, disruption of family ties, poverty, residential mobility, suburbanisation, changes in economic structure, and the generational effect in the pattern of social capital decline.

However, there are some difficulties in concensus in definition. Blaxter and Poland's (2002) research into the relationship of social capital to health – the context in which it is most commonly defined – found ambiguity, complexity, and conflict in the definition and concepts of social capital for the researcher, community and individual as well as the relationships within communities and the state. It is difficult to identify any precise notion of community social capital, and it is commonly represented as personal social capital. It is about conflict as well as negotiation. It is essential that networks are not measured in crude terms, as this would present crude results. The importance of the social, political, economic – and also dynamic – context of the group being studied should be considered.

Campbell et al (1999) and Sixsmith and Boneham (2002) suggest that in areas abundant in social capital:

- individuals feel an obligation to help others, and those in need, as personal networks support link individuals, households and peer groups;
- there is a willingness and capacity to make use of community resources, especially where provided by the state, evidenced for example by health service systems;
- individuals exhibit more trust and less fear in interacting with others in the community, manifested in positive attitudes toward personal interactions, and the use of communal facilities, with a sense of belonging;
- communities rich in social capital are also socially cohesive, co-operative and caring as people work together for mutual benefit.

Social capital and health: developing an evidence base

Social capital has the potential to explain how community factors may influence health and buffer against the worst effects of deprivation (Swann and Morgan, 2002), although the evidence base for this is minimal. The possible links between social capital and health are defined in terms of grassroots participation in local community networks and how social exclusion affects social capital (Campbell and McLean, 2002), but there is insufficient research and evidence into the lived experience of deprived and disadvantaged UK communities (Sixsmith and Boneham, 2002). Indicators of communities low in social capital can be isolated, suspicious, reluctant to participate in social, economic and political life. They may exhibit a breakdown of social fabric (Sixsmith and Boneham, 2002).

The decline of social capital: implications for health

It has been argued that social capital is in decline (Putnam, 2000, Cattrell and Herring, 2002). If social capital has declined over generations, are there implications for health? Cattrell and Herring (2002) argue that the effect of a pleasant environment on health in breaking down barriers and facilitating integration must not be overlooked. They also report the limits to mutuality and the crucial need for sustained state services. People need to be seen as active agents, not just passive objects in their environments, who hold variations in attitude, value and aspiration, with some better equipped to resist the negative health effects of poverty and adversity than others. Facilities and services are important to the generation of social capital over a lifetime. The needs and potential contribution of younger people have already been discussed. Older people value clubs and other organisations in preventing loneliness and isolation.

Building a thriving community takes time, opportunities, facilities, motivation and effective empowerment. Social capital can be exclusionary and active people can be demotivated by bad experiences (Cattrell and Herring, 2002). However, social capital is currently favoured as a policy tool. It needs to be carefully nurtured, taking into account different cultural needs in respect of age, gender, ethnicity and indeed class. The policy drive to re-engineer social capital is key to driving participation in health promotion strategy.

Community development

The term 'community' has become increasingly important to the public health agenda and communities – with appropriate support – are key to addressing inequality. However, the recent Public Health Skills Audit (cited in Beishon, 2002) indicated that health professionals involved in delivering change are not sufficiently skilled in community development. Community development projects have traditionally been run by the voluntary sector, although this is not now felt to be sufficiently mainstream.

Beishon (2002) suggests that community development needs to be able to incorporate the following features:
- making contact with people in communities where there has traditionally been little contact; and
- deciding which community agendas should take priority and how to consolidate groups, or when to deal with them separately.

Many of the issues involved in community development are dealt with elsewhere in this book, including sections on health needs assessment, community profiling, community empowerment, partnership processes and strategic development. Community development is essentially about working together at the community level. At the time of writing the HDA is developing courses for health professionals to improve their skills in this area.

Health Needs Assessment

Health needs assessment (HNA) is research into the current status of health and health need within a community – as a geographical area or social group of people – as a basis for decision-making. It is about profiling a community to determine which health issues should be tackled and how they should to be tackled (Lock, 1999). A needs-assessed approach is emphasised for both existing and new organisations charged with delivering public health through partnership arrangements – notably LDPs, community strategies and local strategic partnerships – with an emphasis on ensuring that identified, evidence based health inequalities are addressed. HNA is becoming increasingly important in attracting resources to an area or community in an increasingly competitive funding environment that requires almost constant justification with regard to value for money. (see figure 3.4).

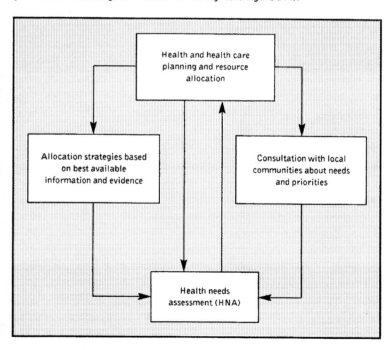

Figure 3.4
Principles in planning and resourcing health and health care

HNA involves looking at the health problems that have a major impact on the health of the population and the recurring factors so that better services can be provided locally (Lock, 1999). It helps to provide accurate information about:

- baseline or supporting evidence in developing innovative, partnership-based strategies that are comparable over time;
- current health-based activity and potential activity based on resource allocation, bidding or prioritisation, or to influence, justify or review policy, service or practice;
- acceptability and feasibility of policy changes;
- impact maximisation in relation to resource used;
- community participation and involvement in health activity;
- organisational and individual activity in health delivery and its impact on a community's health; and
- local health issues to raise consciousness, or in advocacy work.

Unravelling the definitions: health, need, community

Before getting started on an HNA, it is important to achieve consensus among partnership organisations (statutory, voluntary, community, etc) with regard to what is understood by the concepts of 'health' and 'need' as these terms can mean different things to different people. It is also necessary to determine the 'community' subject to assessment, which may be geographically based or a more dispersed social group. The research and analysis methods selected need to be valid, reliable, objective and rigorous enough to withstand scrutiny (Payne, 1999). At the earliest stage, the organisation(s) commissioning the HNA research must decide its purpose so that it can be appropriately directed and managed.

Health

HNA seeks to identify, measure and source health information in its widest sense – (See table 3.10), unravel the causes and find out what action to take to best address it. Although much of the literature on HNA is placed firmly in the remit of the NHS, it is clear that improvements need to reach far beyond the NHS. It is also about those charged with delivering positive change to address the underlying causes of ill health – notably environmental and public health specialists – to help prevent both the development and maintenance of poor health in the first place. But it must be centred around communities that need support, many of which have already filled the gaps in state provision and begun to find their own health solutions. HNA – and resulting policy – not about public sector organisations domineering and taking over such grassroots organisations, but about looking at why and how they work and providing appropriate support.

Demography	Office of Population Census and Surveys Transport infrastructure	**Table 3.10** Sources of Health Data
Quality of the physical environment including pollution, quality of the infrastructure and housing	Transport and planning data House condition surveys Housing Investment Programme returns Neighbourhood Renewal Assessment Air and drinking water quality monitoring data	
State of the local economy including unemployment levels	Unemployment figures Deprivation indices Benefits data	
Quality of the social environment, including levels of psychosocial stress and quality of social support services, strength and nature of local culture(s)	Health profiling Health and social needs assessment	
Personal safety	Crime statistics Accident statistics	
Aesthetics of the environment and quality of life	Health questionnaires	
Appropriate education	School league tables OFSTED reports	
Extent of community power and participation	Community profiling	
Health promotion indicators – participation in physical exercise, dietary habits, alcohol and tobacco use	Health and lifestyle surveys	
Quality of health services	Primary Care Trust data Department of Health statistics	
Mortality and morbidity	Director of Public Health's annual reports Epidemiological data	
Equity	Local Black reports Deprivation indices	
Public health	Public health observatories	

Source: adapted from Ashton and Seymour (1988: 161)

Need

A health need can seen as a subjective, relative concept, identified by a professional or community. Needs defined by professionals reflect a professional judgement and may be very different to those identified by the community. It is essential that those most in need of information, support or services are able to express their needs and have them taken into account. Community profiling can result in a wish list, but not all needs can be met as resources are limited.

It has been argued (Maslow, 1954; Doyal and Gough, 1991) that there are universal needs and fundamental rights and that in order for individuals to find self-fulfillment and participate in society, the need for food, water and adequate housing, for security and a safe environment, for health care, education and family planning and for social support and self-esteem must be met.

Whether subjective or objective, the purpose of identifying health needs is to assist in prioritising action to secure health improvements and to reduce inequalities. Action must be based on qualitative and quantitative data with medical, environmental and social data overlayed. Information on health status, the community itself and on the determinants of health is needed ie on lifestyles, quality of housing, levels of employment and access to health services.

Community

Invariably, much HNA is related to the population or 'community' in a geographical area – such as a local authority, a neighbourhood, or ward – as this normally relates to funding regimes and initiatives (eg New Deal for Communities, see Box 2.2). HNA on a geographical basis is relatively straightforward – the boundary is clearly defined, easy to understand and a community is either included in the assessment or it is not. Most population information is geographically specific and it is relatively easy to compile socio-economic, environmental and health information about a particular area.

However, there are some difficulties in a geographically specific approach. Not all vulnerable people live in deprived areas, and not everyone living in a deprived area is vulnerable. The impact of globalisation, personal mobility, cultural evolution and evolving class differentials means that lifestyle has become increasingly important in health determination. The fact that health status in an area has changed may be more to do with gentrification than actual improvements in the health of existing residents. Recorded trends in health – as well as individual perceptions about health – may not provide an accurate picture of what is really going on as data may be skewed and distorted.

A more accurate and thorough understanding of a community's health also needs to consider groups of people. Examples of social groups include ethnic minorities, households headed by women in bed and breakfast accommodation, gypsies, or those sharing some similarities in health status and experience, such as those with a particular disability, or with AIDS, or older people leaving hospital and returning to their homes alone. However, although professionals may group those with similar perceived 'needs' for their own purposes, it does not follow that the same group will recognise itself as a community with common interests or features. (see Figure 3.5)

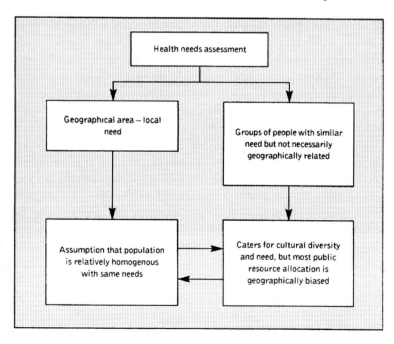

Figure 3.5
Issues in HNA

HNA must increasingly collate, map and report specific physical and social health information relating uniquely to ethnic minorities – such as sickle cell disease or cross-cultural tension arising from forced marriage and isolation from family – so that appropriate service provision can be developed. Additionally, refugees and asylum seekers – an ethnic minority sub-group – may have specific health needs arising from earlier trauma and persecution that has led to their current living environment and financial status, with exclusion compounded by language and communication, cultural barriers and frequent moving, as well as racism (Barnardo's et al, 2000). The overlap of ethnic-specific health status also needs to acknowledge any relationship of illness to poverty and exclusion experienced, represented by poor housing conditions and access/barriers to appropriate health care.

HNA: Compiling the data

HNA is essentially a research project carried out at multiple levels and perspectives involving the assessment of the health of a community and planning how to improve it. Besides regionally and nationally collated data sources, organisations like local authorities and primary care trusts (PCTs) already collate and map (eg. through geographical information systems) many sources of data that can provide the information needed in the initial stages of an HNA. Since health and social care delivery organisations do not always share coterminous boundaries, consideration needs to be given to possible duplication or distortion of compiled statistics. Statistics and communities may or may not overlap, are not always comparable and are not necessarily mutually exclusive.

Community profiling helps provide a systematic, objective needs assessment rather than a health worker's subjective view. It provides a comprehensive overview of a community and its resources as a basis for health improvement planning. Community profiles vary according to circumstance. Naidoo and Wills (2000) suggest that they involve the following key elements:

• composition of community, including, for example, the age profile, organisation and capacity;
• socio-economic environment, such as economic activity and unemployment, car ownerships, housing, transport, pollution;
• availability, effectiveness and impact of health and social service provision; and
• local strategies for health, including LDPs, local regeneration schemes, etc.

Initial profiling involves asking a broad range of people and professionals what they consider to be the key health problems, as well as collecting data about an area. The information obtained will contain interrelated issues such as asthma, TB, traffic pollution and the lack of an integrated transport system which will begin to reveal how medical, environmental, social and economic factors influencing health are linked and how an integrated approach is needed to tackle them (Lock, 1999). In this way medical and environmental data are mapped with socio-economic data across boundaries to identify common patterns and to achieve an integrated, partnership-based approach to seeing where the gaps occur, identifying the links and solving the problems.

Compiling information about an area normally involves collating statistical data – numerical indicators of health that are readily measurable (quantitative) from various sources. It confirms in numbers what is already there, but also implicates what might be missing from an area as expressed through deprivation indices, medical data, etc. Quantitative data needs to be backed up with qualitative data from the local community to help explain a situation from the perspective of the statistic. The HNA focus on both quantitative and qualitative data reflects the wider shift in thinking in public health away from the traditional medical model and toward a socio-economic model that recognises the underlying causes of ill-health that environmental and associated health specialists deliver on a daily basis.

Qualitative data is the 'why?' in social research and provides valuable understanding and insight into why a situation is as it is and enables patterns of interrelated issues to be made clearer. Qualitative data can be compiled from questionnaires, focus groups, and community networks. It provides personal and community perceptions which give valuable insight into the impact of a policy that may not be fully revealed by statistical the data alone, rather than just concentrating on what the overall statistics are (apparently) saying about an area. It is becoming increasingly important to the social agenda as communities are engaging with policy-makers in making decisions locally – a fundamental part of developing inclusive and bottom-up partnerships so that communities themselves can self-identify need and how it can be met. It may raise policy issues that had not even occurred to people making decisions affecting communities. It provides decision-makers with the data to support or refute policy and implementation processes.

HNA is not just about finding out what is not adequate or suitably sufficient in a community, but is also about recognising the potential of what is already there in the form of social capital – and how important it is to the way the community resolves its own issues. A HNA needs to be local and contribute toward this as part of problem solving and democratic participation (Sirianni and Friedland, undated). However, communities may be experiencing 'survey fatigue', or have had bad experiences of governmental organisations in the past, leading to some uninterest in current health research activity. HNA therefore needs to be approached with sensitivity and tact, valuing the contribution that many communities already provide themselves.

Uses and presentation of HNA

In an age when mountains of reports seem to be filling every available office space – and there is so much information that no one has the time to read most of it, let alone develop a viable way forward as a result of its findings – any HNA needs to be presented – orally or in written form – in such a way that something positive will actually come of it. What is important is to consider the key message of the research and to communicate it in the right way to the right audience. What was the research for? Is it accurate and contemporary? Has it been successful and useful? Has it confirmed or refuted earlier perceptions? Who is going to read it and in what format? Why? What is its current and future use in policy change or advocacy? Do we recognise the issues and move forward?

The final document may take several drafts before it is acceptable for public scrutiny and it may be appropriate to publish interim findings to help maintain momentum and interest, particularly if a very long time delay is anticipated between collating and analysing the data. The expected audience needs to be able to actually understand what is being said and to be sure that what is being said is factual and accurate. There is no point in pouring resources into a HNA that goes nowhere or that is so complex or secretive that no one can make sense of it. It may be that the results need to be reported in a variety of formats suited to each recipient and a summary report is extremely useful.

The report presentation should be interesting and eye catching with an appropriate amount of text explaining the situation supported by suitable and sufficient graphs, pie charts, etc and notable (anonymous) quotes from the qualitative research (Payne, 1999). Sufficient resources should be set aside so that that the final document can be professionally prepared. It should be a document that provides evidence-based data that is comparable over time.

Summary

HNA provides a basis for partnership working by connecting medical, environmental and socio-economic factors that affect health. It identifies what needs to be done, by whom and how. A lot of data is already available, but the patterns, links and connections need to be seen and understood, particularly as there are many small-scale projects underway that could be incorporated into a wider common aim to improve health. HNAs are going to continue to become important in identifying and sourcing resources to respond to health need. They need to be carefully considered prior to commissioning and closely managed. The resulting report needs to suit the purpose and audience – so that viable and sustainable change can be delivered in some of our most vulnerable communities.

Health impact assessment

Health impact assessment is a concept that has been around for a number of years but it is only recently that it has attracted wider interest and application. It is a tool which combines a number of methods 'by which a policy, programme or project may be judged as to the effects it may have on the health of a population' (WHO, 1999). Essentially, it is about identifying health impacts or outcomes with the aim of minimising adverse health effects and maximising beneficial health effects. In particular, health impact assessment emphasises the need to work towards sustainable development, aims for fairness and equity, targets disadvantaged and marginalised groups and encourages community participation. Health impact assessment is based on the premise that achieving better health is not entirely dependent on effective health services but is also reliant on action focusing on the determinants of health (WHO, 2002).

The scope for the application of health impact assessment is vast, since policies and projects of any nature may affect the health of a population either directly or indirectly through their influence on, or alteration of, health determinants. The World Health Organisation views health impact assessment as one of the key elements in advancing multisectoral strategies to tackle the determinants of health and thus achieve the objectives of 'Health 21' (WHO, 1998). (see Table 3.11)

Categories of influences on health	Examples of health determinants
Biological factors	Age, sex, genetic factors
Personal/family circumstances and lifestyle	Family structure and functioning; primary, secondary, further, higher, adult education; occupation; unemployment; income; risk-taking behaviour; diet; smoking; alcohol and substance misuse; exercise; recreation; means of transport
Social environment	Culture; peer pressures; discrimination; social support (neighbours, social networks); community, cultural, spiritual participation
Physical environment	Air; water; housing conditions; working conditions; noise; smell; visual amenity; public safety; civic design; shops (location, range, quality, value for money); communications (road, rail, 'bus networks); land use; waste disposal; energy; local environmental amenity
Public services	Access to (location, disabled access), and quality of: primary, community and secondary health care, child care, social services; housing; leisure facilities; employment; social security services; public transport; policing; other health-relevant public services; non-statutory agencies and services
Public policy	Economic, social, environmental and health priorities, policies, programmes and projects at national and local level

Table 3.11
Influences on health

Source: Adapted from Scott-Samuel et al (2001)

The European Union too recognises the need for the Commission to ensure that proposals for policies and their implementation do not have an adverse effect on health or create conditions which undermine the promotion of health (Article 152, Amsterdam Treaty).

The UK government acknowledges the value of health impact assessment methodology. Health impact assessment is identified in the health White Paper *Saving Lives: Our Healthier Nation* (DoH, 1999a) where a commitment is made to the need for the health impact assessment of all policies, plans and projects at local, national and governmental level. In keeping with the Labour government's joined-up approach, elements of the concept of health impact assessment can be identified in the sustainability White Paper *A Better*

Quality of Life: a Strategy for Sustainable Development for the UK (DEFRA, 1999), the local government White Paper *Modern Government: In Touch with the People* (DETR, 1998d) and the urban regeneration White Paper *Our Towns and Cities: The Future – Delivering an Urban Renaissance* (ODPM, 2000). Perhaps, most significantly, The Public Health White Paper *Choosing Health: making healthier choices easier* (DoH, 2004b) clearly signals the government's committment to health impact assessment in respect of government initiatives and policies, and identifies the need for routine consideration of the health impacts of non-health interventions. The government is also committed to building a consideration for health into new legislation through the inclusion of health as an element of regulatory impact assessment.

The outcome of the health impact assessment process will be a recommendation or a series of recommendations that can be used to inform decision-making processes within the context of, for example (Taylor and Blair-Stevens, 2002):

- policy development and analysis;
- strategic development and planning;
- commissioning and provision of services;
- resource allocation and capital investment;
- community development and planning;
- the preparation or assessment of funding bids.

Researchers at the University of Birmingham (HIARU, 2002) argue that health impact assessment does not and may never have answers to the key questions posed by policy-makers and go on to propose that health impact assessment should be viewed as 'a mechanism to make life easier for decision-makers'. Joffe and Mindell (2002) note, however, that one of the early obvious outcomes of health impact assessment generally is that potential impacts on health are beginning to be considered systematically across different policy areas and by those who may not traditionally link their work with impacts on health.

The benefits of health impact assessment

Health impact assessment permits a systematic assessment of the health implications for any policy or project. The WHO (2002) identify the following benefits:

1. Protection of human health
2. Reduction in the burden of ill-health
3. Improved cross-sectoral co-operation in improving health
4. The promotion of greater equity in health
5. A reduction in the costs, borne by the health sector, of dealing with the health outcomes of a policy or project.

Health impact assessment is thus presented as an essential tool in protecting and promoting public health, although there should be no assumption that a consideration of the health issues is the only priority in critically evaluating a policy or project (National Assembly for Wales, 1999).

If the benefits of health impact assessment are so tangible, why is it that only recently has there been a concerted effort in the UK to develop and promote a suitable methodology? Perhaps one of the most obvious reasons is that at present there is no statutory requirement, unlike the requirement to perform an environmental impact assessment where certain prescribed forms of development are proposed. Others would argue that to date, an evidence base and the expertise to perform health impact assessment is missing. There are also competing interests. For cash-strapped local authorities, the financial gains as a result of introducing a new policy or project are likely to be of far more interest that the health gains. The actual process of performing a health impact assessment may also be complex and resource intensive.

What is a health impact?

Very simply, a health impact is a change in the health status or the determinants of health of an individual, group or community. Adverse impacts on health tend to affect those communities and individuals that are more socially and physically vulnerable. Health impact assessment is thus a socially inclusive construct.

In common with health needs assesment, it is essential at the outset to agree on a common understanding of health. The London Health Commission (2001), for example, uses as a starting point the model of health endorsed by the WHO, ie *health is a state of complete physical, mental and social well-being, and not merely the absence of disease or infirmity*, and then goes on to ask the questions:

- Which determinants of health are likely to be affected?
- How may health determinants change?
- How might the expected changes affect the health of people?
- What might be the outcomes for health?

Consensus on the relevant determinants of health is perhaps more difficult to achieve, although models such as those proposed by Dahlgren and Whitehead (1991), the DoH (1998a) and Scott-Samuel *et al* (2001) provide a good basis for discussion.

The principles

Barnes and Scott-Samuel (2000) have identified some key principles embodied in the approach to health impact assessment:

- *Multidisciplinarity* – public health issues can be complex and the scope of a health impact assessment will require the involvement of many different professionals, not all of whom will be traditional health professionals. In many ways, health impact assessment embodies the essence of 'partnership' working.

- *Participatory* – the involvement of stakeholders, including those from defined groups or communities, is an essential part of the process.

- *Equity-focussed* – health impact assessment should be concerned with addressing health inequalities and consistent with this should be open to public scrutiny throughout.

- *The use of qualitative and quantitative information* – ideally health impact assessment should be based on sound, scientific information which can be used to determine quantifiable outcomes. It is recognised, however, that until a firm scientific evidence base is established, much of the information used during health impact assessment will be of a qualitative nature. Qualitative information is, however, valuable, particularly in achieving the perspective of those most directly affected by a proposal. Multi-method approaches are therefore advocated.

The process

Health impact assessment may be conducted prospectively, concurrently or retrospectively. Clearly, there are key advantages in carrying out a prospective health impact assessment, particularly at an early stage in the policy-making or project-planning process, when action can still be taken to mitigate adverse health impacts and enhance health gains. Health impact assessment conducted concurrently with the implementation of a policy or project can identify and characterise health impacts that may or may not have been anticipated, and will facilitate early intervention Retrospective health impact assessment is, in common with any activity conducted with the benefit of hindsight, much easier to perform and its conclusions may serve to guide policy-makers and project managers in the future.

The procedures for carrying out a health impact assessment are still being developed and refined. Some of the early methodologies reflected those processes employed by environmental impact assessment (see, for example, British Medical Association, 1998; Birley, 1999), and in Australia, health impact assessment as an explicit element of environmental impact assessment is endorsed (Commonwealth Department of Health and Aged Care, 2001). It is recognised, however, that health impact assessment conducted through the environmental impact assessment process does not necessarily offer the best approach to identifying and reporting health impacts unless specific guidance is given (Commonwealth Department of Health and Aged Care, 2001). In the UK, health impact assessment is viewed as a methodology in its own right and there now appears to be a general agreement emerging as to the key steps (eg Taylor and Blair-Stevens, 2002; Scott-Samuel *et al*, 2001; WHO, 2002), as follows:

Screening is undertaken to determine whether policies or projects are suitable for assessment. Obviously, a degree of selectivity and prioritisation is required since resources will not support the assessment of every proposal. Parry and Stevens (2001) draw attention to the lack of criteria for selection and argue that those proposals where the health impacts are less obvious or may take time to emerge should be the focus of attention. They note, however, that the identification of such proposals in itself requires a health impact assessment and call for strategic screening of single-sector and cross-sectoral activities (Parry and Stevens, 2001). The

HDA guidance (Taylor and Blair-Stevens, 2002) provides some help by suggesting that a proposal should be screened out if it is likely to have little impact on health and equity issues, where impacts are already well-documented or where decision-makers are unlikely to be receptive to evidence-based recommendations.

Scoping is conducted to identify how the health impact assessment should be undertaken and what issues should be addressed. At this stage a decision will be made as to the level of appraisal. A consideration of the scale and importance of the proposal, together with the resources available, will inform a decision as to whether the health impact assessment will be conducted at a rapid, intermediate or comprehensive level (also known as mini, standard and maxi health impact assessment (West Midlands Directors of Public Health Group, 2002)). The scoping exercise will often be carried out by a steering group comprising representatives from the various organisations, agencies and communities with an interest in the proposal. The emphasis is on partnership working.

Appraisal or assessment – The evidence is appraised or assessed to determine the potential impacts on health. Parry and Stevens (2001) stress the need for robust methods during this stage to secure the validity of the health impact assessment process. Rapid appraisal is likely to be a desk-top exercise lasting a matter of hours, and usually less than a day. There is a reliance on readily available data, scope for limited consultation and minimal quantification. The outcome is likely to provide an indication of the overall positive and negative impacts of the proposal. An intermediate appraisal allows for more detailed appraisal, conducted over a period of days or weeks. It will consider a wider range of readily available or routinely collected data, allows for wider and more detailed consultation and a degree of quantification. Comprehensive appraisal is a major investigation lasting over an extended period of time. It may entail the collection of new data and sophisticated analysis of the evidence to quantify the outcomes. It is especially resource-intensive and likely to be employed infrequently. Intermediate and comprehensive health impact assessment will require a multi-disciplinary approach.

The HDA guidance identifies examples of evidence and data-collection methods that might be employed. These include key informant interviews, focus group discussions, surveys and questionnaires, community profiling, health needs asssessment, expert opinion and documented sources, including evidence from other health impact assessments (Taylor and Blair-Stevens, 2002). Concerns about the evidence base, however, remain.

Joffe and Mindell (2002) highlight a lack of good and complete information as a limitation on carrying out a rigorous health impact assessment, noting that information needed to form a strong evidence base is patchy. This in turn may undermine the conclusions and hence lead to inappropriate recommendations. Joffe and Mindell (2002) argue that this may result in health impact assessment being percieved as ineffective, a waste of resources and, in the longer term, a methodology which is not advocated.

As an example of the approach to appraisal, the London Health Commission has developed a standardised approach to health impact assessment in respect of the development of all statutory mayoral strategies (London Health Commission, 2003). A key feature is the policy appraisal workshop, that provides an opportunity for key stakeholders to 'bring their own experience and knowledge to bear on key questions about the draft strategy, and to share their views with other participants' and to 'explore evidence linking the focus of the strategy to health, and, where appropriate, relate this to their own experience and recommendations' (London Health Commission, 2001). Stakeholders attending these appraisal workshops include representation from PCTs, local authorities, strategic health authorities, then health action zones, and other non-governmental organisations.

Developing Recommendations – Recommendations are developed through the identification of options for achieving optimal health gains and minimising adverse health impacts. It is important to consider priorities, particularly where resources are limited or there are competing priorities such as employment or economic gains (Taylor and Blair-Stevens, 2002). Recommendations are usually presented in the form of a report – see, for example, the report by Cambridgeshire Health Authority (2002) following the health impact assessment conducted to examine the future redevelopment of the former airbase at Alconbury.

Reporting re-engages the stakeholders and decision-makers through the communication of the anticipated health impacts and the proposals for their enhancement or mitigation. This stage can help decision-makers and, arguably, help to improve the quality of decision-making (Taylor and Blair-Stevens, 2001).

Monitoring and evaluation considers the extent to which recommendations have been implemented and what effect they have had on the proposal. This is particularly useful for identifying the accuracy of the predictions made during the appraisal and expanding the evidence base. It also serves to improve the process of a methodology still in its infancy.

A database of documented health impact assessment case studies is beginning to emerge (see, for example, the web-based 'Health Impact Assessment Gateway'). Predominantly, these health impact assessments are being initiated and led by those with a traditional health or medical background, and with local authorities only tangentially involved. Some exceptions do exist, for example the health impact assessment of the proposed development of a container port in Harwich (Kitcher and Jathanna, 2003).

Why is it, then, that the environmental health function of local authorities is not leading the way in health impact assessment when their work is so intrinsically focused on changing health determinants to bring about health gain? Arguably, the environmental health practitioner engages in mini assessments of health impact as part of their everyday work but without naming it as such. Examples might include assessing options for an appropriate course of action to abate noise nuisance (see Box 3.4); the provision of suitable facilities for disabled persons or the development of strategies for the purpose of an air quality management action plan. The environmental health practitioner needs to transfer these skills to the assessment of policies and projects in the broader context of public health. The environmental health profession has long argued that one of its strengths is the holistic perspective of health – an ideal position from which to make a significant contribution in the development and execution of health impact assessment in partnership with other health professionals.

Box 3.4 – partnership working in health impact assessment

The London Borough of Bromley are working in partnership with Oxleas Mental Health Trust to deal sensitively with domestic noise attributable to those with mental health difficulties.

The initiative is part of a wider programme of activity led by the Anti-Social Behaviour unit within the Environmental Services Division of the London Borough of Bromley. The local authority has identified that in some cases of domestic noise that is the subject of complaint, anti-social behaviour, such as shouting or banging, is caused by individuals suffering from a mental illness. On the basis of their observations of the nature of the noise, environmental health professionals liaise with the Head of the Community Mental Health Team at Oxleas Mental Health Trust. The Community Mental Health Team follow up the referral by determining whether the individual has a history of mental health difficulties and, where appropriate, an assessment of that individual is carried out by the community mental health team. The local authority and community mental health worker for that individual then jointly decide on the most appropriate course of action to deal with the noise or anti-social behaviour. Although Abatement Notices are served under the Environmental Protection Act 1990, more commonly, the person concerned enters into an 'Acceptable Behaviour Commitment', supported by their mental health worker. This is a set of guidelines/rules that the individual must follow. The initiative has proved to be successful in dealing with noise complaints and anti-social behaviour where mental health is a factor.

Case study provided by Peter Sibley.

In summary, the process of health impact assessment establishes health as a concern for all. Policy and decision-making is informed by a systematic consideration of health and proposals subjected to health impact assessment are enhanced to optimise the health gain for the population. For the public bodies involved, the process provides greater transparency and accountability. Action can be taken towards meeting community, local or national aims, objectives or priorities. Over time, a common understanding of health determinants can be developed. It is clear, however, that there is a continuing need to develop and refine a methodology for health impact assessment both as a strategic tool and as a project-based tool. The ongoing monitoring and evaluation of health impact assessments will identify and help to operationalise good practice. Environmental health practitioners need to engage with the methodology more proactively since it complements the range of other tools available to them for health improvement. Finally, it should be noted that health impact assessment is not a panacea but part of a wide range of approaches to improving public health.

Chapter 4
Food and public health

Food, Nutrition and Health

Introduction

A real understanding of the impact of food on health must take into account the broad definition of health, and the interrelationships between the different factors, ie food quality and safety, food production and distribution, nutrition including deficiency disease, increased susceptibility to infectious disease and diseases of excess such as cancer and coronary heart disease. Not having enough quality food has an impact not just on physical health, but also on mental, emotional and social health.

A term that embodies a multi-disciplinary approach to nutritional interventions, across the environment, health, food and nutrition interface is 'food security'. Food security is a goal of the Food and Agriculture Organisation. Its Committee on World Food Security states (1996):

'Food security means that food is available at all times, that all persons have means of access to it, that it is nutritionally adequate in terms of quantity, quality and variety, and that it is acceptable within the given culture. Only when all these conditions are in place can a population be considered food secure. We aim to achieve a lasting self-reliance at the national and household levels. In order to succeed, our initiatives must be founded on principles of economic viability, equity, broad participation, and the sustainable use of natural resources.' (cited Lang, 1996)

The World Bank defines food security as ' access by all people at all times to enough food for an active and healthy life.' (World Bank, 1986, cited in Lang, 1996).

The right to have adequate food is one of the most neglected human rights. Investing in nutrition reduces health care costs, reduces the burden of non-communicable diseases, improves productivity and economic growth and promotes education, intellectual capacity and social development (James, 2000). In particular, an investment in foetal nutrition is a highly effective investment because of its likely reduction in chronic disease in later life.

The WHO Regional Office for Europe launched its first Action Plan for Food and Nutrition Policy in 2001 and stressed the need for policies which reduce the burden of food-related ill health by protecting and promoting health while contributing to socio-economic development and a sustainable environment. The WHO Regional Office provided a framework of three interrelated strategies: a food safety strategy, nutrition strategy and sustainable food supply strategy, as a way of promoting public health through food. A multisectoral approach, including agriculture, the environment, food industry, transport, advertising and commerce is seen as essential to place the policy high on the political agenda. Meanwhile the EU Common Agricultural Policy has been working against public health nutrition through: withdrawal and destruction of tonnes of fruit and vegetables (117 million EUR/yr); aided consumption of milk fat (460 million EUR/yr); aided consumption of high-fat milk to schoolchildren; promotion of high-fat milk products and wine (10 million EUR/yr)(Schafer Elinder, 2003).

In the UK, the Independent Policy Commission's report led by Sir Don Curry(2002) led to the Government's Strategy for Sustainable Farming and Food:Facing the Future (2002) and in England, the Department of Health is taking the lead in the development of a Food and Health Action Plan. There are concerns that an under-resourced and overstretched Department of Health is not up to the job of addressing the huge public health crisis of diet-related disease, has not placed nutrition and health in the context of sustainable development and is focusing too much on nutrition to the exclusion of more imaginative strategies (Spear, 2004). Unlike Scotland and Wales, England has a more complex government structure and many departments are involved in food and health policies and strategies, ie DEFRA, FSA, DoH and Department of Culture, Media and Sport. This can lead to interdepartmental rivalry, duplication and problems with co-ordination, coherence, delivery and monitoring (Warburton,2004).There have been calls for an overarching food, nutrition and physical activity council to bring together the government departments and agencies, along the lines of the Scottish cross-cutting food and health council (Spear, 2004).

Physical health
Food has an impact on physical health in terms of survival, growth and development. It also has an important role in the ability of the body to fight disease. There is a link between diet and disease because of the importance of nutrition to the immune system, and a poor diet leaves people at risk

from infections which in turn have a role in chronic disease and cancer (Melikian *et al*, 2001). It is estimated that around one-third of cancers are related to diet (Doll and Peto, 1981, in Health Development Agency, 2002c). Cancers of the stomach, colon, breast, ovary and prostate have all been linked specifically to diet (Barker, 1996). Obesity has also become a major public health issue and is a major risk factor for coronary heart disease (CHD) and diabetes. Excessive intake of sugar can contribute to dental caries and excessive salt can lead to hypertension (WHO,2001).

Food-borne diseases associated with contamination of food and drinking water are a continuing public health problem causing symptoms ranging from diarrhoea and vomiting to kidney failure and death. Some people can experience an allergic response or hypersensitivity based on an abnormal immunological reaction to food (Garrow *et al*, 2000). When any adverse reaction is delayed, an association with food may go unrecognised, eg there is evidence that gluten sensitivity without accompanying signs of coeliac disease could be involved in causing neurological disease (Hadjivassiliou *et al*, 1996).

Mental and emotional health
Adequate nutrition is important for the developing brain and intellectual potential of the next generation. Diet has an impact on behaviour, appetite, satiety, cognitive development and emotional stability (Garrow *et al*, 2000). The role food plays in mental health includes mental retardation, lack of concentration and psychological disorders such as bulimia and anorexia. Eating disorders are a major source of morbidity among young women in western societies and are linked with body image, control and a tendency to judge self-worth in terms of shape and weight (Garrow *et al*, 2000). Some people experience a psychological reaction to food or an aversion involving unpleasant bodily reactions caused by emotions associated with food (Garrow *et al*, 2000).

A wide range of foods, including food additives, may be involved in causing attention deficiency and hyperactivity in susceptible children. Dickerson (1998) suggests that there is sufficient evidence to justify attention being given to a link between adverse responses to food or nutritional deficiencies and truancy, expulsion from school and anti-social or violent behaviour which may result in criminality.

Social and societal health

Food has enormous social importance and spiritual and cultural significance. It is a central part of celebrations, religious festivals, welcoming of guests and family sharing. Not having access to culturally acceptable, safe, adequate, nutritious food through lack of money, education or geography is a major part of social exclusion. Government messages about healthy eating fail to address cultural and behavioural issues or the problems associated with poverty and access.

Food habits are established in childhood and are often resistant to change because food means more than meeting nutritional needs. Food intake is heavily influenced by social, cultural and psychological factors (Holmes, 1985). Religion may be particularly important in determining food acceptability and be associated with particular eating practices. Consumption of specific foods or specific methods of food preparation may demonstrate religious faith. Also, adherence to familiar food habits may create feelings of security and stability. Familiarity is one of the most important factors underlying food selection but general health, mood, convenience, sensory appeal, natural content, price, weight control and ethical concerns are also important (Steptoe et al, 1995).

Poverty

With the money left over each month after bills are paid, poorer families have limited dietary choice and may lack adequate cooking and food storage facilities. People on low income also tend to eat around half the amount of fruit and vegetables that professional groups eat (MAFF, 1998, in Health Development Agency, 2002c). Vegetables and fruit contain many of the protective factors for CHD and cancers, but the British eat fewer vegetables than any other European country and this is reflected in the UK's record of ill health (Lang, 1996). Therefore increasing the average intake of fruit and vegetables to at least five portions a day is an important strategy in reducing rates of chronic disease (Health Development Agency, 2002c).

The availability of affordable, good quality food also depends on geography. Out-of-town supermarkets are inaccessible to those who cannot afford transport, the elderly and the sick. Older people may be particularly nutritionally vulnerable, as in addition to low income and lack of transport, they may have impaired mobility, a fear of crime if they leave the house and may not feel like cooking or lack the confidence to do so (Health Development Agency, 2002c). The National Diet and Nutrition Survey of people aged 65 and over highlighted low intakes of dietary fibre and high intakes of saturated fat and sugar (Health Development Agency, 2002c). The National Service Framework for Older People, has highlighted the benefits of improving nutrition, such as improved well-being, mental health and self-esteem (DoH, 2001c). Changes in the availability of nutritious food may therefore have a profound effect on the health of the population (Shaw, 1999).

There is a relationship between livelihood and nutritional status in that people need food to have the energy to work and need to work to be able to afford the food. We do not need to look to developing countries, however, to find poverty, malnutrition and low birth weight babies. Britain's infant mortality rate is the second highest in the EU and infant mortality is regarded as an indicator of poverty, poor nutrition, low educational standards and low standards of healthcare during pregnancy and childbirth (EHN, 2001).

The fact that many hospital patients are malnourished on admission suggests a substantial incidence of malnutrition in the population as a whole. Malnourished patients remain in hospital for significantly longer periods, experience higher rates of mortality and morbidity and experience more complications and infections than the adequately nourished (Holmes, 1999). Healthy Eating interventions may be appropriate for the overweight or for the uninformed, but are inappropriate for the sick or malnourished (Allison, 1999). High fibre foods are bulky and difficult to eat, low fat foods are low in energy and often do not taste so appetising. Even when people are consuming apparently adequate amounts of food, they may still be suffering from micronutrient deficiencies caused by dietary imbalance or vitamin losses during food preparation and storage (Holmes, 1999).

Conclusions

If a health needs assessment in an area has identified food poverty as a public health issue to be addressed, the appropriate agencies need to work in partnership. The barriers to access to culturally acceptable, adequate, affordable, healthy food, knowledge of how to prepare it and skills to grow it need to be identified and removed. Local authorities spend considerable amounts of time meeting targets for inspections of food premises and preparing for Food Standards Agency audits, but the Food Standards Agency under the Food Standards Act 1999 has as its essential aim the protection of public health in relation to food. An integrated approach to improve food security can have a significant impact on public health and, the environment and a reduction in healthcare costs.

Obesity – a role for local authorities

Introduction

The alarming rise in obesity, its associated physical, psychological and social health effects and cost to the National Health Service requires a more integrated approach. There have been some small-scale projects and single-issue programmes, but a lack of an effective, comprehensive obesity management system. Obesity is more prevalent among deprived groups who through poverty, poor transport and cooking and storage facilities, lack of choice, geography, lack of time and cultural factors do not have access to affordable, healthy food and leisure facilities. Health promotion initiatives need to address cultural, social and psychological functions of food and barriers to change associated with poverty and access. Activities must be appropriate and planned with the target group, and may need to involve specialist advice.

Local authorities have a significant role to play in schools, local communities and the workplace by enabling access to a range of healthy foods, increasing opportunities for physical activity, developing skills and reducing social isolation. Workplaces, schools, hospitals, community centres and meals on wheels services prepare a significant proportion of meals, so they offer a major opportunity to gain access to a large percentage of the population and offer healthy food choices. The larger unitary authorities have introduced food mapping to highlight food deserts, community growing schemes, food co-ops, breakfast clubs and cooking skills programmes, and have created food networks. To increase physical activity, they have improved transport links, subsidised exercise classes and provided safe cycling and walking routes. They are also responsible for environmental improvements, which have regenerated areas, revitalised the local economy, supported local food suppliers and reduced the need for transport.

Obesity is a complex issue which requires a multi-disciplinary partnership approach at the individual, community and environment levels. This public health approach to tackling obesity relies on a reintegration of the environment and health after years of separation.

Obesity

Obesity levels in England have almost trebled in the last 20 years and currently 8 million adults in England are obese (Commons Public Accounts Select Committee, 2002; National Audit Office, 2001). Obesity is claiming 30,000 lives annually in England, it shortens a life by nine years on average and unless drastic action is taken, one in five men and one in four women could be obese by 2005 (Commons Public Accounts Select Committee, 2002; National Audit Office, 2001). The most likely causes are a sedentary lifestyle and changes in eating patterns. However, obesity is predominantly a social and environmental disease and political, socio-economic, cultural and physical factors promote obesogenic environments (International Obesity Taskforce, 2002).

There are wide variations across the country in treatment and knowledge. Although by 1999, 83 per cent of health authorities had identified obesity as a public health risk, only 28 per cent had taken any action (National Audit Office, 2001). There are limited effective obesity management systems in place in contrast to other chronic diseases and it has been regarded in the past as a self-inflicted condition. However, obesity costs the National Health Service (NHS) at least £0.5 billion a year in patient care and £2 billion to the wider economy (Commons Public Accounts Select Committee, 2002). Heart disease, diabetes, high blood pressure and osteoarthritis are conditions linked to obesity, and 18 million sick days a year are lost to the condition (National Audit Office, 2001; Health Development Agency, 2001). It is estimated that almost all the coronary heart disease (CHD) in those under 65 is preventable (Wanless, 2002). A 10 kg reduction in weight can lead to a 20 per cent fall in total mortality, a 30 per cent fall in diabetes –related deaths and a 40 per cent reduction in obesity-related cancer deaths (Jung, 1997).

Obesity is measured using the Body Mass Index (BMI), which is a person's weight in kilograms divided by their height in metres squared. A BMI of 20 – 25 is normal, more than 25 is overweight and more than 30 is defined as obese (Commons Public Accounts Select Committee, 2002). It occurs when energy intake exceeds energy expenditure. People are using up less energy due to more labour-saving devices, an increase in car usage, more time watching TV and using computers (Health Development Agency, 2001). Socio-economic and ethnic factors also play a part. People in lower income groups find it more difficult to lose weight and are most at risk of gaining weight, along with South Asians, African-Caribbeans, smokers who are planning to quit and people with disabilities (Health Development Agency, 2001).

Obesity and health

Obesity is increasing and has become an important nutritional disease globally. Not only is obesity a major risk factor for coronary heart disease, but there is social discrimination against the obese and psychological penalties (Garrow et al, 2000). The social stigma can lead to low self-esteem, anxiety, depression, victim-blaming, bullying and social isolation. There are genetic and environmental components to obesity. It tends to run in families due to shared genes, common behaviour traits and common environmental factors (Webb, 2002).

Obesity often masks underlying deficiencies in vitamins and minerals. People are eating larger quantities of cheap, processed, convenience food that is high in salt and fat, and deficient in micronutrients, particularly iron and vitamin A (International Obesity Taskforce, 2002). A poor diet leaves people at risk from infections, which in turn have a role in chronic disease and cancer (Melikian et al, 2001; Barker, 1996).

Health inequalities

The Chief Medical Officer's recommendations for better health include eating a balanced diet with plenty of fruit and vegetables, keeping physically active, managing stress by talking things through and taking time to relax (DOH, 1999a).

Alternatively, if there was a choice, better health could be achieved by not being poor, not living in a deprived area and not working in a low paid, stressful job (Shaw, 2001). Obesity is 65 per cent higher among poorer women than affluent women (Wanless, 2002). Poverty, rather than lack of knowledge, appears to be the main factor in preventing certain socio-economic groups from selecting a diet conducive to health (Shaw, 1999). The rich can choose from a wide range of foods on the hypermarket shelves including ready meals, organic produce and new products which cater for customers with food allergies and intolerances (real or imagined). There are gluten-wheat-and dairy-free products and convenience foods packed with fruit and vegetables for the health conscious.

Deprived groups are twice as likely to be sedentary as the most affluent groups, and a high proportion of men and women in non-manual occupations participate in sports and leisure activities compared with those in manual occupations (Health Development Agency, 2001). In addition to a lack of understanding about what 'physical activity' is, barriers to lifestyle change include access, cost, lack of time, negative perceptions, concerns about body shape, racism, cultural inappropriateness (lack of single-sex provision), importance of family responsibilities and language issues (Health Development Agency, 2001). Activities must be appropriate, planned with the target group and may need to involve specialist advice.

Promotion of healthy eating

Improving knowledge about a healthy diet does not necessarily lead to behaviour change. Government messages about healthy eating need to address cultural, environmental, psychological and behavioural issues and the problems associated with poverty and access (Health Development Agency, 2001; Commons Public Accounts Select Committee, 2002). There have been many mixed messages about food and its relationship with health, and this undermines credibility and leads to confusion.

To ensure that an intervention will succeed, it is important to look more closely at our relationship with food. We need to examine our food selection and exercise patterns and determine what needs to be done to enable and support a change in lifestyle. Changes are difficult to achieve in a climate of greater choice of food, lower prices, urban work demanding less physical exertion and lack of time to exercise, shop, prepare and cook healthy meals at home. Long-term dietary treatment of obesity has been unsuccessful. If interventions make people miserable and anxious, they will probably suffer more illnesses and die younger (Webb, 2002). People will weigh up the perceived advantage of change and its observability; its compatibility with existing beliefs, cultural values and culinary style; its complexity and trialability (Fieldhouse, 1998). To be sustainable, dietary changes must be simple, easy and not too restrictive. Instant hedonistic pleasure and relief from anxiety are traded for the slow to achieve increase in self-esteem, health status and weight loss.

Obesity is a chronic problem that takes time to develop. Many treatments achieve short-term success but maintaining the weight loss is difficult and repeated weight loss and gain can lead to metabolic disruption. Food consumption can be improved when people are involved in planning their diet, have some control over food selection and feel responsibility for following advice (Holmes, 1999). Early childhood experiences strongly influence dietary preferences and good eating habits, so parental involvement is crucial and children should be exposed to a range of foods (Health Development Agency, 2001).

Around an eighth of the energy, fat and saturated fat in the diet are from the food eaten away from home (Health Development Agency, 2001). Workplaces, schools, hospitals, meals on wheels, etc prepare a significant proportion of meals, so they offer a major opportunity to gain access to a large percentage of the population and offer healthy food choices. Canteens are often on a tight budget and therefore offer the cheap, processed, fatty and sugary foods, little choice and little waste. Manufacturers need to reduce fat in foods but keep the taste and texture to make healthy eating pleasurable. Food labels and nutritional information are in different formats and claims can be misleading. Foods may be low in fat but high in sugar. Labels should be clearer to enable consumers to exercise informed choice.

Nutritional interventions that do not take account of the cultural, psychological and social functions of food can lead to anxiety and social tensions (Webb, 2002) – see Table 4.1. Major changes in food selection practices can also have economic and environmental repercussions; for example, encouraging the consumption of more fish and fruit could increase problems with depleted fish stocks, marine pollution and more imports mean more transport and environmental damage (Longfield and Hird, 2001).

Table 4.1 Food selection criteria

Cultural	Eating is often a symbolic experience, embedded in lifelong patterns. It tends to be the high calorie foods that are reserved for important or social occasions or used as treats. People have a clear view on which foods are appropriate for which situations and some foods are taboo for certain cultures. There are some core foods that are regularly and universally consumed within the community and have acquired a cultural status beyond dietary and nutritional significance.
Psychological	Adherence to familiar food habits may create feelings of security and stability. Familiarity, general health, mood, sensory appeal, stress, anxiety and self-esteem affect food choice. Food can be used to express a person's individuality. Some people may have a psychological aversion to a particular food or have developed an eating disorder due to a poor self-image.
Religion, morality, ethics	Food plays a part in rituals and religious ceremonies. Religion may be associated with particular eating practices, specific methods of preparation or consumption of specific foods. People may avoid certain foods to demonstrate their ecological awareness or disapproval of animal cruelty. They may boycott food from particular companies or countries to express disapproval of human rights abuses.
Status and wealth	Food can define social status. Some companies have different dining areas for workers of different status. Expensive and exotic foods can demonstrate wealth and sophistication. Affluent groups eat higher prestige and more palatable foods and more wholemeal bread, green vegetables and fruit. At very low income levels, increased wealth leads to increased calorie intake, usually based on starchy staples. Poorer people eat fewer meals outside the home, eat more meat and cheaper meat, less fish and cheaper fish, higher fat milk, more sugar, potatoes and bread.
Interpersonal relationships	Offerings of food and drink are used to initiate and maintain relationships and play a major role in social gatherings. Giving of food can be a demonstration of affection, a reward or an apology, and withdrawal or failure to offer food can be used to signal disapproval or punishment.
Political	Control of food supply and price can be a method of exerting political control.
Folk medicine	Certain foods are associated with healing and are used in traditional treatments.
Availability	Physical (climate, soil, storage facilities, water, transport, season, not local as lack of demand) Economic (money, short shelf life of fruit and vegetables leading to storage problems, cost, time and shopping practicalities) Cultural (acceptability) Gatekeeper (beliefs and preferences of the food purchaser for the family, convenience, appreciation and criticism, introduction of children to a range of foods before tastes established) Personal availability (individual dislike for a food, avoidance due to beliefs or physiological intolerance, allergies, psychological aversion)
Social	More food is eaten away from home, more people are living alone with less incentive to cook and there is more snacking and fewer family meals. Ready-made meals shift control over composition to the manufacturer. Catering managers are gatekeepers for those living in institutions (schools, homes, hospitals, prisons) and in the workplace.

Source: based on Webb (2002); Caraher and Anderson (2001); Holmes (1985); Steptoe et al (1995)

It is difficult to assess the impact of health promotion because of the lag time between intervention and effect. Also, people do not always make permanent or complete changes to their behaviour, and it is difficult to attribute changes in health status to an individual intervention (Wanless, 2002). However, studies show that dietary interventions can reduce CHD risk factors (Health Development Agency, 2001). To achieve success, healthy eating programmes should focus either on diet alone or diet plus physical activity, have clear goals based on theories of behaviour change, involve personal contact with individuals or small groups sustained over time, include personalised feedback and promote changes in the local environment, eg in shops and catering outlets, to help people choose a healthy diet (Health Development Agency, 2001).

Obesity is a complex issue and a range of approaches used in combination work best. Reducing sedentary behaviour in obese children, using diet, physical activity and behavioural strategies for adults, in combination, and using maintenance strategies such as continued therapist contact, were found to be the most effective strategies (Health Development Agency, 2001).

A role for local authorities

After 125 years of medical domination, there is now more of a partnership-based approach to deal with complex health issues. Public health ties with local government are being strengthened after a break of nearly 30 years (Donaldson, 2001). Local authorities (LAs) are recognised as partners in health improvement with respect to CHD initiatives, including the promotion of healthy eating, reducing overweight and obesity and promoting physical activity. LAs have responsibilities as employers and for implementing the preventive aspects of the National Service Frameworks. To avoid duplication and to ensure a multi-disciplinary approach, they need to integrate their workplace, schools environment, regeneration and leisure policies.

Effective strategies to promote healthy eating are those that work at several levels, ie individual, group, community and environment. Interventions should address barriers to dietary change such as dislike of the taste of vegetables and lack of confidence in cooking them, fear of waste and rejection by the family, lack of knowledge, and lack of access due to information, quality, geography and/or money (Health Development

Agency, 2001). Small-scale projects or single-issue programmes often have limited effect. Increasing access and affordability can help but may not achieve appreciable change unless acceptability is considered (Caraher and Anderson, 2001). The efficiency and effectiveness of community-based interventions relies on the involvement of local people.

Some LAs, particularly the larger unitary authorities with a full range of services, have already introduced successful initiatives. There has been a range of nutrition interventions based in schools, local communities and the workplace and a range of contributors to such interventions (Health Development Agency, 2001) – see Table 4.2.

Bradford Council introduced a food mapping project with the health authority (EHN, 2001). It focused on access to and availability of affordable food in the city and used focus groups, one-to-one interviews and surveys to establish the barriers to a healthy diet. It supports existing projects and helps set up community-based initiatives. Some areas of Bradford have a large number of food retailers and good access to fruit and vegetables, but the same areas have low awareness of healthy eating. Other areas of the city have the opposite.

Initiatives have included providing education, improving transport, setting up food co-ops and working with Bradford's retailers. Bradford's healthy food network includes community development workers, nutritionists, dieticians, environmental health officers, health promotion workers, strategic planners and alternative retailers. From the private sector are market managers, business people, caterers and the organiser of the Bradford Food Festival. The network was initiated by the Local Agenda 21 unit, supported by Bradford University. It has developed a healthy food charter to encourage individuals, communities, businesses and statutory agencies to consider food issues. The network aims to promote Bradford as a centre of food excellence, and to encourage people to enjoy locally produced, nutritious food that meets their cultural needs. The network lobbies locally and nationally for healthy, sustainable and ethical food policies. Bradford's Gardening for Health project run with Bangladeshi women has led to participants reporting that they are eating more fruit and vegetables, being more active, losing weight, developing skills and being less isolated (Health Development Agency, 2001).

Table 4.2 Examples of interventions

Workplace	Support and involvement from management Involvement by employees in the planning and implementation Focus on definable and modifiable risk factors Screening and/or counselling Changes to the best selling foods, highlighting healthy choices, modifying recipes Tailoring to the characteristics and needs of employees Using local resources Combining population-based policy initiatives with intensive group and individual-oriented interventions Building in sustainability
Community cafes	Local, not for profit, often part of community centre Affordable meals in social atmosphere
Community owned retailing (food co-ops)	Locally organised, can improve accessibility in areas that lack affordable supplies Allow people to try new foods Increase confidence, self-esteem and develop skills in those running the co-op Social meeting place Empowerment of local community
Community growing schemes	Vary from city farms to allotments or developed wasteland Increase local supplies of affordable fruit and vegetables Participants more active, lose weight, build confidence Reduces social isolation
Farmers' markets	Reduced price Opportunity to buy fresh, local produce, revitalise local economy Social meeting place
Community Shops	Replace closed local shops Improve access Part of neighbourhood renewal
Heartbeat Award	Nationally recognised reward for healthy practices and good hygiene Useful where people eat everyday – workplace, prisons, hospitals
Cook and eat Sessions	Community food projects, learn cooking skills Need to be culturally and socio-economically relevant Reduce isolation, build confidence Forum to discuss other health issues Sessions in women's groups, youth clubs.
Schools	National School Fruit Scheme – free fruit Breakfast clubs – encourage children to eat cereal and fruit Education on healthy eating and cooking skills Healthy snacks Nutritional standards Pricing of healthier choices Sure Start programmes

Physical activity	Promote use of leisure and sports centres Provide opportunities for affordable, accessible physical activity, make it fun and social, involve people in its planning and implementation, address needs of different groups, address political, social and economic barriers Ensure outdoor environment is safe, well designed and pleasant Safe walking and cycling, safe roads, maps, marked routes, play areas, personal safety Community garden schemes Increase physical activity in schools

Source: based on HDA (2001), (2002)

In East Sussex, as part of their work on cancer which is more common in deprived areas, initiatives include: free fruit for school children, promotion of the need for increased consumption of fruit and vegetables and an increase in availability, community action to reduce barriers to healthy food, promotion of local growers and suppliers and support for food markets and community food growing (East Sussex Brighton and Hove, 2001). People who are homeless, lack cooking facilities or who are older and/or single and living on a low income can benefit from community cafes, although the aim is for affordable food in a sociable atmosphere, not necessarily healthy food (Health Development Agency, 2001).

Stockport has a target to ensure over a ten-year period that all residents have access to affordable, good quality food and to maintain and support food co-ops in deprived areas. It aims to make food poverty a key consideration in community transport planning (Bull and Hamer, 2001). Coventry City Council has a health development unit which is also tackling food poverty. Five community nutritionists work with people in deprived areas. They visit them in their homes to help them develop their cooking skills as well as teaching how to budget for a healthy diet on a low income (Brown, 2002).

Manchester has set inequalities targets by area, eg to reduce the number of food deserts in the city by 50 per cent over five years and develop three parental food education projects in poorer areas. It aims to increase consumption of healthy food by increasing access and skills (Bull and Hamer, 2001). South Yorkshire aims to increase the proportion of children cycling or walking to school in certain areas by 80 per cent by 2005 (Bull and Hamer, 2001). Sheffield's award-winning project to reduce cardio-vascular disease is partnership based and includes various projects such as targeting deprived areas and providing subsidised keep-fit classes, line dancing and yoga (Ward, 2002).

Stockton-on-Tees Borough Council has produced a holistic, multi-agency based food policy (LACORS/LGA/FSA, 2002). It aims to improve the provision, safety and accessibility of healthy, nutritious food and help to reduce food and diet-related illness and death. Its objectives include: promoting the provision of a range of food outlets to increase choice and availability; supporting sustainable food production and supply; providing nutritionally balanced meals in schools, workplaces, etc; reducing barriers to healthy eating; promoting healthy and safe food through education; effective enforcement; ensuring clear labelling; and providing advice on consumer concerns.

Legislation now requires school lunches to meet minimum nutritional standards and there is evidence to suggest improvements in school catering standards can help reduce saturated fat intake and increase the uptake of low fat foods among schoolchildren (Health Development Agency, 2001). Schools can ensure through breakfast and after-school clubs that children from low-income families can have at least one nutritious meal a day. Children also need to learn to prepare meals and the Cooking for Kids project has been introduced to increase nutritional knowledge, improve skills, change children's diets and increase self – confidence.

The LGA, LACORS and FSA website (www.foodvision.gov.uk) gives details of local authority initiatives aimed at promoting the production of, and access to safe, sustainable and healthy food. It also provides toolkits on Food Strategies, Allotments , Farmers Markets and Breakfast Clubs.

Table 4.3 Local authority initatives

Local Authority	Initiative
London Borough of Ealing	Ealing Food Matters Strategy is based on partnership working to raise awareness of four interconnecting themes that involve food: food security; food, nutrition and health;food safety and food sustainability.
Warwickshire County, District and Borough Councils	Food for Health Strategy and Action Plan developed through partnership working, to help people improve their food intake through awareness and knowledge (the components of a nutritious diet, weight control, safety and quality of food and food choice) and improve availability of safe and healthy food.
Calderdale and Kirklees councils	Food Futures is a partnership project aiming to further health, community development, environmental and local economic improvements by supporting the development of a more sustainable local food economy.
Bath and North East Somerset Council	Local Producers Award Scheme for pick your own schemes or suppliers to local shops. The produce is sampled for pesticides and organophosphates. The aim is to encourage local people to buy local produce, by indicating it is safe.
Staffordshire County Council	The Safety of Foods for Ethnic Minorities was a project conducted in 2001 to establish the food concerns, eating habits and nutritional value of take-away meals and snacks consumed by Asian residents. A sampling plan was then developed to scientifically analyse the foods of concern to this population group, ie fat content of restaurant and takeaway food, authenticity of 'Halal' food and potential meat contamination of vegetarian foods.
Staffordshire County Council	Training for Consumer Watchdogs on healthy eating and food labelling
Stratford and Warwick District Councils	Food Hygiene Schools Theatre in support of National Food Safety Week. Local performing arts students write and present to primary schoolchildren, a range of plays which deliver food safety and healthy eating messages
Stafford Borough Council	Local Food Links Initiative developed as part of the Local Agenda 21 work. Workshops produced a draft Action Plan from which a range of initiatives have been established such as farmers' markets, shows, demonstrations, awards, farm-school link education pack,allotment promotion, local food directory, support of healthy living, nutrition and diet projects and a Food Festival.
Pembrokeshire County Council	Spade to Fork project comprises a one-day programme to increase school children's awareness about healthy food, emphasising the importance of fruit and vegetables intake, focussing on those foods grown locally and including aspects relating to food history, nutrition and food hygiene. It ran as five separate interactive sessions, repeated over a three day event, held alongside the annual horticultural show. Children were given seeds, recipes and goodie bags to take away. Objectives included encouraging children to create their own garden to grow fruit and vegetables and encouraging them to taste a wider variety of fruit and vegetables.

Newcastle-Upon-Tyne Council	Kids' Cafe Network promotes healthy eating and exercise in a fun and memorable way to children aged 5-11. Volunteers who assist include youngsters 11-16. Sessions run in school holidays and are based on a nutritional theme with games and activities and include the provision of a healthy nutritious meal. Children's cooking skills are developed and they are encouraged to try different foods, increasing their opportunities for choice. It encourages families to learn about food together and promotes community participation in food initiatives supported by expert nutritional advice. It promotes the use of local sources of affordable high quality fruit and vegetables
Armagh and Dungannon Council	My Body is an educational programme with 6 sessions about diet, exercise, hygiene and their impact on health and is designed for children 5-11. It forms part of a larger community food poverty project Decent Food For All which is a 3 year integrated partnership-based programme committed to addressing food poverty issues such as inequalities in access to decent, healthy, affordable food for all. It focuses on low income households. The emphasis is on encouraging healthy lifestyles, raising awareness of healthy and safe eating through education and supporting local regeneration.
Doncaster Metropolitan Borough Council	Activate for Health aims to provide access to community based physical activity opportunities and cook and eat sessions for mental health service users through an 18 week programme. It runs in parallel to the local Exercise on Referral Project. A cook and eat session would include 1-4 participants (with a carer) 2 recipes to prepare and a hand-out. Qualified fitness instructors assess needs and tailor sessions to them. Initial physical assessments are made.
Fermanagh and Omagh District Council	Fit Food is a 6 week weight management programme delivered in 2 leisure centres. Community dieticians facilitate the course with input from fitness staff. It is a holistic approach to weight management including nutritional, behavioural and lifestyle factors. The Programme is about increasing awareness and knowledge about the components of a healthy diet, understanding the benefits of physical activity, finding a suitable activity or exercise, identifying barriers to change, obtaining support and motivation. The target audience were obese men and women on the dietetic waiting list. They had been referred by a medical practitioner and had a BMI over 30. Most had co-morbidities such as hypertension, hyperlipidaemia or type 2 diabetes.

Source: LGA, LACORS, FSA (2004)

Conclusions

Obesity is a significant public health issue and requires an integrated approach. It is a major risk factor for coronary heart disease and causes social discrimination and psychological penalties (Garrow et al, 2000). The most likely causes of the rise in obesity levels are a sedentary lifestyle and changes in eating patterns but as there are higher levels of obesity among more deprived groups, changes in socio-economic inequalities could have a major impact on health-related behaviour.

Health promotion activities need to address cultural, psychological and social functions of food and barriers to change associated with poverty and access. Interventions should include an assessment of food selection patterns and identify actions that could enable and support a change in lifestyle, where the advantages of change outweigh the disadvantages. Instant hedonistic pleasure and anxiety reduction have to be traded for slow-to-achieve weight loss, improved health and increased self-esteem. Behaviour change also has to occur in a climate of increasing variety of foods, lower prices, less physical exertion at work and lack of time to exercise, shop, prepare and cook healthy meals at home. To be sustainable, changes must therefore be simple, easy and not too restrictive, and should not involve mixed messages or lead to anxiety or social tensions. The wider implications for health of a change in eating patterns also need to be taken into account.

To enable people to choose and maintain a healthy diet, a range of approaches at individual, community and environment level is required in combination, as small-scale projects and single-issue programmes often have limited effect. Awareness, acceptability, affordability, availability and accessibility of food and leisure facilities all need to be addressed (Caraher and Anderson, 2001).

Local authorities have responsibilities as employers for implementing the preventive aspects of the National Service Frameworks and for implementing community strategies. Policies on the workplace, schools, environment, regeneration and leisure need to be integrated and their health impact assessed. There has been a range of interventions based in schools, local communities and the workplace and a range of contributors. They have increased access to a range of healthy foods, increased physical activity, developed skills and reduced social isolation. There have also been environmental improvements, which have regenerated areas, provided walking and cycling routes, revitalised the local economy, supported local suppliers and reduced the need for transport.

Obesity requires a multi-disciplinary approach across the environment, health, food and nutrition interface if the problem, causes and solutions are to be effectively identified and tackled. After years of separation, there has been a reintegration of the environment and health, and local authorities are being seen as a vital partner in the public health approach to tackling obesity.

Chapter 5

Housing, community and health

This chapter reviews some current issues in housing, health and c
It particurlarly refers to emotional health, temporary accomoda‌
poverty, home safety and public health issues for gypsies.

Poor housing environments: the impact on anxiety, stress and depressi‌

The exact link between poor housing and health is difficult to make by
empirical evidence. A poor housing environment is frequently the result of
low income, and low income frequently results in a poor housing
environment through a lack of choice. The cycle of inequality is difficult to
break. It can be difficult to directly relate health conditions to poor
housing, as other aspects of inequality – such as unemployment, poor diet,
insufficient health and social care – may be equally responsible for the
physical or emotional poor health experienced. However, there is general
agreement that poor housing and living environments can and do affect
health status (Audit Commission, 1991; DETR, 2000a; Ranson, 1991;
Townsend et al, 1992).

For too many, decent housing is little more than a pipe dream as high
numbers are housed in marginal social housing estates or temporary
accommodation that is frequently inadequate to meet need. It is difficult to
know which of these options is less attractive. Social housing in a marginal
estate can have inherent problems of poor architecture, design and
management with little prospect of further suitable rehousing. Those
housed in temporary private rented accommodation face inherent problems
of uncertainty, overcrowding and over-occupation with generally poor
conditions in the longer term. Neither option offers a particularly viable
route into a socially inclusive lifestyle.

Unsatisfactory living accommodation lies at the heart of excluded
communities since a poor internal and external housing environment can
have a significant impact on physical and mental health and there is
concensus that there is simply insufficient decent quality, locally available
and affordable housing stock in many areas, which is essential if some of
the health issues discussed in this section are to be alleviated. Far too many
have little – if any – active housing choices (Bogard et al, 1999; Cumella et
al, 1998; Vostanis et al, 1998). The situation is summarised in figure 5.1.

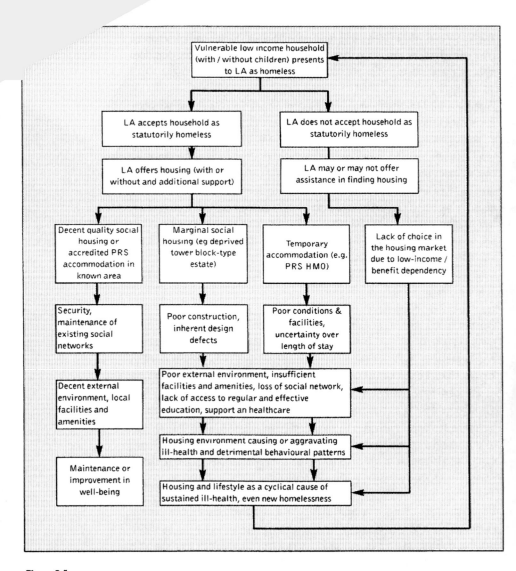

Figure 5.1
Possible fate(s) of the
homeless seeking
assistance: Implications
for public health

Finding solutions to anxiety, stress and depression

Housing policy has its roots in traditional public health and responds to a medical model of physical ill health rather than a wider socio-economic model and policy can invariably miss out on other important issues. While individual housing standards are of course essential, addressing access to affordable housing as well as the wider environment and community development are also fundamental in tackling inequality.

From an environmental health perspective, housing activity has traditionally been about positive change in remedying individual housing conditions – poor conditions include, for example, inadequate heating, external WC, dampness and mould growth and shared facilities in HMOs. Policy has more recently become concerned with area regeneration to help improve access to shops, employment opportunities, transport, etc. But this is only part of the picture, and currently progress is being made in the areas of community development and social capital, seen as the vital part of addressing inequality from the bottom up.

Those charged with developing strategy addressing poor housing need to be able to address the multi-faceted, interrelated issues surrounding anxiety, stress and depression which are caused or aggravated by poor housing, and which Page (2002) refers to as 'immediate environmental stressors', some of which are outlined in Table 5.1. Alone, each issue may cause some degree of stress, but clearly in combination – particularly experienced by communities powerless to effect change – it is not hard to see how severe stress and depression can result. These issues fall clearly within the wider social inclusion agenda, which recognises that traditional 'vertical' strategies are no longer appropriate and that horizontal strategies need to ensure partnership, and cross-cutting strategic intervention to achieve sustainable change.

Temporary accommodation

In April 2002 the Housing and Homelessness Team at the Greater London Authority (GLA) reported that the number of households in temporary accommodation exceeded 53,000, increasing for the seventh consecutive month, amounting to over 3,000 more of London's households in temporary accommodation than in the previous year. They added that the upward trend in the use of bed and breakfast (B&B) accommodation showed no sign of

Table 5.1
Environmental
Stressors: cyclically
interrelated factors
facing residents in poor
housing environments

Factor	Issues involved – features of exclusion	

Individual housing situation	• Cost and 'affordability' (with/without welfare benefits), lack of choice as key determinant of life-chances
	• Tenancy / insecurity / high cost of private sector rents
	• Landlord's behaviour and attitude; lack of tenant control
	• Powerlessness in landlord / tenant relationship
	• Poor housing conditions including:
	   • Disrepair / unfitness / other (e.g. leaking roof, no heating, severe condensation and mould growth)
	   • Overcrowding and over-occupation with sharing of facilities in HMO's
	   • Low likelihood of situation improving in forseeable future; possible homelessness / higher rent / difficulties with landlord if authorities become involved	

Access to community facilities and employment opportunities arising from location	• Private 'low-cost' housing sector (especially B&B type temporary accommodation)	• Peripheral location • Labelling • Stigma • Lack of access to: • Viable, regular work (influence of poverty / welfare trap) in the formal economy • Social support networks
	• Social housing sector tower blocks etc (poor architecture design and construction)	• Healthcare • Community groups • Affordable transport • Decent education • Affordable shops for decent food etc • Advice and advocacy • Other organisations / services / or assistance
Community breakdown	• Isolation, alienation, loss of social network, loss of social capital as 'middle classes' (traditional working class?) withdraw from area • Inadequacy – even failure – of State policy, resource and implementation to sufficiently replace social capital lost in deprived areas (via health and social care personnel?)	
Social behaviour	• Environment aggravates lack of concentration, education etc • Difficulties in supervision, so behaviour learnt from peers, not adults • Crime • Racism (eg asylum seekers) • Cultural and language barriers	
Physical and mental (emotional, psychological) health and safety	• Environmental stressors continue to exacerbate existing poor physical and mental ill-health • Environmental stressors cause poor health or domestic accident e.g. T.B., asthma, stress, depression, fall on stairs, fire etc	

decreasing (GLA, 2002). Added to this is the irony of the term 'temporary accommodation' which is not always particularly temporary — many remain in such accommodation for longer than anticipated through the local authority housing strategy (Ambrosi, 2002a, 2002b; Cumella et al, 1998).

Styron et al (2000) draw together a range of research in suggesting that there are four structural factors that have led to an increase in family homelessness:

- scarcity of decent, affordable low-income housing;
- insufficient income for people receiving welfare benefits or in low-income, unskilled employment;
- inadequate social services and health care; and
- an increase in families headed by women.

In addition, the nature of homeless households is changing and is increasingly associated with mental illness, drug/alcohol abuse, child and adult victimisation, inadequate social support and parenting difficulties. It is unclear whether these are a cause or an effect of homelessness — but certainly the relationship of homelessness and temporary accommodation is not conducive to combating social exclusion.

Households marginalised into such accommodation daily face some of the most basic public health issues they are frequently powerless to tackle. Health and safety issues related to the temporary accommodation living environment — in particular bed and breakfast type accommodation — include the following:

- poor general condition and design; low level of repair and maintenance; cold and damp conditions (Arblaster and Hawtin, 1993; Ballinger, 2002; Conway, 1988; Lowry, 1991);
- overcrowded conditions (inadequate room size for number of occupants), resulting in a lack of privacy, increased likelihood of infectious disease, notably tuberculosis, where levels are 200 higher for homeless people than the rest of the population (Thomas, 2002), difficulties in maintaining relationships and lack of suitable space for child development (Ballinger, 2002; Cumella et al, 1998; Styron et al, 2000; Vostanis et al, 1998);

- sharing insufficient facilities (notably kitchen and bathroom amenities) with strangers (over-occupation), leading to lack of control over personal space in communal areas (Conway, 1988);
- inadequate and inappropriate local health and social care and education services – short-term accommodation may make it difficult to access comprehensive health care, regular education or other support mechanisms (Ballinger, 2002; Bogard et al, 1999; Cumella et al,1998; Vostanis et al, 1998);
- location away from established, known social networks, leading to alienation and loneliness (Bogard et al, 1999);
- increased likelihood of inadequate means of escape in case of fire, thus an increased likelihood of fire injury or death (Home Office, 1989);
- poor external living environment with insufficient facilities such as a good transport system and decent, economically viable food shops;
- feelings of powerlessness about the situation improving – the tenant may be wary of involving the local authority for fear of harassment, or the eviction or rental increase or may not be aware of the potential service (Emmanuel, 1993) accommodation may be part of an 'informal' housing sector where tenants do not want public sector intervention;
- increased physical and emotional/mental health impacts including: home accidents, respiratory disorders, and birth of small babies, as well as increased anxiety, stress and depression arising from uncertainty and poor conditions (Ballinger, 2002; Bogard et al, 1999; Conway, 1988; Cumella et al, 1998; Vostanis et al, 1998).

Temporary acccommodation as an unsatisfactory policy solution
Homeless households in temporary accommodation have the added stress of not knowing how long they might remain there. There has been an increasing amount of research into the mental and behavioural health of homeless families placed into temporary accommodation. Much hinges around how poor health is compounded by the inadequate conditions, insecurity and loss of existing social networks which is faced and how inappropriate some policy solutions to this vulnerable group has been. Homeless families are likely to suffer stress and anxiety before approaching a local authority for rehousing.

Temporary accommodation can be little more than a 'safety net' in the housing welfare system (Styron et al 2000). This increasing supply of 'quasi-social housing' – supported largely by state benefits – is frequently unable to provide an increasing number of homeless families with decent, secure housing in a known area where support is available through existing social networks. Such social networks can never be fully replaced by state services (Arblaster and Hawtin, 1993; Bogard et al, 1999; Cumella et al, 1998; Vostanis et al, 1998). Temporary accommodation may be remote from known facilities, and can cause an untraeceble link in the health and social service bureacracy. GPs may be unwilling to register homeless families, who often end up receiving a second-rate health care service by having to resort to accidents and emergency (A&E) departments rather than maintaining a relationship with a GP (Ballinger, 2002; Conway, 1988; Vostanis et al, 1998).

Homeless mothers and their children may have already suffered ill-health and trauma and have already been exposed to 'risk factors'. These include poor relationship histories, domestic violence, drug/alcohol abuse, parental mental ill-health, physical and emotional ill-health and depression arising from poor housing and socio-economic conditions. The experience of homelessnesss – especially if it is ongoing – can have a particularly negative impact on a child's well-being, leading to delayed communication, can be disrupting to a child's education and lead to an increase in behavioural and mental health problems. This is largely due to insufficient space for learning and development and is aggravated by a lack of social interaction and increasing susceptibility to poor housing as families spend more time indoors for lack of viable alternative. (Ballinger, 2002; Bogard et al, 1999; Brown and Harris 1978; Comella et al, 1998; Conway, 1988; Styron et al 2000; Vostanis et al, 1998).

Homeless households do not easily fit into established health and welfare systems (Vostanis et al, 1998) which can make assumptions that the household is homeless as a result of a 'deficiency' of the individual within a problematic socio-economic community, rather than as a result of a wider system that makes it difficult for households to access the housing market (Bogard et al, 1996). Homeless households have unique and acute health and social care needs – and the services provided need to be co-ordinated (Cumella et al, 1998), sensitive, tailored, individual, flexible and able to follow the household, which is likely to relocate regularly. There is also a notable general lack of specific psychiatric help for homeless families (Styron *et al*, 2000). For these reasons, Ballinger (2002) argues that (then) HIMPs (now LDPs) should tackle the unique health issues facing homeless families. Clearly, these health needs should be based on a rigorous and thoroughly researched HNA of homeless families living in temporary accommodation.

Breaking the cycle of homelessness and poor housing is a difficult challenge when there is insufficient decent, affordable housing stock available. There can be no substitute for decent housing and integration into an established community in the first place, where existing social networks can be maintained. Social services can never replace what is lost to homeless families in terms of security and a sense of belonging, but where provided, services need to be appropriately tailored. Temporary accommodation and marginal social housing can aggravate existing physical and emotional ill-health in some of the most vulnerable communities.

Alternatives to bed and breakfast accommodation

Social costs aside, what is also staggering is the financial cost of temporary accommodation. O'Kane (2002) calculates that direct temporary accommodation cost to central London local authorities approaches £600 million per year, rising at a rate of more than 10 per cent annually. Notably, little of this is invested long term in housing, and housing investment is around half that of many other European counterparts. This is allied to the detrimental health impacts on some 50,000 homeless households (excluding asylum seekers) in London, double the number from six years previously. A major reason for this is the drop of 16,000 per annum in council lettings and housing association nominations available to new tenants in London, the right to buy policy and declining numbers being rehoused. O'Kane (2002: 23) adds that '(e)vidence of joined-up thinking is as scarce as value for money in temporary housing activities'. Many are denied a chance at inclusion from the very start.

'*More than a Roof: A Report into Tackling Homelessness*' (ODPM, 2002d) recognised the complicated nature of homelessness and the need for strategic and practical activities to tackle the acute health issues facing children in B&B hotels and people sleeping on the streets, focusing around why people become homeless and the need for sufficient affordable housing. The Homelessness Act 2002 is central to the approach, requiring local authorities to carry out a homelessness review and develop local strategy to help prevent homelessness and to provide accommodation and/ or support to people who are, or may become, homeless. The earlier two-year time limit granted to unintentionally homeless households in priority need is repealed, so housing is secured for as long as it takes the local authority to find settled accommodation.

Additionally, local authorities should only use B&B accommodation for families with children in an 'emergency' by March 2004. This proposal is supported by some £25 million from the Bed and Breakfast Unit (set to end December 2003) to help increase private sector leasing and lettings alongside changes to the housing benefit system, particularly the 'Supporting People' programme from April 2003 (Jackson, 2002; Ambrosi, 2002a, 2000b). Increased quantitative and qualitative evidence-based policy is envisaged in respect of households in temporary accommodation and partnership arrangements should help ensure reasonable standards (ODPM, 2002d). While this is laudable, it is essential that suitable alternative accommodation is available in the form of decent, secure and affordable housing, particularly in areas where prices are particularly high.

Strategic action to tackle poor B&B accommodation – a form of house in multiple occupation – can be found elsewhere in the publication.

Fuel poverty

Fuel poverty exists where low-income households are unable to afford adequate levels of heating, largely due to inadequate heating appliances and poor domestic insulation. People at home all day – who may already be vulnerable by reason of age (young or old), illness or disability – require additional heating over a longer timescale, which of course costs more. The poorest 20 per cent of households spend 12 per cent of their budget on fuel, whereas the wealthiest 20 per cent spend 4 per cent, and this is aggravated by VAT on fuel (Boardman, 1991).

The scale of fuel poverty – as well as local authority activity to address it – is difficult to ascertain, and estimates vary substantially according to definition. Archer (2002) cites a figure of some 4.3 million households in fuel poverty in England in 1996 and Shenton (2002) cites figures ranging from 2.8 to 7 million households. It is relatively more expensive to heat poor older housing and for private sector housing landlords – where energy inefficient premises are most frequently found (DoE, 1996b) – there is little legal or financial incentive to invest in energy efficiency. Older people in rented accommodation and people in lower occupational groups are less likely to have central heating.

Every winter in Britain, around 30,000 people die prematurely from the cold as a result of poor housing conditions (DEFRA and DTI, 2000). Living in housing that is too cold can lead to:

- physiological changes in the body, leading to an increased likelihood of hypothermia;
- an increase in heart attacks and stroke during the winter months;
- Cardiovascular and respiratory disease (especially in children);
- Asthma and mould sensitivity;
- Stress and depression from the visual effects of mould growth;
- Increased likelihood of accident through changes in behaviour as well as from poor heating appliances; and
- Premature death, mostly attributable to cardiovascular related illness (Arblaster and Hawtin, 1993; Boardman, 1991; DEFRA and DTI, 2000; DETR, 1999a; DoE, 1996b; Ineichen, 1993; Lowry, 1991; Markus, 1993; Ormandy and Burridge, 1988).

Research (Wilkinson et al, 2001) confirms the impact of the winter months on excess ill health and premature deaths particularly for older people, a close correlation to poor energy efficient housing – particularly older housing stock, and reported the substantial public health benefit that could arise from addressing thermal efficiency and heating affordability, reducing costs to the NHS (Shenton, 2002). It is likely to cost £15 to £20 billion to bring houses to required standards, and with current government expenditure, it will take until the 22nd century to combat fuel poverty in the UK (cited in Shenton, 2002, and Spear, 2002a).

Poor energy efficiency of housing stock is the most significant factor influencing fuel poverty (Shenton, 2002) and existing legal controls are not sufficient to combat it. Normally all that can be required is a fixed heater in the main living room and provision for heating (sockets) in other rooms, with minimum loft insulation. Even this requirement is not met in many premises. Older, private sector housing occupied by low-income households tends to be particularly badly insulated – but the private rented sector is even worse, especially where properties are occupied by multiple households (DoE, 1996b).

Clearly, adequate resources are needed to provide additional insulation and improved heating facilities so fuel-poor households expend less of their income on wasted heat. The kind of support needed will vary from simple, low-cost measures – such as covering a hot water tank with a thermal insulation jacket, to a major package of insulation, advice and education provided by skilled personnel. Responses such as cold weather payments are unrealistic, an inefficient use of public expenditure and fail to address the root causes of the poverty which is also key to the fuel poverty debate: what is needed is a proper package addressing poverty, energy efficiency and high fuel costs as the only real way forward (Shenton, 2002; Spear, 2002a), preferably through a known organisation such as a local authority who could hold an overall, consolidated fund for addressing fuel poverty through a unified and coherent strategy.

The Fuel Poverty Strategy 2001 – a partnership approach

Opportunities for assistance available to local authorities dealing with private sector housing have remained sporadic and approaches vary considerably because legislation, funding and requirements to monitor, co-ordinate and report progress have been inadequate, although there have been calls for legal improvements. Local authority environmental health departments (including their home improvement agencies) were previously able to offer limited discretionary grant assistance, but grants are limited as resources are frequently required elsewhere in the private sector housing strategy, such as in tackling unfitness and disrepair, and it is possible that the lack of private sector housing finance ring-fencing will further diminish fund availability for energy efficiency works in this sector (Shenton, 2002). The situation is perhaps clearer-cut for local authorities' own stock, where wider stock regeneration is able to incorporate energy efficiency measures. Indeed, some 80 per cent of (then) HEES grants were paid for local authority and housing association housing rather than private sector housing (Archer, 2002).

Meanwhile, since the government's consultation and the subsequent Fuel Poverty Strategy (see Table 5.2) (DEFRA and DTI, 2001), a number of initiatives – and other players – have entered the scene. These include five warm zone (WZ) pilots based in Northumberland, Stockton, Hull, Sandwell and Newham (see box 5.1). These provide an area-based rather than referral-based mechanism for reaching the fuel poor (Archer, 2002). Funded by national government and the energy utilities, these partnerships involve energy installers, training organisations, PCTs and the business and voluntary sectors – as well as local authorities. If successful, they may be adopted nationwide. In addition, energy efficiency grants have come increasingly from other agencies, notably the EAGA partnership through warm front team (WFT) grants (previously HEES), working with central government, local authorities, charities, and electricity, gas and water suppliers. This latter scheme has been successful for owner-occupiers but has had less impact in the private rented sector. Unfortunately and ironically, many fuel-poor households find themselves ineligible for WFT grants (Shenton, 2002).

While these provide a valuable service, it is difficult for local authorities – who hold strategic responsibility for local housing stock condition – to retain an overview as to energy efficiency status in their areas, particularly for private sector housing, and this is not helpful in delivering and measuring progress locally. The situation could be improved if organisations worked more closely together to develop a package of measures for an individual household – or if local authorities were able to offer a full range of energy improvement works themselves, as part of their private sector housing strategies. With so many agencies and initiatives involved, it is difficult to assess accurately how much will be spent on housing investment (Archer, 2002) and indeed how successful such investment might be, although the Energy Saving Trust (EST) is to evaluate the impact of WFT on vulnerable households over 2001/2.

There can be many obstacles even where a local authority is committed to improving domestic energy efficiency across housing tenures. There have been many high profile cases of civil actions against social landlords where housing stock has been thermally poor and tenants are unable to adequately heat their homes. Litigation costs and staff resource may mean that social landlords are have less resource available to rehabiliate their

Aims to lift 800,000 vulnerable households in England out of the fuel poverty trap by 2004 and to eliminate fuel poverty by 2010. Actions include:

- development of a common, partnership-based approach

- continuing action to tackle poverty, low incomes and social exclusion

- continual review and fine-tuning of energy efficiency programmes and strategies (for

  example, warm front team and warm zones) to ensure an effective,

  comprehensive and co-ordinated approach to fuel poor households

- continuing action to decrease fuel bills and encourage fair treatment of lower

  income households

- ongoing evaluation of alternative fuels, energy technologies and insulation methods

  – particularly for hard-to-heat homes – with continued improvement of energy

  efficiency programmes

- Development of a new advisory group on fuel poverty

Based on DEFRA and DTI (2001)

Box 5.1 The Newham Warm Zone

The London Borough of Newham is currently third out of 354 in the indices of deprivation. There are 96,000 properties within the borough, of which 45,000 are owner-occupied and 15,000 are privately rented. A further 12,000 properties are owned or managed by registered social landlords (RSLS) and 24,000 are council-owned properties. Newham has a population of 250,000 people, of which 30,000 are pensioners. Of the 96,000 households in Newham, pensioners occupy 10,000 households. Six per cent of Newham households do not have access to the gas network and 25 per cent do not have central heating. Approximately £55 million of benefits go unclaimed in Newham (NWZ, 2001).

Over half of all domestic dwellings in Newham were built before 1929 and are of solid wall construction and therefore thermally inefficient. Poor building design and construction can have a considerable impact on its ability to retain heat. Even when all energy measures are applied to a 1900s house, such as loft insulation and draught proofing, the property will still be subject to high heat loss. Installing central heating has the greatest effect on a dwelling's SAP rating 1 (NWZ, 2002).

The Warm Zone concept
The Warm Zone concept forms part of the government's fuel poverty strategy (DEFRA and DTI, 2001) which was officially launched on 21 November 2001. Work on the Newham Warm Zone started in January 2001, and was officially launched in June 2001.

The purpose of each Warm Zone is to evaluate a systematic approach to tackling fuel poverty through economies of scale thereby accelerating the process of eliminating fuel poverty. The government has part funded the development of five pathfinder zones across the country and these are known as Warm Zones. The intention of each zone within its three-year life span is to target those households that fall outside of existing energy efficiency schemes, as well as to develop better links with existing schemes.

Aims and objectives
The Newham Warm Zone's ambitious aims and objectives include:

- the identification of all fuel poor households within Newham in order to facilitate the delivery of energy efficiency measures, and to eliminate fuel poverty through improvements to domestic energy efficiency;

• to reduce fuel poverty by at least 60 per cent with priority given to the most vulnerable groups as identified in the government's fuel poverty strategy (DEFRA and DTI, 2001). It further aims to reduce the number of households spending more than 20 per cent of total income on energy costs by at least 74 per cent by 2004;

• to deliver an estimated £15 million pounds of energy efficiency measures to the most vulnerable households within three-years;

• to develop new funding methods for the zone in order to enable the maximum number of households to benefit from funded energy-efficiency measures.

Identifying the fuel poor through desktop analysis

The methodology adopted by Newham Warm Zone was to identify fuel-poor households using desktop analysis of existing data sources. This was considered the most cost-effective way of identifying fuel-poor

households, with other zones adopting different approaches. Desktop analysis is fundamental to the success of the warm zone and it was not until late January 2002 that a database capable of producing the quality and quantity of data required became available. The evaluation of the five zones is further complicated, because all of the zones use different operating systems.

A potential disadvantage of this approach is the zone's inability to take individual referrals from other organisations or directly from the public who may be put off applying for help altogether. Unfortunately economies of scale can only be achieved by saturating small manageable areas with publicity in order to maximise the take-up of energy measures. There is no intention of tackling individual cases and once an area has been completed it will not be revisited again. While this method of tackling fuel poverty is considered to be cost-effective, many fuel-poor households could slip through the net.

Figure 5.2
Newham Warm Zone: a unified approach

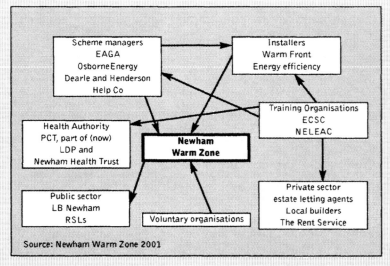

Source: Newham Warm Zone 2001

Figure 5.2 The above diagram shows the complex interactions of Newham Warm Zone and how it interlinks with other organisations.

Engaging the fuel poor

Work in the Warm Zone has revealed that there is some level of mistrust and apathy among Newham's residents, with many not believing their homes will be cheaper to heat following the installation of energy efficiency measures (NWZ, 2001). This may be a result of 'survey fatigue' in the area. Such feelings and attitudes need to be sensitively addressed and overcome in order to successfully engage these hard-to-reach households and to meet the targets as part of an overall strategic approach.

The Newham Warm Zone: one year on

A year after researching this chapter (Page, 2002), the author decided to find out whether the Warm Zone was on course to meet its targets and to assess progress being made.

There are a number of barriers that need to be overcome before a house can be removed from fuel poverty. The assessment team initially has to make contact with the fuel poor household which then has to agree to the assessment and referral process. Once agreement has been reached the household has to be eligible for the scheme and accept the installation of insulation within their home. Finally the installed measures have to be sufficient to remove the household from fuel poverty.

In practice the zone has found it difficult to even gain access to some fuel poor households, despite repeated attempts at various times throughout the day, and it is estimated that as many as one in three fuel poor households are being missed. Of the households that have been contacted as many as a third have been found to be ineligible for Warm Front grant assistance, despite it being the mainstay of the UK's Fuel Poverty Strategy. A significant number of ineligible households are believed to be vulnerable elderly low-income

households who do not claim a passport benefit.

In order to remove a household from fuel poverty it must first be improved to a level lower than the Fuel Poverty Indicator (FPI), which is less than 10. The majority of homes surveyed have a much higher FPI; therefore unless fuel-poor homes receive additional benefits as a result of the screening process all energy improvements will have to come from physical insulation measures alone. It has been found that increasing insulation levels alone only has a modest increase in the warmth of a dwelling. The greatest impact on the warmth of a dwelling is achieved following the installation of gas central heating and cavity wall insulation. However, this is not possible in some hard to heat or poorly designed dwellings and this combined with a low income will not lift these households out of fuel poverty.

The early indications suggest that the Warm Zone approach will only remove a minority of households completely from fuel poverty. The remainder of households will benefit from some additional warmth flowing from the installation of energy efficiency measures. Lessons learned by Newham Warm Zone are constantly under review and need to be adequately addressed to help ensure the government's target of eradicating fuel poverty by the end of the decade

Note. Standard Assessment Procedure – measures domestic energy rating.

References

Newham Warm Zone (2001 and 2002) *Annual Review*. Newham Warm Zone.

Page, D. (2002) *'Cold Comfort'*. Dissertation submitted as part of the BSc (Hons) Environmental Health at the University of Greenwich, unpublished.

stock. Tenants – particularly HMO tenants in the private rented or permission or obligation sector, where conditions are particularly poor – may have inadequate incentive, or permission or obligation, to carry out works themselves and similarly landlords may fail to do anything for lack of return on investment. Older owner-occupiers – in particular those who have never had central heating or loft insulation – may be suspicious about what the grant is for, or not understand the importance or benefits of improved energy efficiency. Strategy needs to recognise and respond to the often complex concerns of those living in fuel poverty and why this is so, before moving forward.

Local authority officers need to be able to offer individual packages of assistance. They have a strategic overview that enables them to direct resource to where it is most needed and to continue to prioritise those in fuel poverty through analysis of local housing stock and income level. Environmental health, housing and social services are well placed to offer assistance, as they routinely visit low-income households as part of their customary work. They can help encourage maximum grant uptake (from their own or a partner organisation), as well as advise on energy-efficient practices in the home, sometimes resulting in improved energy rating with zero financial investment from the householder.

Many local authorities also have databases of information and existing networks of interested parties such as including tenants' groups, residents associations and landlords' forums who already regularly meet and exchange information, as well as databases of interested parties that offer regular mail shot opportunities. Such outlets can help provide a ready audience and help promote the energy-efficiency message, and where to go for help.

The private rented sector remains particularly difficult to reach. A different enforcement and assistance based approach may be necessary for the private rented sector, particularly for HMOs which are especially complex (see box 5.2). Limited energy-based requirements can be incorporated into statutory fitness protocol under the heating criteria, and statutory nuisance legislation may also be applied. Enforcement activity also needs to be closely allied to assistance in developing a more appropriate and viable package of measures that a landlord is likely to undertake which would ultimately provide low-income tenants with more energy efficient housing, helping save limited income from wasted expenditure on fuel. The forthcoming housing health and safety rating system may be able to offer a more rigorous enforcement-led way forward in this sector.

Box 5.2 Luton: Researching fuel poverty in HMOs

About 1.5 million dwelling units in England are in HMOs. With unfitness levels as high as 20 per cent, generally, but not entirely, the worst and least energy-efficient accommodation is in such homes. The 1996 English House Condition Survey (DETR 1998a) demonstrated that energy efficiency standards are significantly worse in the private rented sector with an average SAP1 of 36 compared to 44 for the whole private sector. Additionally, 39 per cent of households in private rented accommodation are classified as fuel poor compared to 16.7 per cent in the owner occupied sector. Research into the energy efficiency of HMOs is limited which prompted Luton Council in 2001 to undertake an HMO energy survey to establish whether they should be adopting a strategy specifically to target energy efficiency improvements these dwellings. The survey sought to determine how the energy efficiency of HMOs compared with the rest of the housing stock in Luton and to further examine the relative energy efficiency of each category of HMO.

HMOs were unlikely to be energy efficient or to meet reasonable standards of affordable warmth. At the time of the study, Luton Council had 358 Category A HMOs, 593 Category Bs, 4 Category Cs, 73 Category Ds and 183 Category Fs. Using the NHER HECA Home Energy Advisor software package from National Energy Services Ltd it was possible to provide a Home Energy Report for each HMO surveyed, recommending the most cost effective energy-efficient improvements for each property. The report shows the cost, savings and payback period for the recommended measures in priority order.

The average SAP rating for a dwelling in Luton is 54, which is well above the national average. Luton's HMO sector comes out significantly worse with mean SAP ratings of 32 for Category F HMOs, 34 for Category A HMOs, 37 for Category D HMOs and 47 for category B HMOs. The presence of many large new-build student halls of residence obviously has a positive effect on the energy efficiency of Category B HMOs as a whole. If the new halls of residence are excluded from the calculation, then the SAP rating for this category falls to 39 (see table 5.3).

Table 5.3: Average energy performance by HMO Category.

Category	Average energy rating	Average estimated cost (£)	Average annual savings (£ / year)	Average payback time (years)
A	34	1,717	364	4.72
B	47 (39*)	1,503	279	5.39
D	37	2,077	358	5.80
F	32	1,908	422	4.52

* Adjusted figure excluding the new university halls of residence

To a large extent, low SAP ratings are a reflection of poorer heating systems. The LHCS found that room heaters are associated with low sap ratings. 59 per cent of dwellings with a SAP rating of less than 20 rely on room heaters for their main source of heat and the majority of these use solid fuel or on-peak electricity which generate high heating costs. In Category F HMOs, 50 per cent of properties surveyed had room heaters rather than central heating as their main source of heating. Category A HMOs also had slightly higher numbers of room heaters than the average for private rented properties, whereas category B HMOs came out better than the average. The survey data has shown that this is the most significant difference between the HMO sectors with Categories F and A having the worst SAP ratings and a higher proportion of inefficient heating systems.

Luton's Private Sector House Condition Survey (2000) indicated that the unfitness rate in the private rented sector, at 12%, is more than double that for owner occupied properties. The 1995 house condition survey identified as many as 37 per cent of HMOs as unfit. Older shared terraced houses, converted flats and bedsits tend to be concentrated in the town centre wards. 40 per cent of category B HMOs are dwellings shared by Luton University students and are concentrated around the University, also in the older town centre wards. There is a strong correlation between the age of a property, the standard of repair of a property and its performance in terms of energy efficiency. The 1996 HECA Report concluded that

Table 5.4: Top 10 recommendation for all HMOs

	% of HMOs	Estimated cost (£)	Annual savings (£ / year)	Payback time (years)
Cylinder jacket	25.8	20	20	1
Insulation (200 mm)	79	200	100	2
Fit cylinder thermostat	13	200	62.5	3.2
Cavity wall insulation	12	540	142.1	3.8
Room thermostat	19	200	47.6	4.2
Dry-lining	84	481	100	4.8
Low-energy lights	100	102.6	16.5	6.2
Draught proofing	32	172	18.5	9.3
Condensing boiler	48	1,473	128	11.5
TRVs	16	238	11.3	21

Table 5.4 lists the recommended measures in order of payback periods, ie the estimated cost of the measure divided by the annual savings. Of the measures with the shortest payback periods, only loft insulation upgrades affect a large proportion of the HMO stock (79 per cent) and have an excellent payback period of 2 years. Although cylinder jackets are only recommended for 28% of HMOs, they are the cheapest measure to install and can pay for themselves from energy savings in a year. They could easily be promoted at the Landlords forum. Low energy light-bulbs are the only measure that is recommended for 100 per cent of HMOs and although the payback is an average of 6.2 years, they are the sort of item that can be successfully promoted at a landlords forum. Condensing boilers were recommended for 48 per cent of the HMOs surveyed at an average price of £1,473 and an average payback time of 11.5 years. While it is acknowledged that heating systems have greatest impact on the SAP rating of a property, the long payback and large initial capital outlay suggest that this item would have to be heavily subsidised in the form of grants or discounts to make it attractive to landlords.

Other improvements that are listed include heating and hot water upgrades including thermostatic radiator valves (TRVs), room thermostats and cylinder thermostats. These upgrades tend to be recommended items for properties with better SAP ratings, ie above 40. They are the sort of measure that could be promoted

via low/zero interest loan schemes or bulk discount schemes.

Despite promotion of HEES and previous HECA Action grant schemes nationally, take-up in the private rented sector has been low in virtually every case where it has not been targeted specifically. The benefits of energy efficiency to landlords are well publicised – lower repair and redecoration expenditure through reduced condensation, damp decay and mould growth, fewer burst pipes in cold weather; reduced management costs due to complaints, and voids and less enforcement action. However the real cost benefit of improvements is not readily quantifiable, as there is little evidence of benefits of increased rent revenue or increased asset value. Most landlords are looking for revenue and/or operational savings from any investments they make in their properties. Additionally, for dwellings with a SAP rating of under 30, approximately 22 per cent have a payback period of more than 10 years (Battersby, 1997). Consequently, many landlords will not be prepared to undertake improvements with long payback periods if their main motivation is financial savings.

Luton has been awarded Beacon status for its excellent work on Energy Efficiency. Its Affordable Warmth Strategy will shortly be in its fourth year. For the private rented sector, the strategy seeks to assist and encourage private landlords to provide affordable warmth in their properties by making presentations to the landlords Forum and distributing Warm Front information, investigating the inclusion of energy efficiency as a requirement for HMO Registration, working with the university on standards for student properties, investigating the feasibility of bulk discount schemes and encouraging tenants to make behavioural changes to implement no-cost / low cost energy-efficiency measures. The strategy has achieved significant success in achieving its objectives in many areas. However, it may be argued that the private rented housing sector, and in particular HMOs has been somewhat neglected.

Since the HMO Energy Survey was completed in early 2002, HEES (now Warm Front) has been promoted at the landlords' forum. However, the overall emphasis has been to raise energy awareness and the promotion of no cost/low cost incentives rather than securing commitment for material improvements from landlords. Consultations with local landlords and Luton University regarding accreditation are still being considered and the feasibility of energy rating within the new HMO registration scheme has not yet been fully investigated. This is an option that could be explored in time for the next five year HMO registration scheme or an HMO licensing scheme.

We know that a higher proportion of people living in HMOs are in fuel poverty than those living in any other type of housing. As Warm Front has not been successful in the HMO sector and enforcement through registration conditions is not currently an option, financial incentives should be considered in the form of energy efficiency grants, loans or bulk discount schemes. A survey of landlords in Luton in 1997 (Graves 1997) found that the incentive most likely to encourage landlords to introduce energy efficient measures was

grant assistance. The average cost of recommended measures for all HMOs surveyed was £1801.25. Clearly, even if grants were only to cover a proportion of the work, there would need to be a precise rationale for prioritising grant aid and the council would also need to consider additional methods of assisting energy-efficiency improvements such as loans or bulk discount schemes

Energy conservation authorities currently have few powers to deal with inefficiency in the private rented sector, especially HMOs. Until such times as mandatory licensing of HMOs is introduced or the Housing Health and Safety Rating System demands higher standards of energy efficiency in dwellings, local authorities, such as Luton, need to be formulating strategies specifically to target energy improvements in their HMOs. Warm Front together with any schemes run by local utility companies must be fully exploited. Best Value and deregulation of the grants allocation policy will allow for a more holistic approach to be taken towards housing renewal with the flexibility to explore new funding mechanisms and target scarce resources where they are most needed and where they can be shown to have been effective.

It is hoped that the study has provided Luton with a starting point for recognising that action is needed in the HMO sector. The landlords forum will provide a base for consultation. There will also need to considerable commitment from councillors, private sector housing managers and EHOs who will need to be motivated if new policy initiatives are to be effectively implemented and landlords are going to be convinced to invest in energy efficiency improvements.

Table 5.8 Summary of recomendations

- 2004 HMO Registration Scheme (or Licensing Scheme) – impose minimum standards for efficiency
- Landlord Energy Efficiency Grants for properties with SAP ratings below 20
- Promotion of low-cost items, for example cylinder jackets, energy-saving light-bulbs at landlords forum
- Explore bulk discount schemes for loft insulation and dry-lining
- Explore possibilitiy of low-interest loans for landlords not eligible for energy efficiency grants
- Adequate resources must be allocated specifically for marketing, promotion and monitoring of activities
- Continued promotion of WFT (previously HEES) and utility company schemes.

Note
1. The Government's Standard Assessment Procedure (SAP) rates the energy efficiency of dwellings on a scale of 1 to 100, 1 being very inefficient and 100 being very efficient.

References
Battersby, S. (1997) 'Home energy conservation', *Environmental Health*, 105 (8): i – iv

Department of Environment, Transport and the Regions (1998a) *The English House Condition Survey 1996*. London: HMSO. Available online at: www.housing.detr.gov.uk/research/ehcs96/tables/index.htm (30 August 2000).

Graves, S. (1997) *Attitudes and behaviour of landlords and tenants towards energy effiency*, Luton Borough Council.

Lewis E (2002) *Improving the energy effiency of HMOs in Luton*. Dissertation submitted as part of the BSc (Hons) Environmental Health at the University of Greenwich, unpublished.

Summary

Fuel poverty is a complex issue – particularly within the private housing sector – requiring a complex range of measures to bring real change. Partnerships potentially offer a way forward, but action needs to be co-ordinated and outcomes reviewed to ensure that real progress is being made and resources are used to maximum impact where most needed, not just where most easily provided – and to ensure local authorities do not lose a fundamental part of their private sector housing renewal strategies to other organisations. The strategy itself recognises that local authorities know their areas and private sector residents better than anyone else to enable effective fuel poverty strategies – particularly when personal involvement can be crucial – and are uniquely placed to develop partnerships, including with the new warm zones.

Safety in the home

A person's, or community's, housing can have a substantial positive or negative effect on their risk of suffering domestic accidents. Poor home safety – defined as domestic conditions or behaviours that might give rise to harm – can be aggravated by inequality. The Home Safety Act 1961 is now largely defunct and despite the fact that there are more accidents in the home than many other environments, such as on the road or at work, although there is no national strategy to address the problem.

Home safety – the evidence

The Department of Trade and Industry (DTI) – through then Homes Accident Surveillance System (HASS) – collated statistics on domestic and leisure accidents recorded at A&E units in UK hospitals from 1997 - 2002. (See http://www.dti.gov.uk/homesafetynetwork/gh-stats.htm). The data was used as part of a wider government initiative to identify preventable accidents and to make proposals for change (DTI, 2000; DoH, 1999a). HASS statistics included fatal and non-fatal home accidents. Male deaths tend to exceed females deaths across all age bandings, and risk generally increases with age. For 1998, the DTI (2000) recorded 3,946 home deaths resulting from:

- falls (1,650 people)
- accidental poisoning (649 people)
- drowning, suffocating or choking (356 people)
- fire or burns (340 people)
- poisonings, other accidents and undetermined events (951).

Non-fatal accidents are collated by HASS on a UK wide basis from people attending A&E departments. The DTI (2000) recorded that these accidents at home comprised approximately:

- 1.08 million people falling – mostly children and older people on the stairs, children because they are inquisitive or inadequately supervised (Connelly, 1999; DTI, 1995, Ransom, 1999), older people because of decreased mobility, eyesight and sensory responses – one older person suffers a fatal home accident and dies every five hours (DTI, 2000),
- 650,000 people being struck or colliding with a person or object (usually older women);
- 102,000 being burnt (mostly in the under five age group – eg by kettles, hot fat) ;
- 41,000 people being poisoned (mainly cases include pills, bleach; etc);
- 14,000 suffering choking in 1998 (increasing trend).

See also Tables 5.6 and 5.7.

The cost of home accident injuries has been estimated at £25,000 million annually (DTI, 2000), but there is little media interest in the subject (RoSPA, 2000). Ironically, many accidents are preventable by low or no-cost measures. Adequate supervision can help prevent accidents. Alternatively, remedial measures can be simple and relatively inexpensive and include the provision of non-slip flooring, safety catches to cupboards containing cleaning fluids, medicines, etc, electrical circuit breakers, stair or fire gates, cupboards at suitable heights, safety catches to windows, grab rails to baths and so on (Ranson, 1999).

Table 5.6
Accidental deaths in
the home for 1998
(England and Wales)

Age	Male	Female	Total
0 – 4	47	29	76
5 – 9	9	7	16
10 – 14	18	5	23
15 – 19	78	34	112
20 – 24	138	35	173
25 – 29	192	42	234
30 – 34	220	65	285
35 – 39	167	68	235
40 – 44	143	80	223
45 – 49	153	78	231
50 – 54	141	83	224
55 – 59	96	51	147
60 – 64	115	58	173
65 – 69	124	85	209
70 – 74	140	102	242
75 – 79	157	156	313
80 – 84	163	204	367
85+	212	451	663
Total	2,313	1,633	3,946

Note: Accidental deaths caused by drug poisoning, other poisoning, falls, fire/burns, natural
factors, drowning/suffocation/choking, other accidents or undetermined.
Source: Based on ONS statistics cited in DTI (2000)

Table 5.7
Summary of (non-fatal)
home accidents by type
from UK A&E statistics
1998

Category	Numbers of people
Fall	1.08m
Striking	650,000
Burn	102,000
Poisoning	41,000
Choking	14,000

Source: statistics cited in DTI (2000)

Accident prevention was a key area in the government's *Health of the Nation
Strategy* (DoH, 1992). However, the last ten years' home accident statistics
cited above reveal fluctuations rather than general trends in the reduction
of the major injury categories of falls and striking leading to A&E
attendance over the period 1989 – 1998 (DTI, 2000). Statistics reveal that
home accidents due to falls fluctuated rather than declined, those being

struck or colliding in the home rose fairly steadily from around 400,000 to 650,000, while burns, choking and poisoning accidents generally decreased (DTI, 2000).

Housing conditions and home safety

Poor housing conditions lead to an increased incidence of accident (DTI, 1995) and there is a significant correlation between domestic accident statistics and social class, unemployment, overcrowding, tenure, education and so on. Accident levels are higher in temporary accommodation – where homeless families are often placed – which can be poorly designed, equipped and maintained, often with inadequate means of escape from fire (Arblaster and Hawtin, 1993; Conway, 1988; Lowry, 1991). Childhood injuries are closely linked to social deprivation. Research by the DoH (1998) illustrates that children from poorer backgrounds are five times more likely to die as a result of accident than a better-off child and this incidence can be increased by stress, homelessness and anxiety.

Gas heating appliances pose a particular likelihood of injury if improperly maintained and ventilated due to the risk of carbon monoxide poisoning. Every year around 30 people die from carbon monoxide poisoning by inadequately installed or maintained gas appliances and flues (HSE, 1999). The Gas Safety (Installation and Use) Regulations 1998 – enforced by the Health and Safety executive – place duties on gas consumers, installers, suppliers and landlords. Landlords are responsible to ensure that flues are maintained and checked annually, and that records are made avaiable to existing and new tenants. Anyone working on gas appliances must be CORGI registered. No one is allowed to use appliances known to be unsafe.

Fire safety can be improved by providing smoke detectors to provide early warning. Forty-six per cent of all fatal accidents to children occur through house fire (DTI, 1995). Fire safety is a particular concern in houses in multiple occupation (HMOs), which include houses converted into bedsits, some shared housing, etc, where residents are ten times more likely to die in fire than residents of other dwelling types (Home Office, 1989). There is a particular risk in such rented accommodation because the landlord may be unwilling to carry out necessary works to provide adequate means of escape in case of fire and other fire precautions, and tenants would have not have the power, or incentive, to do so. HMO accommodation is unique in that it is the only domestic accommodation where adequate fire safety measures can be enforced.

Home safety – the need for strategy

In the absence of any UK-based duty or strategy, home safety promotion tends to be distributed sporadically and by a variety of organisations, with no consolidated, national programme for delivery in what comprises a major safety issue. In a climate of decreasing local authority resource, discretionary powers, such as those vested in the Home Safety Act, are normally first to go so that statutory duties can be met. Education and promotion rarely seem to attract the same status as enforcement-led work in many local authority departments – even though it represents a major public health function and may have a major impact on accident statistics.

Non-statutory organisations have filled this gap. Organisations such as the Royal Society for the Prevention of Accidents (RoSPA) and The Institute of Home Safety (IHS) are campaigning for a new Home Safety Act to give local authorities a statutory duty to investigate accidents and provide education and advice as part of an adequately resourced National Home Safety Strategy (NHSS) founded on empirical evidence and training for those involved so it becomes a central – rather than a side-line activity. RoSPA has developed partnerships with interested organisations, producing a NHSS that sits alongside wider government policies such as *Saving Lives – Our Healthier Nation* (DoH, 1999a). Through this, RoSPA hopes to broaden the scope of home safety by linking it to the wider public health agenda and the underlying social, economic and physical factors influencing well-being, with local authorities as key players. Their recommendations include developing a new Home Safety Act containing a duty for local authorities to investigate home accidents and to provide good education and advice.

Many statutory and non-statutory organisations have a role to play in promoting home safety. Local authority environmental health, housing and social service departments, the fire service, PCTs and voluntary organisations have regular contact with the public in their homes and are in a position to review home accident data and to develop appropriate strategies for their areas. By working in partnerships, organisations can share and exchange knowledge, as well as prevent duplication, thereby saving resources (see Box 2.3). Initiatives to help improve home safety might include:

- proactive action, eg building control and planning stages;
- enforcement activity targeted toward at-risk accommodation/ households, eg HMOs, low-income older people;
- recognition of link with healthy housing, eg fuel poverty, and developing individual solutions to low-income households to improve both health and safety;
- home safety awareness campaigns (specific, eg fire safety, or general);
- free home safety audits;
- information leaflets, videos and advice targeted to higher risk groups;
- partnership working with other social care organisations to cascade information; and
- equipment loan schemes for low-income households, eg stair gates for young families, stair lifts for people with limited mobility or disabilities;

Gypsies and travellers: special concerns

A gypsy is defined as a person of nomadic habitat, whatever race or origin, and normally incorporates people travelling for work, but excludes members of organised groups such as travelling circuses, etc. A New Age traveller is a more recently used term with no legal definition, but normally includes those leaving established settled communities. Government publications refer to gypsies and travellers together, acknowledging some similarity in a nomadic lifestyle that, though lawful in itself, presents some concerns in locating suitable 'legal' sites, frequently manifesting as 'civil trespass'.

In January 2002, the ODPM (2002e) reported that there were around 325 local-authority-owned gypsy sites in England providing sites to 5,005 caravans, providing accommodation for just under 50 per cent of gypsy caravans. Sites are also provided privately, and gypsies prefer to provide their own sites. An estimated 1,000 to 2,000 residential pitches and between 2,000 to 5,000 additional transit sites or stopping places will be required over the next five years (Centre of Urban and Regional Studies, University of Birmingham, cited in ODPM, 2002f). Local authorities had a duty to provide sites with capital funding until the Criminal Justice and Public Order Act 1994 repealed this duty, but around two-thirds of English local authorities still failed to provide sites (Ormandy, 1999).

The level and adequacy of site provision varied nationally and some 25 per cent of local authorities with recent experience of unauthorised camping had no sites in their area, with extremely limited provision for transit or emergency stopping places in most areas (ODPM, 2002g). Many traditional sites used by gypsies for generations have been redeveloped and other land 'protected' from use. As a result, by January 2002, some 2,774 gypsy caravans – or 20 per cent of all gypsy caravans – were found to be on unauthorised sites (cited in Spear, 2002b). Such unauthorised sites tend to be less suitable and more visible, causing growing concern about disruption caused by unauthorised camping from local authorities, the police, settled communities and gypsies and travellers (ODPM, 2002g).

The lack of sites allied with growing numbers of gypsies and travellers invariably means no immediate access to basic public heath provision, such as drinking water, toilets and refuse disposal, but also difficulties in accessing education and healthcare services.

Access to sites and facilities etc
The then DoE (1994) issued Good Practice Guidance suggesting that local authorities should 'tolerate' unauthorised sites and identify suitable stopping places with basic amenities. More recently, the government has encouraged local strategies to respond to the needs of gypsies and travellers – as well as settled communities, with relevant stakeholders (including the local authorities and the police) working in close partnership to help manage unauthorised camping in a more flexible and realistic way. It is increasingly recognised that evictions alone do not resolve gypsies' and travellers' need for somewhere to stay or their access to public health provision.

Local authorities are advised (rather than required) to make adequate management and maintenance arrangements for gypsy sites in their area, and to consider making further provision for sites. Local authorities should also consider providing emergency stopping places with basic public health facilities including provision for refuse, water and temporary toilets (ODPM, 2002e).

Although there remain calls for more sites to be provided, the government has no proposal to introduce a legal requirement or central subsidy, preferring that individual local authorities take decisions locally (ODPM,

2002f; Spear, 2002b). However, local authority response to the Good Practice Guidance (DoE, 1994) has varied enormously. Many strategies have been influenced as a direct result, but only around half of local authorities had a written strategy in place. Only a quarter had reviewed their strategy in light of the Human Rights Act 1998, with others still uncertain about its implications. Benefits of the Guidance were reported as being the taking of a more holistic partnerships and generally more consistent approach to gypsies and travellers, but a need for an agreed protocol with advice on which agency should take the lead was also expressed (ODPM, 2002g).

Government has announced £17 million is to be made available to local authorities as part of the Spending Review between 2001/02 and 2003/04 for temporary sites and authorised encampments in order to discourage unauthorised camping and its associated problems (ODPM, 2002e, 2002f, 2002g; Spear, 2002b) and at the time of writing, policy continues to develop rapidly responding to continued concerns about damage, waste disposal and nuisance arising from unauthorised camping (Spear, 2002b). Additional duties, resource and guidance are required to ensure a consistent and national approach to gypsies and travellers.

Chapter Summary

Intervention in hosuing has for far too long taken a physical focus and failed to address social, community and needs-based issues adequately. While it is encouraging that socio-economic and emotional issues are being increasingly addressed, efforts are frustrated by a lack of decent and affordable accommodation for many already vulnerable and lower-income households. For those occuppying the poorest end of the housing stock, or those at the very margins of society, the situation looks grim and is not sustainable. Gypsies provide their own accommodation, and although there are inadequate sites and facilities, some progress is being made in this area.

It is not just physical housing conditions per se that are important, but also how people are able to access and remain in their homes, and feel physically and emotionally safe and secure. Policy and strategy need to be able to respond to community health issues to maximise a reintegration of health and housing.

Chapter 6 continues the housing theme and looks at the positive steps being taken to help promote healthy living conditions.

Chapter 6
Local strategies for area regeneration

Sustainable living environments

Jonathon Porritt, Chair of the Sustainable Development Commission (cited in Ounsted et al, 2001a: 1), argues that:

'Sustainable development isn't a difficult idea. It means doing right by people today without trashing people's prospects for tomorrow. Housing is one of the key areas where this simple but powerful precept can make the biggest difference to people's lives – strengthening communities, building local economies, improving their quality of homes and surroundings, reducing energy bills, protecting the local environment, and so on.'

In other words, inclusive societies are founded on decent quality housing across tenures within suitable and appropriate environments, where active and vibrant communities can have full access to societal amenities and facilities that help to maintain and promote health for all in its widest sense. In contrast, excluding, non-sustainable environments and their communities suffer the high social and economic cost of empty homes, hard-to-let estates, vandalism, anti-social behaviour and criminality (Randall, 2002).

Government has placed sustainability at the core of 'decent' housing delivery in providing a healthy living environment with access to facilities and services, as fundamental in promoting good health and well-being while preventing illness (DETR, 2000a, 2000b, 2000c). Housing should increasingly take its rightful place at the heart of an inclusive society, with the communities it houses becoming active rather than passive factors in the housing delivery process (Homeless International, 1998).

'Decent housing' is defined to statutorily fit, to be in reasonable repair with reference to the property's age, to have reasonably modern facilities and services, to have adequate insulation against external noise, to have adequate size and layout of common areas in flats, and to have a reasonable degree of thermal comfort, incorporating both heating and insulation (DETR; 2000b, 2000c). Priority is to address poor social housing in the most deprived local authority areas, although it has recently been reported that many local authorities do not expect to be able to meet this target (Evans, 2002). The standard also applies to private sector housing, subject to appropriate local authority strategic intervention within existing regimes.

Housing and the Communities Plan

The recently published *Communities Plan* (ODPM, 2003a) lies at the heart of government proposals to create thriving, sustainable communities in all regions. It encompasses social and private sector housing, and seeks to ensure that community needs (economic, social and environmental) – not just housing delivery – are tackled through lasting, dynamic solutions. The Plan proposes a continuation of partnership approaches, particularly through LSPs, as part of the wider public health agenda. The Plan has received wide general support not least because it draws together programmes and regimes to help revive poor neighbourhoods and build sustainable communities, with additional housing funding across sectors.

The Communities Plan is wide ranging and encompasses:
- providing more quality affordable housing that recognises and responds to regional differences, housing demand and changing social trends, while recognising the housing need of key workers;
- designing attractive towns, cities and public places, making better use of previously developed land for possible redevelopment and more efficient use of greenfield sites;
- regenerating declining communities and recognising regional differences in housing demand as well as urban/suburban and rural priorities;
- tackling social exclusion and homelessness, tackling empty homes, responding to the demand for decent homes for all by 2010 and recognising neighbourhoods and environmental problems (eg neglect, vandalism and vacancy) as key contributors to the quality of life;
- improving the planning system so that it is faster, fairer and more efficient; and
- empowering local and regional government and improving performance standards.

Reintegrating health and housing: the local authority role across tenures

For environmental health practitioners, just about every aspect of housing law, practice and wider strategy in a public health context is set to change to reintegrate housing and health. Housing should be a key component of the public health agenda, with a renewed emphasis on joined-up solutions through community participation as part of local strategy. Local authorities are being given new powers in the private housing sector to find new solutions to meet need, and must ensure that they do not lose out on funding to social housing within their areas with 'single pot' housing capital (Merron, 2002). Environmental health practitioners need to continually champion their cause at a time of such rapid change.

Jointly, the Community Plan, the Regulatory Reform (Housing Assistance) (England and Wales) Order 2002 (see also ODPM, 2002a, 2002b and 2002c) and the Housing Bill 2003 (ODPM, 2003b) change the face of intervention across housing sectors. The Regulatory Reform Order supersedes the power to provide housing grants with a general power to provide assistance, overturning decades of grants as a policy tool in ensuring required housing conditions. The Housing Bill also brings radical change to assessing stock condition and taking enforcement action. Its relevant clauses:

- replace the current fitness for human habitation provisions with the new evidence-based housing health and safety rating system together with a new enforcement protocol;
- introduce a national mandatory licensing scheme for high risk HMOs, with discretionary powers for lower-risk HMOs and a completely new enforcement regime;
- give local authorities powers to license landlords in areas of low housing demand or similar, where a poor quality private housing sector adversely impacts strategy to secure sustainable communities.

(The Housing Act 2004 received royal assent literally as this book was going to press. Readers can therefore refer to the CIEH website for the CIEH Brief on the Housing Act, available at http://www.cieh.org/about/policy/bnotes/2004-11-HousingAct.htm for latest updates.)

Local authorities have responsibilities for housing stock across tenures. Although some still tend to focus on managing their own stock (Goss and Blackaby, 1998), most are recognising the growing political importance of an increasingly self-regulating private housing sector. Strategic action is now about meeting wider strategic socio-economic objectives (such as area regeneration, bringing vacant properties back into use, tackling fuel poverty etc — see box 6.1 for an example) not just in physically maintaining, repairing or improving existing housing. Social and private sector area regeneration strategies now need to address complex, inter-related issues of social exclusion represented by multiple deprivation indices.

Box 6.1 Gadebank: Horizontal strategies in housing renewal

Addressing poor private sector housing conditions, and finding solutions that suit all interested parties, can be extremely complex. This is particularly so where there is mixed tenure – privately rented and owner occupied – because households frequently have different objectives and interests which need to be recognised. While owner-occupiers might be pleased to have the works done, particularly with the benefit of grant aid', increasing their capital asset but not their mortgage, tenants may feel differently if faced with an inevitable increase in rent, especially if on an assured shorthold tenancy where they may already feel insecure. Addressing such issues can comprise as big an issue as the renovation project in itself.

Allied to this is a local authority's responsibilities to meet legal and strategic requirements in its area's housing stock, including ensuring statutory fitness, as well as making inroads to addressing fuel poverty and enabling more effective use of available private sector housing stock in meeting homelessness and other local housing need, such as bringing vacant properties back into use, as well as making sustained efforts to engage a new relationship with communities.

Nature of the renovation project
Gadebank comprised 16 private sector dwellings that were statutorily unfit by reason of substantial disrepair. In addition, the poor thermal quality of the construction gave rise to condensation and massive heat loss, aggravating fuel poverty for many of the low-income households living there. Three of the properties were long-term vacant and difficult to let which was having an impact on the feeling of the area and adding to a general downward spiral that had not been tackled (see Figures 6.1 and 6.2).

These dwellings were not a common construction type and were not designated under the Housing Defects Act. Step one, therefore, was to employ a structural engineer to identify the particular type of construction and whether it was even feasible to renovate them, and extensive concrete tests had to be carried out. It was found that the properties were structurally sound and

could therefore be overclad to provide a serviceable life of at least thirty years. This information enabled initial discussion negotiations with the private sector landlord who owned 14 of the 16 dwellings (including the vacant ones), the remaining two being in owner occupation.

It was also important that all residents were involved in discussions about the present situation and future options for the site. Visits were arranged to each household individually allowing the opportunity for

Figure 6.1

Figure 6.2

Notes:

1 House renovation and other grants have recently been superseded by the power to provide assistance for private sector housing renewal.

2 The statutory standard of fitness is to be imminently replaced by the Housing Health and Safety Rating System

initial discussion. Officers attended with samples of the overcladding material, information on comparable renovated sites in the area and an information sheet containing details of useful contacts such as housing advice. It was clear that most residents were sceptical about whether the project would take off. However, all were keen for the works to go ahead, despite the fact that it might mean an increase in rent. It was a useful opportunity to discuss many related issues and what residents would like to see in the future.

We discussed with the landlord their possible eligibility for renovation grant aid toward the cost of works and raised issues discussed with the residents regarding works falling outside the scope of the fitness standard. The tenants had some good ideas which were incorporated into the scheme, such as partitioning the master bedroom, locating the bathroom there and thereby maintaining three bedrooms with more living space downstairs. The landlord was also willing to decant tenants to the newly refurbished vacant properties if this was necessary. The landlord proved to be extremely co-operative and agreed in addition to fund some additional works falling outside of the fitness regime, particularly in the vacant properties which presented greater potential for internal redesign. This included relocating the bathroom/WC upstairs, creating a large and modern kitchen/diner downstairs and installing full central heating. Efforts were made to keep the residents informed and feel they were involved throughout, although it was difficult for a relatively short-tem project where there would not be a long-term relationship with the local authority on completion.

Notices were served and the landlord made a grant application for each of their properties which was closely tied to the owner-occupier's grant applications. For uniformity, the scheme was to be dealt with as one project, despite the mixed tenure. Following discussions, the landlord's site manager was keen to oblige in overseeing all works once the financial contributions were established.

Internal works and external works had to be kept separate due to the specialist nature of the overcladding. Internal works were carried out first, with more extensive works to the vacant properties. Some residents chose to enhance the upgrade, for example by paying the difference themselves for a higher specification front door. Once the internal contractors were offsite, the specialist contractors were instructed to commence overcladding under a separate site manager.

Outcomes of the renovation scheme

One of the main objectives of the scheme was to enhance the poor thermal standard of the construction. External walls were prepared to receive the insulating board and rendering was carried out in two coats, using a traditional coloured top-coat pebbledash finish of a colour that residents had jointly agreed. Issues like resiting drainage pipes and residents' satellite dishes also needed to be taken into account (see Figures 6.3 and 6.4).

Figure 6.3

Figure 6.4

Taking the building as a whole, it was calculated that the typical U value for a dwelling was 0.40W/M²K. The overcladding works increased this value to 0.77W/M²K, taking the thermal insulation above current building regulation requirements. Double glazing with trickle vents combined with insulation to all loft spaces (with necessary additional ventilation provided to the roof) made an important contribution to addressing fuel poverty.

This scheme provided a valuable and timely scheme of works to improve the housing conditions, thermal efficiency and local environment for 16 dwellings. The scheme met many of the council's private sector housing strategy objectives, particularly in respect of the authority's obligations under housing legislation, as well as bringing vacant properties back into use and implementing anti-poverty and energy efficiency initiatives at a relatively economic cost to the local authority with a specific targeting of limited resources.

Sorce: Stewart and Nunn (1999)

The majority of housing is in the private sector, and the proportionately worst housing is in the private rented sector, particularly in HMOs. This sector is generally older stock than local authority dwellings, so it is of no surprise that conditions can be worse, such as the lack of internal WC in pre-1919 dwellings, etc. As improvements have taken place along with new build over successive years, numbers requiring standard amenities have declined and the main reason for unfitness is now substantial disrepair (ODPM, 2003c) – see Tables 6.1 and 6.2. Some three fifths of low-income households in England live in poor conditions in this sector (cited in Wilcox, 2001), with increasing numbers of vulnerable households finding accommodation at the bottom end of the privately rented sector through lack of alternative (Cowan, 1998). There remain fundamental problems in housing supply, quality and delivery that is both inadequate and increasingly insufficient to meet need.

For social housing, identifying a boundary for strategic intervention is relatively clear-cut and resource regimes well established. However, it is not quite so straight-forward in the private sector where ownership and responsibility for renewal works is more complex. Private sector housing regeneration strategies have long been criticised for their inability to be able to incorporate some of the issues that social housing sector regeneration strategies take for granted, although there has been an increasing move toward sustainable private sector regeneration. Private sector housing renewal law – and associated funding opportunities – lies at the heart of the problem as it is frequently limited and reactive, and not able to address many of the wider issues in physical housing conditions – let alone environmental improvements – comprehensively, or the reasons for people living in poor quality accommodation in the first place. Current changes in legislation and local strategy seek to address such issues, with a new emphasis on evidence-based and area activity to bring wider socio-economic regeneration.

Area action

Renewal areas provide a focus for intense housing and area renewal over a ten-year period and once established enable local authority environmental health practitioners to consolidate regeneration activity with an emphasis on increasing personal responsibility for housing conditions (DoE, 1996a; ODPM, 2002a, 2002b). Part of setting up a renewal area involves carrying

Table 6.1
Findings of the English
House Condition
Survey 2001

- 21.1 million dwellings overall, with 20.5 million households, an increase since 1996 survey
- 39% (8.1 million) housing stock built before 1945; 21% (4.4 million) before 1919
- 70% stock owner occupied, 10% rented from private landlords, 7% owned by registered social landlords; profile of stock differs substantially between tenures
- HMOs comprise 1.1 million dwellings, providing homes for 1.3 million households; over half of these are self-contained flats, 82,000 have been converted into bedsits providing accommodation for 27% households (363,000) living in HMOs
- 43% (700,000) dwellings are vacant, a decrease since 1996 survey, about half of these being 'problematic' vacants
- 7 million dwellings are non-decent (33% of all dwellings), a fall of almost a quarter since 1996 survey; main reasons for non-decency are:
  - 5.6 million dwellings (26% total stock) fail to meet thermal comfort criterion
  - 1.9 million dwellings (9% total stock) fail to meet disrepair criterion; least progress has been made here since last survey
  - 0.9 million (4% total stock) fail to meet fitness standard
  - 0.5 million (2% total stock) fail to meet modernisation criterion
- The average cost to make homes decent is nearly £7,200, representing a total cost of £50 billion.
- 6.7 million households live in non-decent homes (33% of all households), compared to 8.9 million (45% households) in 1996; of these:
  - the majority of households are owner occupiers (63%), with RSL 22%, private landlords 15%, but private sector tenants are most likely to occupy non-decent housing
  - 49% households comprise people living alone, sharing with others or lone parents
  - ethnic minority households comprise 9% of all living in non-decent homes; 40% ethnic minority households live in non-decent homes
  - poorest fifth of all households (42%) around twice as likely (42%) to live in non-decent homes compared to highest fifth (24%)

Note: Detailed results for the 2001 English House Condition Survey are now available online at: http://www.housing.odpm.gov.uk/research/ehcs/continuous/index.htm

Source: ODPM (2003c)

Table 6.2
Survey of English
Housing

Continuous ODPM survey reporting on:
- Trends in tenure
- Composition of households, mobility and accommodation across all tenures
- Attitudes of tenants toward their landlord
- Mortgage payments and arrears
- Housing benefit receipt, rent payment and arrears
- Factors affecting rent levels
- Results are analysed using the Index of Multiple Deprivation

Note: For Survey of English Housing see
http://www.housing.odpm.gov.uk/statistics/publicat/summaries/009/index.htm

out a neighbourhood renewal assessment (NRA) to decide the best way forward, taking issues such as socio-economic status, environmental infrastructure, community opportunities and housing condition into account in consultation with residents.

Local authorities are increasingly encouraged to adopt area-based renewal strategies as a wider strategic framework for regeneration, responding to the local need to demonstrate commitment to the area. This is seen to stimulate further partnership investment and build confidence. The Regulatory Reform Order relaxed earlier renewal area designation criteria which is allied to the new power to give assistance in renewal areas. The ODPM has issued substantial guidance to support the new Order (see for, example, ODPM, 2002a, 2002b).

Some concern has been expressed that there is no explicit requirement to assess 'health' within the community before initiating area-based activity. As a result, the Rhymney Health Study (Jones, 2002) was established to help inform a partnership approach to community regeneration as an additional component to the NRA in December 1999, an integral part of a wider process of health and social needs assessment across the county borough area. The exercise was found to add a health improvement focus to the declaration of the area, with private sector housing renewal providing the impetus to a real opportunity to engage with communities thus enabling partnership working and improving local health. The key recommendation arising was to make health needs assessment pivotal and integral to the process of renewal area declaration.

Strategically, local authorities need to be able to optimise their legal duties and powers to ensure that activity is properly and effectively targeted to areas where it is most needed. This is allied to a wider vision of economic development, social inclusion and cohesion, enabling better use of the privately rented housing sector to meet local need. Environmental health practitioners must not lose sight of what they are trying to achieve overall: an improvement in healthy housing and communities, not just the continual delivery of segregated services that fail to tackle the root causes of social integration through a betterment of housing and environment.

Houses in multiple occupation

A house in multiple occupation (HMO) is legally defined as a house which is occupied by persons who do not form a single household. CIEH (1994) guidance classifies HMOs largely by design and living arrangements to include the following general categories:

- houses occupied as individual rooms, bedsits, etc with some exclusive use and some sharing of facilities;
- houses occupied on a shared basis;
- some degree of shared facilities where occupation is allied to employment;
- hotels, guest houses and bed and breakfast establishments;
- registered care homes and similar establishments; and
- buildings converted into self-contained flats.

Defining a property as an HMO is not always clear cut and legal advice may be necessary in cases that are not clear cut. Additionally, the differences in definition – alongside renowned difficulties in identifying the sometimes fluid nature of HMOs in the first place – are in part responsible for the differences in statistical accounts of HMOs.

Poor conditions in HMOs in relation to other housing stock are well documented (Audit Commission, 1991; ODPM, 2003c, DETR, 1998a). Environmental health practitioners working in local authorities currently have a range of legal powers to address conditions in HMOs. These include requirements related to all dwelling houses in respect of statutory fitness and nuisance, repair and overcrowding but controls also extend to the increased risks inherent in sharing accommodation with other households, notably in respect of the additional necessity for extra amenities and/or the reduction of households living there, management and fire safety. Local authorities are also able to introduce discretionary registration schemes for HMOs in their area and – in extreme cases – are able to take control of HMOs to protect the health, safety and welfare of tenants.

However, despite extensive legal controls, conditions in HMOs remain poor in relation to other types of housing accommodation. They are notoriously time consuming and difficult to identify, and there can be difficulties in obtaining the required legal standards, particularly when dealing with some of the most deprived households who in many cases are understandably concerned about harassment, eviction and rent increases.

The HMO sector can comprise the lowest-cost accommodation for those already disadvantaged and not able to seek preferable and more suitable accommodation elsewhere in the housing sector, particularly for those who do not qualify to be accepted as 'statutorily homeless' and could have no where else to go. For many, the situation is compounded by language and cultural differences, but most acutely by poverty and consequent lack of choice.

Many asylum seekers are reported to be 'drifting back' to, or 'disappearing' in London (Hefferman, 2002; Marr, 2000) following dispersal through the National Asylum Support Service (NASS), to be with family and friends – many living in unregistered and poor-quality HMOs (Hefferman, 2002). NASS has said that it will not share details of all known poor HMOs – where local authorities hold enforcement responsibility – with those local authorities (Hatchett, 2002a), creating a vacuum in a potential partnership approach both to homelessness and housing conditions, despite the new local authority duty under the Homelessness Act 2002 to identify the causes of and develop solutions for reducing homelessness in their areas.

At the very bottom end of the HMO sector, housing need and conditions are at their most acute and multiple disadvantage needs to be addressed.

Partnership working to improve HMOs

Many working in the HMO sector already work in close partnerships within and outside of their local authorities, dealing regularly with housing benefit and homeless officers as well as external agencies and organisations, including fire authorities, homeless charities and advice workers. Many local authorities already have good strategic processes in place to respond to the unique conditions in HMOs, including well-trained, dedicated staff working to practise protocol guidelines backed up by sound enforcement and assistance strategies.

Wider partnerships have also become necessary. Statutorily homeless households are sometimes housed in another local authority due to pressure on housing availability, where that authority is responsible for private sector housing conditions. The HMO housing situation became particularly acute in London, leading to the Bed and Breakfast Information Exchange

(BABIE) being established in 1988. BABIE (see box 6.2) was formed to co-ordinate action and agree recommended prices. It has prepared a common grading system for hotels, which environmental health practitioners inspect. BABIE centrally collates details relating to location and condition, including amenities, etc. This has led to a gradual improvement in some B&B establishments and disuse of accommodation that remains unsatisfactory.

Environmental health practitioners and housing officers involved in HMOs have also established the National HMO Network (see www.nationalhmonetwork.com) which meets regularly to share knowledge, practice and experience of HMOs. This group also comprises representation from tenants' and landlords' groups and as such helps provide invaluable insights into the various parties involved and their objectives. The Network invites key speakers as well as enabling professional interchange in seminars relating to current issues in HMOs, such as debate on proposals to license HMOs, asylum seekers and the government position on the use of B&B accommodation for families.

HMOs: proposals for licensing

Many involved in HMOs have called for a national licensing system for some time to enable proactive, mandatory standards – rather than largely discretionary and reactive standards – to apply across the HMO sector (DETR, 1999b). Some local authorities already have a voluntary licensing system in place in preparation for the mandatory system. The scheme will be a balancing act that seeks to maintain good relations with decent landlords, but one which is able to identify and remove rogue landlords in some areas (Ellery, 2002).

Box 6.2 Housing the homeless: Islington and the Bed and Breakfast Information Exchange

The London Borough of Islington is located in north London. It has a very cosmopolitan population, is vibrant in nature and is generally considered one of the more desirable London boroughs to live in by the comfortably well off. However, in common with all of the other London boroughs it has pockets of deprivation, poverty and social exclusion and a community of homeless people.

The Bed and Breakfast Information Exchange (BABIE) is a non-statutory scheme whose function it is to collect and disseminate information on bed and breakfast establishments and hostels used to temporarily accommodate statutorily homeless households in London (BABIE, 1995). Originally this scheme was set up in January 1988; it is currently run by the Greater London Authority.

The rationale behind this scheme is that hotel accommodation by its very nature is not suitable for housing homeless people, and the allocation of grades provides housing professionals, such as Homeless Persons Officers with an index of unsuitability: 'A' graded premises provide the best and 'E' the worst accommodation (see Table 6.3).

Table 6.3 A summary of the BABIE grading system

Grade	Meaning of grade
A	Premises that provide satisfactory temporary accommodation to a high standard.
B	Premises that provide satisfactory temporary accommodation.
C1	Premises suitable for short-term placements.
C2	Premises suitable only to house childless households.
D	No further placements should be made at these premises and existing placements should be re-housed as soon as possible.
E	Completely unsuitable to house homeless households. Existing placements should be re-housed as a matter of urgency.
P	Premises awaiting assessment or no longer used to house homeless households.

Source: BABIE (1995)

Environmental health officers (EHOs) are required by BABIE to inspect properties once every six months against the criteria listed below and then allocate an appropriate grade:
- fire precautions and means of escape;
- health and safety;
- management, repair and cleanliness;
- overcrowding;
- occupancy levels;
- provision of baths/showers and wash hand basins;
- provision of kitchen facilities.

Typically, bed and breakfast accommodation in Islington is inspected annually by officers of the Residential Team. The standards fall short of the borough's Code of Practice for houses in multiple occupation (HMO) and is therefore simply viewed as an information gathering exercise. The grading is returned to the owner of the hotel together with details of any defects. Formal action may be considered if there is a history of non-compliance.

Chadwick Villas (name changed here, henceforth called 'The Villas') is representative of the bed and breakfast premises used to temporarily house homeless households in Islington. It is located in the north of the borough in a residential street just off a main thoroughfare. In the surrounding area there is a very limited selection of small shops. Most of the buildings in this and adjacent roads are large three-storey Victorian villas and are in varying degrees of decay. The Villas consists of three adjacent villas converted into a 29-bedroom bed and breakfast hotel. It is owned by a limited company and only accepts referrals of statutorily homeless households from local authorities. It had a current BABIE grading of C1. This hotel typifies the standard of temporary bed and breakfast accommodation most homeless households are placed in.

At the time of the BABIE inspection in June 2001 it was home to 63 homeless people, 46 per cent of whom were children. The permitted number of residents was 60 and at the current occupancy levels there was 5 per cent overcrowding. Both the ratios of the provision of baths/showers, WCs and kitchens exceeded the minimum standard. Only the occupants of two rooms had exclusive use of a shower. Residents had no access to a washing machine. There was no lounge or children's play area and no facilities to allow residents to receive a visit from a GP or social worker. One public telephone was the only means by which residents could contact the outside world. There were two protected escape routes from fire plus one secondary route. There were some minor defects in fire precautions such as a large gap between a fire door and door threshold and a self-closer missing on one door. There were sporadic instances of minor disrepair to rooms and a lack of cleanliness in some areas, mainly common parts. Additionally, there was evidence in two rooms of a current infestation of German cockroaches. Records had shown that previous attempts had been made by a pest contractor to treat this infestation. It maintained its BABIE grading of C1.

Figures in 2002 showed that 70 per cent of homeless households either included dependent children or a pregnant woman (GLA, 2002) – see Table 6.4.

Table 6.4 Priority need profile of those households accepted as homeless in 2001/02

Dependent children	59%
Pregnant women	11%
Mental illness	10%
Physical disability	8%
Other special reasons	5%
Old age	4%
Domestic violence	2%
Vulnerable young people	1%

In 75 per cent of cases where relationship breakdown with a partner had occurred, domestic violence was given, as the main reason for homelessness (GLA, 2002). Clearly, this group of people has very specific healthcare needs, and access to both physical and mental health services is essential for the recovery process to begin. Additionally, asylum seekers who according to GLA (2001) made up 14 per cent of the homeless population in London, are traumatised individuals who also have very specific healthcare needs. Reactions from residents to EHOs conducting the BABIE inspection at The Villas clearly demonstrated that there was a fear of anyone who was perceived as representing 'authority'. This fear was particularly acute in those residents that were asylum seekers. Potentially, this fear could develop into a barrier against these individuals' ability to access much needed healthcare and other support services.

The Villas clearly demonstrates that it is unable to provide an environment and the facilities that enable people to access health and social services. For example, there were no facilities such as a private room to enable a GP or social workers to visit residents. This is not an uncommon situation as only five per cent of homeless households are placed in hotels with the top grade that would provide such facilities. Seven per cent are placed in those with the worst grade, while the great majority are placed in C graded hotels (GLA, 2002), neither of which can provide the necessary facilities or support that these homeless households need.

In conclusion, this means that some of the most vulnerable people in our society – children, victims of domestic violence and asylum seekers – are excluded from the healthcare system and other specialised practical and emotional support services that they so desperately need. In fact they are housed for the most part in places that are healthcare exclusion zones.

Despite some of these difficulties, BABIE has led to a gradual improvement in some B&B establishments and a disuse of accommodation that remains unsatisfactory.

Case study provided by Nicola Wilson

References
BABIE (1995) London boroughs bed and breakfast information: The BABIE hotel grading system The London Research Centre

GLA (2002) Homelessness in London 38 Electronic sources [Online] Available: http://www.london.gov.uk/approot/mayor/housing/homelessness_bull/docs/200=2/bull_38_2002.rtf [18 December 2002]

GLA (2001) Homelessness in London Electronic sources [Online] Available: http://www.london.gov.uk/approot/mayor/housing/homelessness_bull/docs/bul=l_27a_2001.rtf [18 December 2002]

The Housing Act 2004 (ODPM, 2003b) to some extent improves controls for HMOs by introducing a mandatory licensing system to tackle poor physical conditions and management standards for higher-risk premises, where the HMO is three storeys or more with five or more occupants. The Act also provides for the discretionary designation of additional licensing areas. The new HMO definition and high-risk designation contained in it is crucial to the success and coverage of the new regime and – at the time of writing – it is likely that some 1.5 million homes will fit this definition, mainly ex-hotels, bed and breakfast establishments and hostels of three storeys or more housing five or more unrelated people, with local authority and housing association properties excluded. It is likely that the scheme will be self-funded (Ellery, 2002; Hatchett, 2002b; ODPM, 2003b).

Not surprisingly, many environmental health practioners are disappointed that the proposed definition will exclude many smaller HMOs (Hatchett, 2002b) and there have been calls for practitioners to become more closely involved with the proposed legislation. However, the introduction of HMO licensing is seen as a positive step overall in improving some of the nation's worst housing stock. Licensing legislation is likely to be backed by an approved Code of Practice on HMO management currently being commissioned by the ODPM.

Additional information and guidance continues to be published and should be referred to for latest information.

Statutory fitness and the housing health and safety rating system
Current statutory standards of fitness and nuisance
Currently, a key housing activity for local authorities is addressing housing fitness under the Housing Act 1985 (as amended). A dwelling-house is deemed fit for habitation unless it fails to meet one or more specified criteria and for that reason is not suitable for occupation. The criteria include structural stability; serious disrepair; dampness prejudicial to health; adequate provision for lighting, heating and ventilation; a wholesome water supply; facilities for preparation of food – including a sink with hot and cold water; provision of a WC (internal); bath or shower with hot and cold water; foul and surface water drainage. The fitness standard also applies to houses in multiple occupation (HMO), where an extended standard includes means of escape from fire and amenities for the

number of occupants in response to the increased likelihood of fire and accident by overcrowding and discomfort caused by inadequate numbers of amenities. The fitness standard is well recognised and interpreted and fits neatly into existing enforcement and assistance regimes.

Statutory nuisance provisions under the Environmental Protection Act 1990 also provide a legal resolution for poor housing conditions, where the effect of the defect on health rather than just the presence of the defect is important. Statutory nuisance legislation may be a better course of action in some instances where the fitness standard is not sufficiently extensive and action can be instigated across housing tenures.

Proposals for change

A review of the current statutory standard of housing fitness has been underway for some time. It has been criticised as being subjective and limited in scope, excluding many domestic health and safety issues likely to cause harm, such as insufficient requirements for fire safety, internal arrangement, energy efficiency and indoor air quality. The standard is static, finite and non-progressive, being enforcement-based and unable to distinguish between degrees of unfitness. Initial consultation focused on expanding the standard to incorporate items such as internal arrangement and energy efficiency, and on whether a more fundamental review of evaluating housing conditions, based on empirical evidence, was required. Additionally, many other public and environmental health standards have moved toward forms of risk assessment which can help provide a more dynamic approach.

A complete rethink on housing safety data (see Tables 5.6 and 5.7) (DTI, 1995 and 2000) allied to an increasing use of risk assessment techniques elsewhere in environmental health activity confirmed that existing housing legislation was failing to tackle many domestic conditions likely to give rise to harm and that a change in intervention was necessary (see, for example, Battersby and Ormandy, 1999; Battersby et al, 2000; DETR, 2000d) in the form of the Housing Health and Safety Rating System (HHSRS).

A new approach – the housing health and safety rating system

The HHSRS is a completely new method of comprehensively assessing evidence-based domestic health and safety issues. It measures and ranks the severity of risk by considering the effect of a defect, not just the presence of defect. It is medically and scientifically valid, practical and modern in application and legislatively based, seeking to protect the occupant most vulnerable to a particular defect.

The HHSRS considers the effect of the defect and provides a rating. The ideal standard is established and the actual condition compared with this ideal and conditions falling short of this (faults) are assessed for their potential to cause harm. The assessment is based on the likelihood of occurrence (an event or period of exposure) multiplied by the range of harms or outcomes, which provides a hazard weighting score. The person most vulnerable to the hazard is taken into the equation. The numerical score calculated represents the risk, which may be deemed acceptable or unacceptable, and would then trigger appropriate action.

In practice, applying the standard involves identification of the 29 hazards, to be assessed and recorded individually. These are in four groups focusing around health requirements, which are then sub-divided as follows:
  • Physiological requirements (including hygrothermal conditions and pollutants)
  • Psychological requirents (including space,security, light and noise)
  • Protection against infection (including hygiene, sanitation and water supply)
  • Protection against accidents (including falls, electric shock, burns and scalds, and building related conditions)

This involves a two-stage assessment considering the likelihood of occurrence and the range of probable harm outcomes that may result. The combination gives a hazard score.

The most appropriate action can then be determined from ranges of possible hazard scores (DETR, 2000d, and 2000e).

The HHSRS can compare different types of hazard, taking into account the likelihood and severity of occurrence and providing a numerical score for each hazard. This allows for improvements to architectural features that can give rise to accident, such as the design of stairs, windows, kitchen and so on. The HHSRS is a system or an approach, not a fixed standard, which enables it to be progressive.

The government has continued to produce guidance as the system is tested and refined. Worked examples have shown how the standard applies to all dwellings. These examples range from system-built tower blocks to addressing major condensation and mould growth and individual hazards arising from steps to an owner-occupied 1930s dwelling (see DTLR, 2001a). This is particularly important so that all tenures of housing stock within a local authority area can be considered and compared, with resources increasingly allocated according to risk.

Additional information and guidance continues to be published. At the time of this book going to press, the ODPM (2004), has published HHSRS Guidance (version 2) which should be referred to for latest information. It is available online at http://www.odpm.gov.uk/stellent/groups/odpm_housing/documents/page/odpm_house_032782.pdf

Tower blocks and health: the unique health issues in the social housing sector
Mass municipal housing schemes – the rise and decline of a new ideology

The UK has a distinct mass housing estate situation because it urbanised earlier than the rest of Europe. This early urbanisation meant that poor private sector housing conditions had become acute by the mid-20th century. The UK response tended to favour replacement of private stock with public sector housing, built and managed by local authorities. This, combined with increasing owner-occupation and, some argued, over-regulation of the private rented sector, ensured that local authorities acquired and maintained the major proportion of rented tenure. By the 1960s and 1970s, housing policy was one of almost unquestioned clearance and municipal rebuild on a scale quite unlike any other European counterpart (Power, 1993, 1999).

The legacy of mass local authority house-building programmes has been the creation of high-rise, volume-built estates closely tied to slum cleared areas, which originally received cross-party government support. However, these utilitarian – even utopian – modernist estates were designed by architects (partly inspired by Le Corbusier's vision of 'Towers in the Park'), developers and politicians, not housing managers or potential residents. They stood out in sharp contrast to surrounding urban landscapes and were frequently inhumane, harsh and forbidding in appearance because they were made up of flattened concrete blocks and had bare, unusable open spaces. With pressure to build quickly, their construction was often unsupervised, poor and cheap. Although initially designed with communal local facilities in mind, such as heating and lifts, which were fundamental to the new design, many never functioned properly from the start. The scale of such large contracts and potential cost of delays sometimes meant that fundamental construction features were neglected and poorly funded and managed.

Initially seen as the answer to the nation's housing crisis, such estates have created a new set of socio-economic problems. Fundamental issues of their design, architecture and construction made them difficult to manage. There was an initial skewing of new tenants through a slow, cumbersome, divisive process which led to social and racial segregation, establishing a new process of exclusion (Power, 1993) and many were traumatised at being forceably removed from known communities (Coleman, 1990). High-rise flats proved both unpopular for tenants and unsuited to the UK climate as the concrete and flat roofed structures were prone to damp and condensation and were poorly insulated.

The rapid downward spiral made them increasingly difficult to let, creating an imbalance in an increasingly welfare-dependant population, with high ethnic concentrations and an unmet, increasing need for services. The large units created an imbalance of young families not suited to such design and communalised environment. Such estates, funded and created by the state, have led to marginal, polarised and visual foci of social exclusion that can be socially fraught, turbulent and very difficult to manage. Many have argued that divisions in UK housing tenure have caused tension and division (Balchin, 1985; National Federation of Housing Associations, 1985; Coleman, 1990; Power 1993, 1999).

Problems of estate management were exacerbated by local government reorganisation in 1965, around the time that such high-rise construction was starting to decline, and some new administrations suddenly had high levels of local authority housing stock. The late 1970s fuel crisis led to heavy local government cut-backs, notably affecting council house-building and maintenance programmes. There was no national overview of housing management, as rapidly expanding stock had taken priority over issues like maintenance, and local authorities were not sanctioned if they performed poorly as landlords (Power, 1993). Housing managers were based in remote town halls, generally offering a low level of direct service provision (Power, 1993).

Until the 1980s, such housing estates were almost a part of the national culture and little had been done to address the emerging problems. This was an era of rapid social upheaval: demographic change, increasing unemployment and family breakdown which led to further poverty, alienation, social unrest and a growing marginalised 'underclass' dependent on benefits and even rioting. Cole and Furbey (1994: 86) reported that by 1979, council housing consumers 'were increasingly drawn from the ranks of the economically inactive, dependent on social security benefits – a group yielding far less political or economic power than the skilled and semi-skilled working-class households which constituted the original council tenants'.

Design disadvantagement and the new housing management

The physical characteristics of many mass housing estates can not only fuel social problems, but also concentrate them, with a cyclical and repetitive effect for parent(s) and child (Coleman, 1990; Power, 1999). This has been found to reinforce insecurity, low self-esteem and underachievement because of an already polarised environment and restricted social contacts outside of the estate (see table 6.5).

Aspect of decline	Characteristics
Physical	Includes design, layout, structural and repair problems
Management	Includes letting problems, voids, high turnover, difficulties with care-taking, staffing problems, poor liaison with tenants
Financial	Includes higher costs than income, high rents, rent arrears, inadequate resulting resource for repairs, rent loss through voids, turnover, vandal damage
Social	Includes poor facilities, concentrated need, breakdown of control

Table 6.5
Aspects of (social housing) estate decline

Source: Based on Power (1999)

Pioneering research carried out in the 1980s sought to investigate and analyse the effect of 'design disadvantagement' in housing on behaviour (Coleman, 1990). This work was based on earlier research by Jacobs and Newman (cited in Coleman, 1990). Jacobs argued that adult 'eyes on the street' were needed to maintain social stability, and where absent, the immature would learn only from their peers, so gain no sense of ownership or respect. This view was extended by Newman who found that criminal behaviour became easier where a lack of 'defensible space' that provided some sense of ownership enabled criminal behaviour due to anonymity, lack of surveillance and the presence of alternative escape routes. Coleman's research team explored the effect of design features on civilised behaviour, measuring the impact that specified design features such as overhead walkways, child density, spatial organisation, blocks per site and the number of storeys had on a 'socially stabilising environment' (Coleman, 1990: 3) and the likelihood of encouraging social malaise such as graffiti, excrement, littering, family breakdown and criminal behaviour.

The team concluded that design disadvantagement ultimately causes higher public expenditure for policing, courts and prisons as well as social costs. Their scoring system showed how some features, such as overhead walkways, could be designed out, having an effect on the disadvantagement score and the level of criminal behaviour subsequently expected, but that each estate needed to be separately assessed. Coleman (1990: 173) argued that 'all these discoveries add up to the fact that it is the Utopian design imposed upon post-war Britain that appears to be the chief factor in many aspects of social decline in new or redeveloped areas'.

Area regeneration with community participation
By the 1980s, it was clear that many of the new estates needed substantial regeneration investment (see, for example, Stewart and Rhoden, 2003) but local authority capital budgets were simply inadequate to address not only the poor housing but also the wider socio-economic decline. Government had no major programmes to deal with issues in such estates and central/local government relations, particularly concerning housing management, were not helpful. Until then, local authorities held a near monopoly position as social housing provider (Malpass, 1992; Cole and Furbey, 1994), but this was set to change dramatically as the radical Conservative government set about introducing 'public choice' by seeking alternative housing providers and

Date	Key event, policy, etc
1974	Government postal survey reveals serious problems on modern, difficult-to-let estates
1976	Department of the Environment investigates reasons for difficult-to-let housing, finding that decline can become extreme, with social problems and council services management problems
1977	Greater London Council tackles hard-to-let problems through advertising campaign
1979	Election of Conservative government, to run for three terms
1979-84	**Priority Estates Project** established in attempt to rescue unpopular estates, with money available from Housing Investment Programme – scheme extended in 1984 and 1987; other initiatives funded through **Urban Programme**
1980	**Right to Buy, Urban Development Corporations, Competitive Tendering**
1981	Enquiries following the Toxteth and Brixton riots identify social, economic and policing problems of run-down estates with unemployment and discrimination as major causes of disorder
1982	Social security and housing benefit reforms
1985	**Estate Action** set up by government to target capital at run-down estates with the condition that management is localised and tenants are consulted. 350 estates are upgraded over five years. Local authority stock generally decreases and becomes increasingly polarised due to **Voluntary Transfer, Estate Management Boards**, etc
1988	**Housing Action Trusts** and **Tenants Choice** are introduced to break up council housing. Private finance for housing associations
1989	Ring fencing of the Housing Revenue Account
1989-93	**Housing Associations become the major developers of new social housing**, using partly private finance for the first time in Britain. Needs-based lettings are encouraged by government funding and local authority nominations, so polarisation quickly emerges. Increased emphasis on tenant-led initiatives, such as Tenant Management Organisations, with government funding
1991	**City Challenge** established to create new partnerships of public and private involvement for inner-city areas in decline, which involves housing as well as economic and training initiatives, encouraging competition and company structures into housing organisations. Some new HAT schemes are introduced

Table 6.6
British social housing policy from 1974

Table 6.6 (cont)
British social housing policy from 1974

1992	**Compulsory Competitive Tendering** is introduced for housing management to 'improve' management performance, causing further concern for the future of more marginal estates as private sector proprieties become paramount
1992	**Private Finance Initiative** introduced to increase the involvement of the private sector in the financing and management of services that had been traditionally supported through private finance
1993	**Single Regeneration Budget** introduced to consolidate separate social, economic, training and housing regimes – it supersedes Estate Action and is seen by some as a cut in estate regeneration funding
1994-95	Proposals to develop selected urban estates by autonomous local housing companies
1997	Election of Labour government
1997	**Social Exclusion Unit** established
1998	**New Deal for Communities** launched
1999	**Best Value** launched – a new duty requiring local authorities and registered social landlords to review all services which they provide for local people and improve them by the best means available
2000	**Rent restructuring** – patterns of rent should be restructured over a ten year period so that rents are affordable, reflect the qualities which tenants value in properties and can be seen to be fair
2000	**Supporting People** – funding support to enable people to live in the community

Source: Based on Power (1993, 1999)

managers. Meanwhile, residents, frustrated with the local authority response, had began to set up associations and boards to take a more pioneering role in estate management. Social housing policy is summarised in table 6.4.

Emerging estate problems made it politically difficult, if not impossible, for local authorities to fund regeneration from existing financial regimes and investment income from rental income alone could not even start to address the situation. Local authorities were therefore faced with uncomfortable questions about how to rehabilitate poor high-rise housing stock and its local environment, combined with the acute need to help move tenants from social exclusion to inclusion. Some examples of how local authorities are addressing this can be found in Boxes 2.2 (see chapter 2) and 6.3.

Box 6.3 Regenerating the Chalkhill Estate, Brent

The Chalkhill estate – based on Park Hill in Sheffield – was designed and constructed in the late 1960s and received design awards for its innovative architecture. However, the utopia was short-lived and major concerns arose about poor security due to the walkways interconnecting the 30 Bison blocks of flats (see Figure 6.5). Early top-down schemes failed to consult residents, who found the strategically installed security doors along the walkways inconvenient. Following a murder in 1986, an Estate Action funded pilot scheme was implemented on two newly isolated blocks which were given their own entrance with security features including an entry phone, magnetic keys, surveillance equipment, lighting and – crucially – a receptionist.

Figure 6.5

Estate Action was initially focused on the most problematic urban estates, targeting central government funding through the Housing Investment Programme for improvements in security, the environment, and the construction of local offices and some buildings, on the condition that local authorities set up local management offices and consulted tenants. The Estate Action programme for Chalkhill totalled £11

Figure 6.6

million, but while this provided increased security through design modification (see Figure 6.6), it did not provide the major regeneration required to turn the estate around.

A new opportunity for redevelopment was made available through the Single Regeneration Budget (SRB), introduced in 1993 to unify earlier government-funded schemes. Bids were competitively assessed with an emphasis on partnership between the public, private and voluntary sectors. In return for government funding, the partnership had to deliver certain outputs such as the number of people finding work and the number of new businesses established. The three main partners for Chalkhill SRB are Brent Council, the Metropolitan Housing Trust and Wimpey Homes (Chalkhill SRB Programme Team, 1999). The main objectives of Chalkhill SRB are:

- to enhance the employment prospects, education and skills of local people, especially the young and disadvantaged, and to promote equality of opportunity; and
- to encourage sustainable growth and wealth creation by improving competitiveness in the local economy for new and existing businesses.

It was seen that these could be achieved by encouraging construction-related employment through the £60 million building work scheduled for the estate, on-site security and catering during redevelopment. In addition, other training outside the SRB should be provided such as basic skills, English as an additional language and women's vocational training, with childcare support offered during training and regularly advertised to residents. Currently, the majority of training and employment opportunities in the construction industry locally are funded through the SRB. The training programmes that are currently available are fairly expensive compared with the amount that is currently spent on similar training programmes elsewhere. This is because the training programmes on Chalkhill tend to last for a longer period of time – around 18 months – compared to other similar programmes. The training is at National Vocational Qualification (NVQ) Level II and is provided in five different trades. Part of the wages paid to the trainees come from SRB funds.

The current redevelopment process started in 1992 with extensive consultation (the Foresight Survey) with Chalkhill residents about a possible way forward. The options offered to tenants included doing nothing, demolition, refurbishment or a mixture of these. This process helped inform Brent Council about what to do, and how. Funding was a prime concern because of existing commitments elsewhere. It was clear that the necessary resources needed to be drawn from other existing sources, which caused concerns elsewhere in the borough.

Competition had become key to redevelopment proposals and funding opportunities, so Brent Council's Housing Committee decided to conduct a Design and Development Competition in 1993. The intention was to appraise issues including design, employment, tenure mix, income generation and private finance, security and space standards and increasing energy efficiency, while ensuring that residents would remain pivotal to the whole process. Applications for redevelopment were shortlisted and more detailed technical and planning aspects considered. Most people interviewed preferred demolition or part demolition as opposed to options such as continued linkway removal and refurbishment. In 1994, the competition winners, judged by a jury of local residents, independent experts and council officers, were a consortium of Wimpey Homes and the Metropolitan Housing Trust, who subsequently formed New Horizons (Brent) Ltd, with this partnership programme remaining key to the redevelopment of Chalkhill and keeping public expenditure to a minimum.

Since 1995, rehousing tenants of some 1,274 flats, temporarily or permanently, has been fundamental to the scheme's success in allowing for redevelopment from 1997. Tenants have been given the option of remaining at Chalkhill and becoming housing association tenants, or of remaining as council tenants but moving to live elsewhere within the borough. All had to move away at least temporarily to make way for their new homes. Finding alternative accommodation for so many has been one of the more complex aspects of the redevelopment, which has caused knock-on delays in the programme, although 90 per cent of flats awaiting demolition had been vacated by the end of 2000. Overall, the development will result in a net loss of affordable housing because of the high original density (see Figure 6.7). This may present Brent Council with further problems in the longer term in finding accommodation for statutorily homeless households.

A major part of the funding strategy came from selling some of the land identified by New Horizons to a retail project in 1998. This was won by bids and totalled approximately £24 million. Of the total amount £6 million was paid to the local authority and the remaining

£18 million was used for a variety of projects such as subsidising rents, helping the local Chalkhill primary school develop a park and establishing a five-year programme with the private sector in order to set up a local craft centre. In 1999 a new superstore was constructed, with many jobs being advertised through the SRB-funded employment agency. This helped many local residents into employment. The superstore has also supported community events such as the Healthy Living Day and Community Week.

Figure 6.7

Brent Council is working in partnership with housing organisations such as ASRA to develop a number of specialised units for people with special needs. These will be situated among the general needs properties on Chalkhill. In addition, a Healthy Living Centre is planned which will be funded by a private land deal with the private sector. The proceeds will be used to build the centre. The local Chalkhill primary school has benefited from the works on site and to date has received £250,000 from the New Horizons partnership. Some of the money has been used for the development of an information and communication technology suite that is both used by the pupils and by Brent Adult Education Services.

New Horizons aims to maintain consultation via the Joint Development Board established in 1996 (the main consultative forum for redevelopment proposals with a wide membership base), its subcommittees (Management Subcommittee and Social and Economic Subcommittee), tenants and residents associations and new build design groups. A regular newspaper (New Horizons) is also produced, which is published bi-monthly to maintain consultative momentum. There are two Tenants and Residents Associations on Chalkhill. Consultation is soon to take place about the Community Trust Fund – a fund set aside by New Horizons to provide neighbourhood community developments following the physical regeneration. The Metropolitan Housing Trust plans to have a local estate office on Chalkhill, which it intends to pay for from its own funds. There is also a possibility that a library will be built on the site, possibly through funding by the New Horizons partnership.

The public image of Chalkhill has gradually improved, having been considered a dangerous place with a high number of robberies, drug-related problems, muggings and car thefts. This image tended to criminalise the residents and resulted in many having no desire to live on Chalkhill, preferring instead to move elsewhere. However, the redevelopment has resulted in a reduction in the level of crime on Chalkhill and a consequent change of image. Initially, when residents had been informed that they were allocated a property on

Chalkhill, they were often very wary; however, once they actually saw their new homes they were happy to accept.

Acknowledgement
This is part of a paper that was first published in Stewart, J. and Rhoden, M. (2003) 'A review of social housing regeneration in the London Borough of Brent', *Journal of the Royal Society for the Promotion of Health*, 123 (1): 23–32.

Further reading
Chalkhill SRB Programme Team (1999) 'Chalkhill Single Regeneration Budget'. Unpublished.
Brent Council (2001) Chalkhill Database. *Welcome to the Chalkhill Redevelopment Project.* Available online at: http://www.brent.gov.uk/chalkhill.nsf?OpenDatabase [17 May 2001].

It would be easy to assume that such estates had such physical problems and an over-concentration of deprivation that it may be better to simply demolish them and start again. However, many such estates had also been found to have enormous potential, seemingly against many odds, and Power (1999: 312) has found that many notorious estates across Europe 'seemed likely to be destroyed by their very reputations', but that the 'turnaround was as dramatic as it was unforeseen'. Power suggests that the success of rescue schemes comes through highly responsive, variable and localised programmes, but with many shared patterns of renewal. What seems to be key is the extent to which authorities and residents can re-engage relationships to help encourage and retain constant interest and ongoing involvement and a new concept of estate management.

Funding is no doubt key to the process to enable physical renewal – a visible display that government is committed to, and serious about, estate renewal. Combined with the creation of activity centres such as shops, social facilities, recreation areas and so on, physical investment can have a major impact in helping ensure a sense of belonging, ownership and commitment and making the estate feel more humane to live in (Power, 1999). Allied to this is organisational and management changes which fundamentally involve residents to regain a sense of estate control. Locally based management is key, with enhanced caretaking responsibilities and new relationships with front-line staff to help address issues at early stages and forge new, more personal relationships with residents. The estates also had alien environments and this was overcome to some extent by recreating communities through local economic and social activities, such as by upgrading or introducing facilities, training and social networks. Power (1999) has suggested that it is likely to take around ten years to bridge the gap between such marginal communities and wider society.

The current approach in each estate shows how important partnership approaches, with residents taking a pivotal role, are in ensuring sustainable regeneration potential. This squares with Power (1999), who identifies three areas of concensus as to the causes of exclusion and that a combination of strategies is required in moving forward:

- the need for combined strategies to tackle estate problems, not single, simple solutions;
- localised operations to reverse poor conditions; and
- creating a sense of community by involving residents and building confidence in the area to help enhance conditions and prospects and to reduce the threat of social breakdown.

Summary
Many estates have been transformed in recent years through pioneering innovative changes in housing management, resident involvement and massive resource injection.

Early attempts at rehabilitation such as Estate Action were not a major success because they failed to address some of the key issues, despite considerable government expenditure. In any estate regeneration programme, it is essential to improve design, or in effect demolish and start again, with the residents at the centre of the process. This helps remove dependency on bureaucrats making remote decisions, and brings creative, innovative housing management to the fore to promote change that is sustainable physically. It also encourages active citizenship in housing through greater access and choice for those currently excluded or not greatly involved. It is also about housing quality and supply.

Lessons have been learned about what is going to work in both housing and community regeneration. It is crucial to find a unique and relevant regeneration programme for each individual estate and its residents' needs through resident involvement from the earliest stage. There must be engagement with initiative, reworking the role of the professional and assessing the overall working of the strategy from needs assessment to the direction of policy implementation and to how success is accounted for and how sustainable it is in terms of the real difference the regeneration has been able to make to people's lives.

Encouraging home-owners to maintain their homes and the Regulatory Reform Order 2002

The owner-occupied sector comprises the predominant tenure requiring the majority of resource available in its renovation, but the privately rented sector contains proportionately more unfit homes. Figures on the cost of private sector renovation vary considerably, and if early maintenance and repairs are not carried out, the cost will rise substantially.

Homeowners carry out the majority of repairs to private sector housing themselves, annually investing around £16 billion in their properties. However, many are not in a position to maintain and repair their homes. For this reason, local authorities currently invest some £250 million in supporting private sector renewal, assisting more than 70,000 households annually (ODPM, 2003c).

With declining capital expenditure and a return of personal responsibility for home repair and maintenance to owners, local authorities are having increasingly to seek new and innovative ways to lever private finance into existing housing regeneration strategies rather than continue with various housing grants as a main thrust of their private sector housing renewal strategy (DTLR, 2002). English and Welsh local authorities currently invest almost £400 million on improving conditions for 100,000 households per year and provide support to Home Improvement Agencies (HIA) (DTLR, 2001c).

Local authorities have traditionally held an invasive role in the privately owned sector – particularly since the Housing Act 1969 in financing various grants (see also Table 6.5) which may have created some culture of dependency on grants (DETR, 2001c; Mackintosh and Leather, 1992) and may to some extent be responsible for the reduced likelihood of home-owners themselves maintaining their homes. Grants are essentially a one-

Table 6.7
Initiatives (legislation)
in private sector
housing regeneration

Act/Policy	Key regeneration purpose
Housing Act 1969	New powers for repair; General Improvement Areas introduced
Housing Act 1974	Housing Action Areas introduced
Local Government and Housing Act 1989	Previous grant provisions superseded; Act introduced mandatory means-tested house renovation grants based on revised fitness standard; introduced home repair assistance; introduced renewal areas and group repairs schemes; redefined clearance areas and action for individual dwellings; Greater emphasis placed on role of Home Improvement Agencies
Housing Grants, Construction and Regeneration Act 1996	Switch from mandatory to discretionary grant aid for renovation; further proposals for renewal areas and group repair schemes; home repair assistance extended
DoE Circular 17/96 (DoE, 1996)	Provided detailed guidance on private sector renewal activity, emphasis on relevant local housing strategies and home-owners' responsibilities for repair and maintenance
Consultation Paper 2001 (DETR, 2001)	Consultation Paper on Private Sector Housing Renewal reviewing the role of housing grants, etc
The Regulatory Reform (Housing Assistance) England and Wales Order 2002 (DTLR, 2002)	Repealed existing grant legislation (except DFGs); introduced new local authority power to provide assistance for housing renewal, requiring that local authorities publish their policy
Housing Renewal Guidance (ODPM, 2002)	Non-statutory guidance supporting above, encourages increasingly strategic context and approach aligning with other corporate objectives

Source: Based on Stewart (2001)

off injection of funds to enable dwelling fitness and repair, but do not in themselves encourage regular maintenance as they are mainly concerned with an owner's deemed ability to afford works. There has been little progress in marrying grant policy to adequate resource in tackling private sector housing conditions and policies to assist low-income home-owners tend to lack direction (Leather, 2000) as grant budgets decrease.

There has been increasing emphasis on providing a broad power to provide financial and other assistance for home repair and improvement (DTLR, 2002, ODPM, 2002a, 2002b). This raises several key issues in seeking:

- more discretion for authorities to address the specific needs of their area;
- more opportunity to target help effectively to those at risk from poor housing;
- more effective use of resources;
- less dependency on grants and reinforcement of homeowners' responsibilities toward their properties; and
- more choice for homeowners between grants or loans.

As a result, many local authorities have already been actively seeking new ways of encouraging and enabling home-owners to routinely invest their own resource in their homes before they fall into substantial disrepair, rather than continue to rely on public sector funding through housing grants.

The Regulatory Reform (Housing Assistance) (England and Wales) Order 2002

The Regulatory Reform (Housing Assistance) (England and Wales) Order 2002 and supporting *Housing Renewal Guidance* (ODPM, 2002a; ODPM 2002b) repealed earlier grant provisions for renovation under the Housing Grants, Construction and Regeneration Act 1996, and introduced a new wide-ranging and flexible power enabling local authorities to improve living conditions in their area by providing 'assistance' – rather than grants – for housing renewal. Local authorities had to research and publish a policy for private sector housing by July 2003 consolidating wider strategic objectives and grant alternatives, and firmly setting objectives for private sector housing within a wider strategic context of furthering personal responsibility for private housing conditions. Local authorities must have regard to a person's ability to repay any assistance.

Maintenance, repair and improvement – whose job is it?

There are many reasons why homeowners fail to invest inadequately in their homes. In the owner-occupied sector, many simply cannot afford to, despite owning a major capital asset. Older and younger people, and some ethnic minorities, are the most likely to live in poor housing conditions (Macintosh and Leather, 1993; Revell and Leather, 2000). Older people – frequently occupying some of the worst stock – may not wish to have the upheaval or stress associated with major repair, or may hold valid concerns about trusting some builders. Many have such high outgoings, including mortgage repayments, that they may not be in a position to afford necessary repairs. Younger homeowners, in a position to afford repairs, may simply prefer to spend their income elsewhere on something frankly more interesting than home repair. Additionally, regional house prices may be a disincentive for a mobile population to invest substantially in repairs, as house prices may increase, regardless of an owner's investment level (Leather and Reid, 1989).

There is little accurate information available on the extent to which individual householders use their own resources for maintenance and repair. Homeowners tend to spend more than other tenures, although the figure shows regional variation. The amount spent rises with income (Leather and Reid, 1989; Revell and Leather, 2000). The EHCS probably provides the most accurate estimate of expenditure; an aggregate £31.5 billion spend by householders, some £28 billion of this (89 per cent of total) by owner-occupiers. During the 1987-91 period, 86 per cent of owners completed major works, but estimates for landlords are not available for improvement, repair or internal decoration (Revell and Leather, 2000). Homeowners tended to spend more on improvements (53 per cent) than repairs (30 per cent). Do-it-yourself (DIY) represents an important contribution in influencing the state of stock repair – normally for minor rather than major repairs, and generally carried out by younger, higher-income homeowners. It is estimated that since there is no labour cost involved, four times the work is possible at the same price, although it is difficult to accurately assess either the quality or quantity of works undertaken (Davidson et al, 1997).

What is clear is that a source of money, advice, support and sometimes compulsion is required, which local authorities are already well placed to deliver and/or support.

Stock condition and grant expenditure

Not all private sector housing investment comes in the form of grant assistance. Many owners are financially able and willing to maintain their homes, but some are not interested and others not able to afford – or perhaps cope with the upheaval of – necessary works. In a complex South East housing market, homeowners are not always 'rewarded' for regular maintenance and repair and their properties would increase in capital value regardless of condition. Many potential grant recipients were excluded from all local authority assistance and are deemed eligible to afford works as a result of the means test, although in practical terms this may not be so, particularly in areas where mortgage repayments are so high. Others regularly maintain and improve their homes and these groups are not normally offered any form of assistance from the local authority.

Homeowners and local authorities may have differing objectives about where housing investment is best spent. Homeowners already secure their own repairs and improvements outside of the grant regime, such as through saving schemes, loans, insurance, social fund loans and so on. However, owners and the authority's strategic housing duties and objectives do not always coincide. Homeowners, for example, may invest in improvements such as central heating, redecoration or a new kitchen which may not affect fitness, while local authorities may prefer to concentrate resources on a strategic enveloping scheme to help prevent further stock decline.

Government policy continues to favour the private sector as housing provider, with almost 70 per cent UK home ownership in 1999 (Wilcox, 2001), but the increase in this sector has not been matched by a parallel increase in renovation funding. Renovation is generally promoted as a lower-cost alternative to demolition (Macintosh and Leather, 1993). In addition, the stock is ageing and in need of continued investment as poor housing is closely related to age of stock as well as household income.

Despite considerable expenditure, recorded disrepair has remained relatively static, and is still a key cause of unfitness. Problems remain even in areas where substantial grant expenditure has been paid (Leather and Reid, 1989; Wilcox, 2001). Disrepair is particularly crucial as nearly a third of all dwellings require urgent repair and swift works are required to arrest further decline. Local authorities – with government encouragement – have sought to concentrate resource on area activity in attempt to stimulate private sector investment, but there is little local data analysing the impact of grant investment over time or the profile of householders receiving assistance. For example, Group Repair Schemes – introduced to enhance the external envelope of dwellings – were encouraged on the assumption that owners would then be prepared to invest further, but there was no real evidence to support this. Information tends to be property based with, for example, 75 per cent of approvals for pre-1919 stock (Revell and Leather, 2000).

So why do owners fail to invest in their housing? There is a significant correlation between household income, unemployment and poor housing conditions (DETR, 1998a; Macintosh and Leather, 1993; Revell and Leather, 2000). In England, 1 in 10 households where income was less than £4,000 per annum lived in unfit dwellings, compared to 1 in 25 who had an income of £24,000. Some three-fifths of low-income households live in poor private sector housing conditions (Wilcox, 2001). As recorded levels of disrepair have remained relatively static over subsequent house condition surveys despite grant expenditure over the period, it is reasonable to assume that a viable, cost-effective culture of home maintenance is somewhat lacking.

Households typically respond to rather than anticipate repair requirements, and tend to favour low-cost solutions that may fail to tackle underlying problems (Leather and Reid, 1989). The previous grant regime to a large extent reflected this, essentially being a one-off injection of funds with no conditions attached requiring the owner to take a more proactive role in future maintenance. Some see this as a fundamental flaw in the earlier grant system, which essentially rewarded those who have failed to invest – either deliberately or through lack of resource – and did not assist those outside of the grant system at all. A fundamental shift in culture is required to encourage – and to enable – owners to regularly maintain their homes before they fall into substantial, and expensive, disrepair.

The private housing sector needs to become essentially self-regulating, with local authorities financially or otherwise assisting those in need. A new proactive and reactive approach is required to help prevent the need for assistance in the first place, and also to preserve diminishing funds for the worst stock.

Can homeowners be encouraged to invest?

Government emphasis is increasingly about homeowners taking responsibility for their own homes (DoE, 1996a; DETR, 2001c; DTLR, 2002). It is fundamental that local authorities develop realistic strategies based on local circumstance that draw together a range of in-house services and external providers (DETR, 1998c) that provide the right things to enable homeowners to maintain their homes. Many local authorities already have strategies in place that incorporate several initiatives.

Financial investment aside, local authorities already have substantial house renovation expertise, experience, organisational arrangements and systems in place which could be readily adapted to encourage and enable homeowners to arrange for and fund necessary works outside of local authority expenditure to protect their investment. Authorities increasingly operate Home Improvement Agency Services, in-house or via a partnership arrangement with another organisation, which operate to a variety of levels and suitability. While many are established to support 'vulnerable' groups such as older people, their role and expertise could be increased to cater for the needs of others. Similarly, existing direct service organisations (DSO) or suitable local building companies, could take on a new role to carry out repairs at a more cost-effective price, possibly on a self-financing basis.

Several existing schemes have been identified which are of increasing interest to local authorities in levering in private sector finance (Mackintosh and Leather, 1992; DoE, 1996a; DETR, 1998c). These include targeting grants more effectively, home improvement loans and increasing emphasis on equity release schemes (see summary in Table 6.8). The government is keen to promote interest in the effective use of these relatively new schemes, though it recognises some of the problems of working with the private sector, including possible repossessions and the impact on the borrower's benefit entitlement, and the market has been slow to develop, can be localised and expensive (DETR, 1998c). The government is asking local authorities to take a fresh look at such initiatives in partnership with the private sector (DETR, 2001a). Few new initiatives have been proffered since, and few have made major leaps forward in the intervening period, although a combination of them may help reduce pressure on local authority capital expenditure.

Local stock condition surveys are fundamental in deciding how best to administer available resources. Local authorities increasingly need to spend money they have available efficiently, effectively and on dwellings that most require investment as part of a wider strategy. Successful strategic development requires honest appraisal of housing stock and the make-up of local residents so that maintenance strategies can be sensitively and appropriately targeted, possibly by the development of existing schemes in the area or the development of new partnership-based schemes with advice from operational schemes elsewhere. The DoE (1996a) suggests that those least aware of problems with their homes are older people, those with mental health

Table 6.8 Initiatives in encouraging personal responsibility in home maintenance, repair and improvement

Initiative	Comments	Organisation responsible
LA Home Improvement Loan	Currently permitted in legislation, but effectiveness could be improved to enable preferential LA rates and terms of interest	LA (private sector would expect preferential interest rate return)
Equity release scheme (as form of loan cited above)	Use of capital rather than income to repay loan; avoid the need for borrower to make repayment from income, so access capital without affecting income	Private sector
Handy person services	Free or low cost service (available on request or referral) for minor repairs – may have limited contribution to stock condition, but early intervention many help prevent more serious problems. Increase in such services, but likely to remain specialist for vulnerable groups.	Scheme facilitated by local authorities, housing associations, HIAs, voluntary sector etc.
Subscription-based emergency repair services	Nationally available, for provision of accredited builders and available 24 hours. Seen to offer the greatest potential for developing wider demand as already has a growing membership and high satisfaction with service provided; encouraging more work through awareness	Private companies, funded by charging client
Subscription based maintenance service	Includes exterior survey and maintenance plan, with free emergency call out and fees charged. Little interest currently – tends to be for more affluent householders and related to age. 40% scheme members use it for works.	Local building companies – local authorities may initiate such a private sector scheme with appropriate personnel
Money advice	Owners – particularly those on low income – may require advice concerning increased spending on loans, benefits, savings, etc.	Local authority, citizens advice, voluntary sector etc
Advice and information	Verbal, visual and literature advice and guidance on repair and maintenance issues and wider issues eg energy efficiency – eg leaflets, videos, exhibitions, demonstrations. Many schemes exist, eg may give schedule for necessary works to someone not eligible for grant	Local authorities, HAs and HIAs, particularly associated with applications for, or completed grants, community associations, residents groups
Home maintenance surveys	Written or verbal survey plus report on short and long term repair and maintenance requirements, how to tackle the problem, likely costs – may help with owner prioritising works required and employing suitably priced builder with LA inspector checking quality of works. May form part of home maintenance strategy, encouraging and enabling works owner would not otherwise tackle.	Local authorities, HAs and HIAs – either free of charge, or fee to cover costs
Tool loans	Including loan of specialist or expensive items, eg cement mixers, scaffolding, ladders, power tools – saving owner money in enabling them to carry out works	Local authority or community based organisations

Home maintenance training	Training focus on maintenance awareness of specific maintenance skills; surgeries to discuss common problems, DIY, targeted focus. Could be tied to capacity building through project based employment – not common at present Local authorities as well as possible funding from DFEE, NDC etc	Local authorities as well as possible funding from DFEE, NDC, etc
Volunteering schemes	Encouraging residents to assist with vulnerable persons eg older people etc	Local authority and/or existing community groups
Builders list	Assurance of trustworthy and competent builder	LA or community group
Maintenance strategy	Useful to help protect LA's investment and encourage people to do works to reasonable standard that they might not otherwise tackle. Draws together several above initiatives for all or part of LA area; funding and staffing considerations	LA
Do-it-Yourself (DIY)	Basic maintenance/repair/improvement work by home-owner and unpaid help (mainly cosmetic).	Private sector

problems, those on low incomes and ethnic minority groups, so maintenance schemes need to be developed and targeted accordingly. Local strategies also need to recognise that often older, low-income households are less able to participate in DIY than their younger, often wealthier counterparts, and may have to finance both materials and labour, substantially increasing the overall cost (Davidson et al, 1997; Davidson and Leather, 2000). This has important implications for home maintenance schemes.

Summary
Most housing is in a poor condition because owners cannot afford repairs. The English House Condition Survey continues to report that low-income groups – particularly ethnic minorities – are the most likely to occupy poor housing. A properly targeted and funded grant system could have a substantial impact on maintaining stock condition in the private housing sector. However, local authorities are faced with reducing capital and increasing disrepair in an ageing housing stock and need to find new and realistic ways to move forward.

Alternatives to existing grant-funded regimes need to incorporate new approaches in initiative and attitude of both homeowners and local authorities delivering their strategic housing responsibilities. Fundamentally, local authorities need to develop a variety of resource and support initiatives to encourage and enable homeowners to maintain their homes for the future. Regardless of arguments for and against such initiatives, there is little doubt that local authorities need to find new ways of encouraging homeowners to sustainably invest in maintaining their homes. Additional information can be found in Stewart, Clayton and Ruston (2004).

The Private Rented Sector and Landlord Accreditation Schemes

Government policy continues to drive local housing authorities toward establishing landlord accreditation schemes as part of its stated commitment to increasing both housing availability and standards in the private rented sector. Although many local authorities are ideologically opposed to making increased need in this sector a form of social housing privatisation, and have many valid concerns about its condition and suitability, the sector must increasingly meet growing housing need while offering some potential for self-regulation. However, there remains little systematic information about the extent to which local authorities are working with the private rented sector with many authorities having to do so for lack of alternative accommodation in the social sector.

The private rented sector – who lets, who rents and why?

The private rented sector currently comprises some two million properties and many feel it retains an unfair reputation of poor quality accommodation, insecure tenancies and expensive rents. Its political renaissance began when the Thatcher governments set out to bring radical changes to the nature and extent of the private rented sector, challenging what they saw as the near-monopoly supply of renting provided by local authorities (for more detail, see Stewart, 2001 and 2002).

Following research into the nature of the private rented sector, the DETR (1996) reported that:

- 74 per cent of private lettings are not seen as a full-time business occupation;

- 11 per cent are let by property companies;
- around 25 per cent of lettings are owned by a landlord with one property;
- around 75 per cent of landlords have fewer than 40 lettings;
- the median number of lettings owned is seven;
- there is a dominance of the 'sideline' landlord where 60 per cent of lettings represent less than a quarter of income; business landlords' rent returns represent 75 per cent of income;
- 91 per cent of lettings are owned by landlords of English/European origin; and
- of current lettings, 70 per cent would be relet if they became vacant (ie some 30 per cent would not).

Landlords let for a variety of reasons, but it is suggested that general confidence in letting has increased since the 1980s (DETR, 1996). Much of this increased confidence derives from the deregulated tenancies introduced under the Housing Act 1996 – assured shorthold tenancies (AST). The government believed that such tenancies would increase the supply side of the sector, making it a more attractive opportunity for landlords, thus unleashing an untapped housing supply for rent. ASTs now account for around two-fifths of private lettings (DETR, 1996). The private rented sector is able to cater well for those able to afford market rents, and those who require flexibility in housing location.

However, there is of course another side to the coin – those who are not able to afford market rents, and frequently those households subject to enforcement activity by environmental health departments. Increasingly, those on low income are not able to access social housing and have nowhere to turn but the private rented sector, which proves both expensive and insecure. It has been suggested that the sector's primary client base has been as temporary accommodation for the young and/or mobile who are not able to access social housing (Cowan, 1998) and those in receipt of housing benefit are more likely to occupy poor condition dwellings let by investment-orientated landlords (DETR, 2000f). Those not able to afford market rents may be eligible for housing benefit (HB) and; again, government research makes interesting reading.

Assessed at 1998-9 prices, the housing benefit bill for 1978-9 was £2.3 billion. By 1998-9 it had risen to £11.1 billion (DETR, 2000a). Clearly, the new ASTs had substantial impact on government expenditure as expenditure shifted from bricks and mortar subsidy to personal subsidy during the period. For housing expenditure in 1979, 84 per cent was bricks and mortar subsidy with 16 per cent personal subsidy, and by 1998-9, 27 per cent was bricks and mortar subsidy with 73 per cent personal subsidy (DETR, 2000a). HB expenditure is still expected to rise, even though unemployment is decreasing. Serious questions need to be raised about the economic efficiency of such expenditure, particularly when most homeless households would prefer social housing than the private rented sector (DETR, 1998e).

Government research into the private rented sector (DETR, 1996, 1997) shows that 50 per cent of private sector tenants receive housing benefit, illustrating the considerable demand from lower-income households. Forty per cent of landlords do not wish to let to people on housing benefit, but 50 per cent of their clientele need it. Many on low income are forced into the sector through lack of choice, leaving them trapped into high rents and low security with few opportunities to access other tenures and caught in a cycle of poverty (DETR, 1997).

One key criticism is that despite high levels of housing benefit paid, the private rented sector remains in poor condition relative to other tenures and HB is paid regardless of condition. Most privately rented housing is pre-1919 stock – one of the reasons for its poor condition – which is increasingly occupied by ethnic minorities and low-income groups (ODPM, 2000c). Twenty per cent of private rented housing is unfit, compared with six per cent owner occupation, seven per cent local authority and five per cent of registered social landlord housing stock (DETR, 2000a). Research continues to show that there is not a consistent relationship within deregulated tenancies between dwelling condition and rent charged, although some landlords do have a more responsible attitude toward proactive maintenance. This does not include investment orientated landlords (DETR, 2000f) so tenants may be unwilling – or unable – to pay more for better accommodation. This leaves landlords with little financial incentive to improve condition.

Meeting local housing need through the private rented sector – opportunities for landlord accreditation schemes

Research published by the DETR (2001e) found a vast range of different landlord accreditation schemes – defined as schemes whereby landlords submitted their properties for assessment against a range of condition and management criteria – being developed and implemented by local authorities. Some local authorities saw such schemes as a way to influence standards in the private rented sector, while others saw them only as a possibility for more responsible landlords. A key finding of this and related research (Rugg et al, 2000) was that landlords were more inclined to join such a scheme where there was a surplus of accommodation than in areas of high demand. Schemes were also found to vary in consistency in conditions, facilities, management and tenancy considerations.

Local authorities are faced with trying to house an increasing number of those accepted as statutorily homeless in decent accommodation with a general decrease in social housing stock. But they also have other responsibilities relating to the private rented sector which landlord accreditation schemes may also help address.

Accreditation schemes can also help fulfil a local authority's multiple aims in wider strategic housing objectives, normally related to increasing supply and improving the quality of stock including promoting standards in the private rented sector, bringing vacant properties back to use, addressing anti-poverty strategies, encouraging wider regeneration and finding viable options for homeless households. Many authorities made innovative use of wider government initiatives to help finance local strategies (DETR, 1998e).

Despite the many anomalies of the private rented sector, there is cross-party governmental consensus on the role of the private rented sector, although those involved day to day in trying to regulate the sector may hold an understandably different perspective. Research continues to recognise problems in the sector, especially conditions and management and how these might be tackled (see, for example, Rugg and Rhodes, 2001). There remains a lack of consensus on how to tackle the private rented sector, but the general trend is to focus enforcement attention on the bottom end of the sector, offering assistance to where it currently works well (DETR, 2000a). There is agreement that the private rented sector is performing below its potential in both quality and quantity – but this is hardly surprising considering some of the fundamental dilemmas at its core in terms of problems of affordability for tenants and expectation of return from landlords. The social housing sector simply does not operate in this way.

Many local authorities have found landlord accreditation schemes a more acceptable and viable option than using bed and breakfast hotels for temporary accommodation and costs have reduced in recent years as authorities have learnt to deal with the privately rented sector more effectively (DETR, 1997). While local authorities have tried many schemes in working with the private rented sector – including private sector leasing, housing association leasing and housing associations as managing agents – direct provision through the private rented sector has tended to prove more cost effective as the landlord bears the cost of management, voids, arrears and dilapidation, with most of the cost as housing benefit from central government (DETR, 1997).

Establishing a workable landlord accreditation scheme – the practicalities

Landlord accreditation schemes administered by local authorities attempt to secure a supply of decent-quality privately rented properties for those in housing need. They are also seen to establish a competitive market position for members and encourage others to improve by setting and monitoring standards (DETR, 2000a; Rugg and Rhodes, 2001), although the extent to which this happens in practice is unclear and they can vary considerably in standard. There is therefore much potential for greater partnership working and developing good practice.

Setting up an accreditation scheme requires considerable strategic development and implementation, but authorities already have many organisational systems, personnel, knowledge and information in place to champion them. In order to overcome potential problems before they emerge, it is essential that the interested parties – including local authority officers (housing allocations and advice, environmental health and so on) as well as potential landlords and tenants – meet to determine the aims and objectives of such a scheme. Successful schemes are found to involve landlords from an early stage, for example through a landlords forum, and are likely to take some 12 months to develop and a further six months to launch (DETR, 2001e) (see Table 6.9). Such an approach is not always straightforward as different stakeholders have different objectives (see Table 6.10). While the local authority's objective may be to ensure decent quality accommodation for homeless households, the landlord's may be to maximise rental accommodation and the tenant's primary concern is to ensure an affordable rent with longer-term security of tenure.

• Clear objectives set within overall private sector housing strategy with political support
• Appreciation of the operation of the local housing market
• Thorough development of accreditation scheme with agreement from landlords to ensure that the scheme's incentives are adequate
• Adequate staffing resource and support from partnership organisations
• Ongoing publicity and promotion, supported by clear documentation of the scheme

Table 6.9
Making voluntary accreditation work for local authorities and landlords

Source: Based on DETR (2001e)

While local authorities may wish to help secure better privately rented accommodation and the supporting administrative system, the bottom line is that the letting remains under private sector ownership and the landlord's objectives need to be met if the scheme is to stand any chance of success. Incentives are therefore crucial – such as guarantees on deposits, rent and benefit payments – as landlords will wish to see a market advantage in joining. Landlords may invest further in their accommodation to give it market advantage over other privately rented accommodation (DETR, 2001e; Rugg et al, 2000) with some important strategic implications for the private rented sector elsewhere, eg increased niche letting for students only in university localities, possibly at the expense of other low-income households.

While some schemes work extremely well – and this in itself can encourage further supply to the local authority from other interested landlords – other schemes have been less successful and lessons must be learnt. The constant battle to house homeless households may lead to standards being cut, as any willing landlord may be seen as preferable to a bed and breakfast alternative. Equally, there may be pressure to let to a tenant before inspection by the environmental health department, when standards are not legally acceptable. Schemes must be legally rigorous and an important consideration is liability in case of accident (eg carbon monoxide

Table 6.10 Key players' objectives and considerations in respect of landlord accreditation schemes

	For local authority and/ or housing association as landlord	For tenant /potential tenant	For private sector landlord
Increasingly a requirement of government policy	Meeting government policy by enabling increased availability of PRS and 'choice'	N/A	Increased opportunity for investment and investment return
Financial implications	Pressure to minimise HB expenditure, but may be more financially (and socially) viable than B&B as alternative; 'assistance' with appropriate conditions may prove more cost-effective to LA than B&B as alternative	May not be applicable if HB paid, but may result in poverty trap for tenant	Will seek maximum return on investment
Suitability for housing vulnerable people if applicable (eg statutory homeless)	Letting not owned or managed by LA or HA; loss of social housing management function; enabling overview only; but may be more attractive than B&B alternative		Social issues not part of private sector housing management function; PRS as business enterprise
	LA or HA may be able to manage tenancy – may benefit all parties in securing and maintaining well-managed letting; reduced social housing management workload for landlord but may increase resource input requirement from LA or HA		
Location and suitability of letting, including use of vacant properties	Some LA and HA accommodation may be undesirable or unsuitable for specific need	May wish to live in an area with no LA or HA housing, eg near to family – can offer tenant choice	Most landlords are 'sideline' landlords, location may be variable; may wish to invest in particular locality
	LA may offer assistance to landlord of empty property to bring it back to use on condition of letting to LA tenant; potential for social housing management; important part of community regeneration, etc; mutual benefit to all involved – in particular can facilitate wide LA strategic regeneration objectives		
Security of tenure	May be able to negotiate longer tenancy with landlord – benefits both LA and tenant, but landlord may not agree to more than six month AST		Landlord may wish to retain six month AST for flexibility
Rent level and guarantee of payment	May be paying HB to PRS anyway, so may help to informally encourage accountability of letting condition security, condition and affordability for LA and tenant		Landlord will seek market rent payable throughout proposed letting; LA may be able to respond by offering deposit and rent guarantee to make their tenants a viable option to landlord
Condition of letting and potential for remedial action	May help encourage informal regulation of the sector prior to letting; of benefit to LA in fulfilling wider strategic objectives and tenant in securing a decent standard of letting; retention of enforcement powers and assistance if required		Landlord may withdraw from scheme if LA instigates legal action; no obligation on landlord to continue this or another letting

poisoning) where a local authority placed a tenant in an accredited property. Colleagues have expressed concern as to the cost and sustainability of such schemes, the possibilities for housing benefit fraud due to poor scheme management, and the very real problems of locating decent accommodation on an adequate scale in respect of the local authority resource put into setting up such a scheme. Recent research indicated that only 45 per cent of authorities were monitoring their scheme's success and generally numbers of accredited properties remained small (DETR, 2001e), raising some questions about their viability, particularly where the outcomes, including security for the tenant and the financial and resource cost to local authorities, are considered.

However, there is increasing momentum toward establishing landlord accreditation schemes that work – see, for example, Box 6.4. *Environmental Health News* (2002a, 2002b) has continued to report how environmental health departments are responding to goverment guidance on establishing local accreditation schemes, and partnership approaches are emerging to maximise opportunities for a carrot and stick approach, including opportunities to ensure that higher standards than the legal minimum are met for energy efficiency, etc. The National Accreditation Network has recently been established to provide advice and publications (see *www.anuk.org.uk*), with a partnership-based steering group including representatives from local authorities, landlord associations, higher education institutions, the ODPM and the voluntary sector. At the time of writing, the Network is compiling a national accreditation directory.

Summary

Accreditation schemes are only likely to attract the better landlords and there is still a huge way to go on promoting standards and security elsewhere in the private rented sector. Their establishment requires considerable local authority resource with no guarantee of sustainably increasing privately rented supply and the situation may remain very fluid, but costs to local authorities are decreasing as lessons are being learned and schemes becoming more accountable and more attractive to landlords and authorities alike. While there are differences in opinion as to the viability in theory and practice of accreditation schemes, they at least help promote conditions and self-regulation more widely – and more acceptably – to landlords, tenants and local authorities.

Box 6.4 The Leeds Landlord Accreditation Scheme: working with partners in the private rented sector

Aims of the scheme

The aim of the scheme is to improve the health, safety and welfare of tenants and neighbours in all communities throughout Leeds. Leeds is a relatively prosperous, diverse city, yet it is divided by wealth, with 7 of the 33 wards falling within the lowest 10 per cent of deprived areas within the country. The Housing Strategy and the corporate plan, Closing the Gap, requires that the Leeds Landlord Accreditation Scheme (LAS) must form part of the overall strategy to bring benefits to all the people of Leeds. The LAS recognises where good standards exist and raises the lowest standards by voluntary agreement and market forces.

History of the scheme

The Leeds universities and Leeds City Council, upon representations from landlords, formed the LAS in 1996. Landlords wanted the Unipol scheme, which provides accreditation for the student sector of the PRS, to be adopted for the entire PRS in Leeds. For the first four years it was developed in conjunction with Unipol, but is now diverging and diversifying, serving the entire PRS with Unipol concentrating on the student market. This is typical of the genesis of many local authority accreditation schemes; it seems that a captive, uniform market is needed to 'seed' the scheme.

Resources

The LAS has had limited resources for its development and management, mainly carried out by one Principal Officer within Housing Regeneration working in partnership with the PRS in addition to other duties. The NRF now funds a temporary post for one year for the development of the scheme and about half a post is required to process the administration. There is a considerable printing and distribution cost as documents are of a high standard to reflect the credibility of the LAS. The other resources necessary are the checking of landlords' self-regulation and compliance by field officers; accreditation is integrated into the enforcement procedure.

Leeds PRS

The PRS in Leeds is assumed to be increasing with a growing proportion of 'buy to let' properties. However, a survey of accredited landlords indicated that professional landlords still provide the vast majority of bedspaces (89 per cent). These tend to be members of landlord associations which are active and enthusiastic to enhance the image of the PRS. By their own admission their attitudes towards the council have improved considerably, from hostility to co-soperation, and have recently welcomed being partners in the development of housing strategy. The LAS has many new, small portfolio members, which value the education and training provided. A lack of understanding and commitment among 'buy to let' landlords new to the PRS may cause problems with poor management and eventually, difficulties if they decide to leave the market in significant numbers over a short period. The booming market has enabled many improvements to the PRS, as landlords are able to obtain finance for investment on their increased equity, these being easier in areas of high demand and in the professional market. This has also meant that certain areas are left behind although returns are generally higher in low demand areas. Accreditation has been developed as a useful tool in area regeneration (see below). Some areas unfortunately are irretrievable; in these worst instances accreditation has not yet made any contribution to managing the decline.

Three-year business plan

The LAS has a three-year business plan, which was approved at a level where it gives officers the authority and freedom to develop the scheme within predefined parameters. The plan identifies the four beneficiaries of the scheme – tenants, landlords, the community and the council – and provides the aims and objectives of the scheme for each of these. Sixteen objectives have been identified which have been prioritised and activities have been determined to achieve those objectives. The high priorities for the LAS are:

- tenants – high awareness of the scheme through publicity and increased participation in the development of the scheme;
- landlords – to be a consulted by the council on issues that affect the PRS, and positive promotion of PRS facilitated by the council;
- council – facilitating improvements in the quality of the residential services of the PRS across all segments.

The most pressing issue is to raise awareness of the scheme among tenants and landlords. This will increase the scheme's credibility by increasing the market advantage of accreditation and enable proper regulation of the scheme requirements through tenant awareness.

Partnerships in accreditation

The beneficiaries of the scheme are also its stakeholders and its most significant partners. Scheme management or consultative groups including landlord representatives are created to develop and operate the scheme. Details of the scheme, their requirements, methods of operation and disciplinary procedures are negotiated and agreed by key partners and accordingly local landlords feel that they have a joint ownership of and stake in the scheme. The desire for landlords to work well with the local authority has been emphasised by the standing ovation received by the officer responsible for housing strategy, who invited landlords to be partners in determining housing strategy at a meeting of a landlords association. Managing agents have not been properly represented in the Leeds LAS as only owners could be members. An accredited managing agent scheme is being developed to address this.

Other stakeholders include the Tenancy Relations Service (Housing Advice Centre) which tends to represent tenants' interests and provides legal assistance in developing the scheme.

The participation of housing benefit officers is not always active but their contribution is essential from time to time.

Tenants are the most difficult group to engage, mostly due to their transient nature. Once the public awareness of the scheme has been raised significantly it is necessary to develop tenant participation and eventually to establish a tenants' forum along the lines of the landlords forum.

Community element
The community representation is small but valued and a significant contribution is made to the development of the community elements of the scheme, such as the recently introduced visual amenity clause and the development of the recently launched accredited tenant scheme. A requirement has also been introduced in response to the community representation to restrict the use of 'To let' and 'Let by' boards. The accredited tenant scheme is a landlord-initiated reference scheme which is administered entirely by members. It aims to reduce incidences of nuisances and anti-social behaviour as well as landlord/tenant disputes. A Tenant Code and the provision of a booklet entitled Living in Your Home assists tenants to fulfil their obligations as tenants, neighbours and members of the community. Discussion is also taking place for an 'Undesirable tenant list' for which the Human Rights Act and the Data Protection Act must be considered, and it will take a brave decision to embark on a scheme which may set legal precedent in this area.

Accreditation and enforcement
The scheme relies on self-certification of properties by landlords although a sample of properties of new members is chosen for compliance checks. The LAS is

being integrated into procedures for inspection and enforcement, the enforcement concordat and policy having regard to membership of the scheme, which must be considered in determining the appropriate response. Co-operation in compliance with legal requirements must be total or members will be subject to full legal procedures and will be held to account at a review panel hearing. Enforcement officers, including environmental health and tenancy relations, may refer landlords who fail to reach the standards required by the scheme to a review panel. This is likely to be following representations from a tenant. The review panel has a similar composition to the consultative committee and is supportive rather than punitive, discipline tending to be towards temporary suspension to enable the member to reach the scheme requirements rather than expulsion. A right of appeal to the Chief EHO is built in.

Accreditation and area regeneration
The scheme has been developed as a tool in area regeneration. A dedicated team of officers in the Beeston Hill Neighbourhood Renewal Area has incorporated enforcement, accreditation and grants into their working practices. Resources are available to enable the inspection of all properties within the area. Landlords are encouraged to become members of the Beeston Hill Accreditation Scheme through the availability of an Accreditation Grant. Property accreditation is checked and a property improvement plan is agreed with the landlord. All properties must attain a one-star standard and properties complying with a two-star standard are eligible for grant aid at a current rate of 75 per cent of required works. As many of the tenants within the area are on housing benefit the Rent Service was an active stakeholder in the development of the scheme with a rent differential for accredited properties being agreed. Since then Leeds has been selected as a pathfinder for the new benefit system which will pay the uniform rent directly to the tenant, the effects of the proposed benefit changes on the accreditation grant being closely monitored.

Publicity and promotion
Approximately 15 per cent of the PRS are in the scheme, with perhaps another 20-30 per cent of the total market in the Unipol scheme. This means that about one-third to a half of the PRS in Leeds are in an accreditation scheme. An increase in membership is important at this stage of the development of the scheme. Considerable resources are now required for publicity and promotion of the scheme. A campaign has been developed with the media relations officers, which includes press releases, paid adverts, a poster and

leaflet campaign and a 'Landlord of the Year' competition.

Developing benefits
The benefits to being a member of the Leeds LAS are considerable and along the lines of government guidance. A customer survey revealed that financial benefit is not the biggest influence on membership, training, education, support and partnership being of the greatest importance to members. Members were most satisfied with the quarterly magazine The Network. Benefits are being developed constantly and the Accreditation Network UK (ANUK) has contributed significantly in negotiating considerable discounts with the national suppliers Travis Perkins and Chubb soon to be made available to all accredited landlords in England.

Monitoring, evaluating and developing the scheme
A recent customer survey determined who the members are, why they joined, what they expect, what they like and dislike and what they want developed. This was a large and ambitious survey and preliminary analysis of the results has already assisted in the development of the scheme through the community elements and the accredited tenant scheme. Such a survey has not been done before and full analysis of the results, due by summer 2003, will yield considerable information. When resources become available it will be necessary to evaluate the scheme effectiveness by comparing housing conditions and the management of properties owned by accredited and non-accredited landlords.

The LAS will be used to fast-track members into licensing. Leeds, together with other authorities in the West Yorkshire Housing Group, is bidding for finance to establish and develop accreditation schemes in preparation for the proposed licensing powers.

Future of accreditation
Leeds' representations to government resulted in the establishment and support of the Accreditation Network UK. The consultative paper on the Housing Bill 2003 reaffirms the government's strong commitment to accreditation. The Leeds LAS is regularly providing advice and assistance to other authorities and landlord associations on the establishment of schemes. The scheme is mature and the versatility of accreditation as a tool has enabled its development into areas not foreseen at the establishment of the scheme. It has significant contributions to make in improving housing management and standards, area regeneration, tackling anti-social behaviour, partnership working and other ways yet to be discovered.

Case study provided by Tom Toumazon, Leeds City Council

Specialising the service: The role of Home Improvement Agencies

The home improvement agency (HIA) movement – recognising gaps in existing services – began in the 1970s and grew through the 1980s. Governments have increasingly encouraged their role, providing £2.74 million grant expenditure in 1991/2, rising by 2001 to around £8.5 million (DTLR, 2001b). HIAs are normally small, not-for-profit organisations, managed by local authorities, housing associations or charitable bodies and supported since 2000 by a national coordinating organisation known as 'Foundations' (previously Care and Repair). They are seen as relatively autonomous and independent and therefore able to deliver a people-centred approach that is soft-regulated (DoH and ODPM, 2002; CIH, 2003), although there is a risk that such flexibility could be undermined by too much government intervention.

Hospital discharge projects	Enables older people to be safely discharged from hospital with/following necessary repairs and adaptations
Handy person services	Small repairs service in homes of low-income and people with disabilities; increased comfort and security
Aids and adaptations	As above, to assist independent living
Home security schemes	Provision such as door and window locks, external lighting, etc to reduce crime and fear of crime
Energy efficient projects	Usually tailored to older people for energy efficiency works, including accessing grants etc
Home fitness checks	Client option of detailed check of risk factors likely to give rise to accident and advice on remedial action
Daily living support scheme	Practical help following hospital discharge, equipment advice/loan and installation of minor adaptations

Table 6.11
HIA's: Overview of range of services offered contributing to health and social care agenda

Source: DoH and ODPM (2002)

There are currently around 277 HIAs in England covering 284 local authority areas (DTLR, 2001b), around 230 of which are supported by the ODPM (DoH and ODPM, 2002; ODPM, 2002h), providing impetus to partnership arrangements in meeting local (as well as individual) housing support need and innovative new services in some areas (see Table 6.11). More than 60 local authorities operate without an HIA, and the government argues that this leaves many without the type of support that has been established elsewhere, including:

• helping elderly, disabled and vulnerable people to remain independently in their own homes for as long as they wish to by identifying necessary repairs and improvements and instructing suitable contractors to undertake works;
• helping people access resource for private sector housing renewal; and
• helping people make use of other sources of funding and providing advice on loans, insurance and equity release (DoH and ODPM, 2002; DTLR, 2001b; ODPM, 2002h).

The recent jointly published Consultation Paper outlines proposals to reform the HIA sector to ensure that it is fully able to contribute to health, housing and renewal objectives as part of the Supporting Peopleprogramme as well as placing an increasing emphasis on strategic approaches to service delivery (DoH and DTLR, 2002; CIH, 2003). This programme seeks to introduce new arrangements to commission and fund housing-related support services from 2003/4, recognising the growing interrelationship of health and housing, contributing to the wider health agenda and encouraging further partnership working. At the time of writing, the consultation is particularly inviting comment on issues such as:

- the need for structural and organisational reform to optimise the role of HIAs;
- equity in geographic availability and standard of services;
- clarification of HIA role(s); and
- delivery of services that represent value for money.

The emerging role of HIAs is also closely allied to the Regulatory Reform (Housing Assistance) (England and Wales) Order 2002 discussed earlier, as a broader range of funding options become necessary (ODPM, 2002h). As local authorities are required to adopt more strategic approaches, they need increasingly to work in partnership with allied organisations to help provide tailored, individual services that represents value for money for all parties (see also Box 2.3).

The Consultation Paper (DoH and ODPM, 2002) also makes specific reference to the importance of housing to public health, seeing HIAs as paramount in being able to offer flexible, tailored solutions that meet the individual's health-related housing and care needs at a very personal level by partnering with different organisations and funding opportunities to help provide a streamlined approach. This is seen to physically improve housing conditions, providing health benefits to individuals and neighbourhoods, and – as a combined impact – helps reduce poverty and debt.

Additional information and guidance should be referred to for the latest information.

However, as with any partnership, it can only be as effective as its resource and organisational arrangements allow. Care needs to be taken to ensure that partnership working really delivers what it sets out to and that it is not so constrained by bureaucracy and new rules that it loses sight of its original objective. For environmental health practitioners delivering private sector housing renewal strategy, it is essential that they retain an overview of housing stock so that strategy within a local authority area can be evaluated. Experience suggests that environmental health departments, PCTs and HIAs are not always working toward the same outcomes, or that each thinks that the other is dealing with a specific client need. This is not a helpful position as each organisation vies for its own role, funding and status in a climate of almost constant change. However, if close working partnerships can be developed and maintained, each organisation can provide an essential part of the public health agenda. Early consultation and agreement between all stakeholders is therefore essential

Chapter 7
Conclusions

The role of environmental health in public health has been increasingly recognised as the reintegration of health and environment. Unfortunately, for too many years, environmental health has had an enforcement-led agenda which has more recently been challenged as environmental health practitioners and related organisations have questioned their roles and outcomes, and have been pushing for change in using their skills and expertise to address health inequality and improve health for all.

Environmental health practitioners are uniquely placed and have a holistic approach in areas of food, communicable disease, housing, environmental control and health and safety at work, quite unlike any other profession. They increasingly operate in a variety of statutory and non-statutory organisations including local authorities, private practice, the voluntary sector, the CIEH itself, PCTs and within new organisational roles and functions, taking new strategic responsibilities in an increasingly evidence-based, performance-managed environment. This offers new opportunities, but also new threats.

To improve health, environmental health practitioners and related colleagues need to incorporate strategic interventions that are known to reduce health inequalities as part of their routine workload. Increasing quantities of evidence-based information are available on the HDA website. Many already do this on a daily basis and this should be applauded. However, the opportunity to push this agenda forward is curtailed by audit and reporting requirements that can skew the agenda in more dubious directions, denying opportunities to address substantial health inequalities in the UK.

This book focuses on contemporary research and literature in addressing the past and future direction of the environmental health discipline, notably the break from public health and the current process of reintegration. There are currently many issues affecting the discipline of environmental health, including sustainability, globalisation and social exclusion, the fundamental sources and outcomes of which need to be fully recognised and incorporated into policy and strategy at the global, national and local level. Processes of health needs assessment and health impact assessment can help identify where resources should be directed and intervention activity targeted in a climate of rapid change.

An overview of public health should be taken, needs assessed and services provided in response, which may mean partnership working with appropriate agencies. There is a need to get away from the 'silo' culture and expand the boundaries. Food safety functions should be expanded to address access to culturally acceptable food, nutrition and quantity as well as quality. Local authorities have a role to play in public health issues associated with food such as obesity, which requires a multi-disciplinary approach across the environment, health, food and nutrition interface.

Just about every aspect of intervention into the private sector housing stock is set to change, bringing new challenges to environmental health practitioners. There needs to be new ways of thinking, particularly in encouraging owners to have greater responsibility for their own homes so that public resources are increasingly directed to those on low incomes or even on the very margins of society for whom the need for housing and care services is most acute. However, the sector must not be tackled naively, and it is clear that enforcement, prosecution and works in default will remain the only way forward in the bottom end of the private sector, including HMOs. Environmental health practitioners also need to recognise the roles of the social housing sector and the overall picture of housing supply and demand. Once again, needs assessment and an evidence base become increasingly important in attracting resources.

The very role of the environmental health practitioner is changing, and at a very rapid rate. This had left many discouraged, demoralised and disheartened, and qualifying courses that have existed for many years have been forced to close. The reasons behind this are complex and multi-faceted, and yet the EHP's role continues to be seen by many high-profile figures as key to the public health agenda.

As part of this continuing change, the CIEH has recently pioneered a new core curriculum to respond to the role and skills required for the future of the profession. *Environmental Health 2012* provides a new vision of reintegrating environmental health and public health, with wide recognition and support. But these changes in themselves cannot alter the fact that it is largely down to those of us currently working and training in environmental health who need to grasp the nettle to advance our own roles for the future, recognising and promoting the very unique and holistic skills that we hold.

It is hoped that this book is able to contribute to the future of the environmental health discipline within the public health agenda.

References

Acheson, D. (1988) *Public Health in England.* Report of the committee of inquiry into the future of the public health function. London: The Stationery Office

Acheson, D. (1998) *Independent Inquiry into Inequalities in Health,* Department of Health, London: HMSO.

Allison, S. (1999) in Holmes, S. 'Nutrition: A Necessary Adjunct to Hospital Care', *Journal of the Royal Society for the Promotion of Health* 119 (3) 175-179.

Ambrosi, M. (2002a) 'No time to sleep in B&B challenge', *Inside Housing,* 20 December 2002:11.

Ambrosi, M (2002b) 'Tough line on B&B greeted with scepticism', *Inside Housing,* 6 December 2002:3.

Arblaster, L. and Hawtin, M. (1993) *Health, Housing and Social Policy,* London: Socialist Health Association.

Archer, P. (2002) 'Assessing the UK fuel poverty strategy' *Environmental Health Journal,* August 2002, vol. 110/08, pp. 244-247.

Ashton, J. and Seymour, H. (1988) *The New Public Health.* Open University Press. Milton Keynes.

Ashton, J. (1998) 'Public Health where next?' *For the Common Good. 150 years of Public Health.* An EHJ commemorative issue. CIEH.

Audit Commission. (1991) Audit Commission Local Government Report No. 6. *Healthy Housing: The role of Environmental Health Services,* London: HMSO.

BABIE. (1995) *London Boroughs' Bed and Breakfast Information: The BABIE Hotel Grading System.* London Research Centre.

Baker, B. (2002) 'Health Minister calls for a return to the founding values of public health', *Environmental Health News,* 17, 38, 4 October 2002:3.

Balchin, P. (1985) *Housing Policy: An Introduction (3rd edition),* London: Routledge.

Balchin, P. and Rhoden, M. (2002) *Housing Policy: An Introduction (4th edition),* London: Routledge.

Ballinger, S. (for Shelter and Bradford and Bingley) (2002) *Home Sick,* London; Shelter.

Barker, H. M. (1996) *Nutrition and Dietetics for Health Care.* 9th Edition. Edinburgh: Churchill Livingstone.

Barnes, R. and Scott-Samuel, A. (2000) *Health Impact Assessment:* A ten minute guide. Online. Available HTTP: http://www.ihia.org.uk/hiaguide.html.

Battersby, S. and Ormandy, D. (1999) 'Surveying the system', *Environmental Health Journal* 107 (11) pp. 357-380.

Beishon, M. (2002) 'Healthy Communities', *Health Development Today* June/July 2002. Online. Available HTTP: http://www.hda-online.org.uk/hdt0602/training.html (23 September 2002).

Bernardo's, Centre for Research in Primary Care and Centre for Disability Studies (University of Leeds). (2002) *A Health Needs Assessment of Black and Minority Ethnic Children's Needs: A report prepared for the Leeds Children and Families Modernisation Team and Leeds Health Action Zone* (June 2002), Online. Available HTTP: http://www.leeds.ac.uk/disability-studies/projects/leedshna.htm (30 October 2002).

Bickerdike, J. (1978) 'The Profession, Professionalism and The Way Ahead: A Personal View', *Environmental Health 86* (4): 73-76.

Birchall, J. (1992) 'Council tenants: sovereign consumers or pawns in the game', in J Birchall (ed) *Housing Policy in the 1990s*, 163-189. London: Routledge.

Birley, M. (1999) *Procedures and Methods for Health Impact Assessment in DoH* (1999) Health Impact Assessment: Report of a methodological seminar. Online. Available HTTP: (http://www.doh.gov.uk/research/documents/rd2/healthimpact.pdf).

Blackburn, C. (1991) *Poverty and health: working with families*. Open University: Buckingham.

Blair, A. (1997) *Speech given at Stockwell Park School, Lambeth, December 1997*. Online. Available HTTP: http://www.dfee.gov.uk/socialexcl/newdoc1.shtml (30 January 1998).

Blaxter, M, and Poland, F. (2002) 'Moving beyond the survey in exploring social capital' in Swann C and Morgan M (eds.) (2002) *Social Capital: Insights from qualitative research*, London: Health Development Agency.

Boardman, B. (1991) *Fuel Poverty*, London: Belhaven Press.

Bogard, C. J., McConnell, J.J, Gerstel, N. and Schwartz, M. (1999) 'Homeless mothers and depression: Misdirected policy, *Journal of Health and Social Behaviour*, 40: 46-62.

Bradshaw, J. (University of York) (2002) 'The Scientific Measurement of Poverty and Social Exclusion: Findings of the Poverty and Exclusion Survey of Britain', from *Royal Statistical Society and Social Research Association's Cathie Marsh Memorial Lecture*, Royal Statistical Society, London, 26th November 2002.

British Medical Association. (1998) *Health and Environmental Impact Assessment*. Earthscan Publications.

Brown, G.W. and Harris, T. (1978) *Social Origins of Depression. A Study of Psychiatric Disorder in Women*, London: Tavistock Publications Ltd.

Brown, S. (2002). 'Countless Opportunities', *Health Development Today*, April/May 9-11.

Bull, J. and Hamer, L. (2001) *Closing the gap: setting local targets to reduce health inequalities*. London: Health Development Agency.

Burke, S., Gray, I., Paterson, K., and Meyrick, J. (2002) *Environmental Health 2012: A key partner in delivering the public health agenda*, London: Health Development Agency.

Bush Meat Task Force. (2000) 'Eco-Economics' and 'Health & Disease', Online. Available HTTP: http://www.bushmeat.org.

Cambridgeshire Health Authority. (2002) *Alconbury Health Impact Assessment Final Report*, Cambridgeshire Health Authority. Online. Available HTTP: http://www.phel.gov.uk/hiadocs/alconbury_final_summary_report_February03.pdf.

Campbell, C. and McLean, C. (2002) 'Social capital, social exclusion and health: factors shaping African-Caribbean participation in local community networks', in Swann C and Morgan M (eds.) (2002) *Social Capital: Insights from qualitative research*, London: Health Development Agency.

Campbell, C., Wood, R., and Kelly, M. (1999) *Social capital and health*, London: Health Education Authority.

Cattrell, V. and Herring, R. (2002) 'Social capital, generations and health in east London', in Swann C and Morgan M (eds.) (2002) *Social Capital: Insights from qualitative research*, London: Health Development Agency.

Caraher, M. and Anderson, A. (2001) 'An Apple a day...' *Health Matters* 46: 12-14.

Chambers, D. (1997) *Jacks and Jills of All Trades: From Inspectors of Nuisances to Public Health Professionals.* Inaugural Lecture University of Greenwich. 13th March 1997.

Chartered Institute of Environmental Health. (1994) *Amenity Standards for HMOs*, London: CIEH.

Chartered Institute of Environmental Health. (2003) *Building a Healthier Future: CIEH Annual Report for the year ended 31 December 2002*, London: CIEH.

Chartered Institute of Housing. (1998) Summary Report: *Opening the Door: Housing's essential role in tackling social exclusion*, Coventry: CIH.

Chartered Institute of Housing (2003) *CIH response to ODPM Consultation on Home Improvement Agencies: Development and Reform*, Coventry, CIH. Online. Available HTTP: http://www.cih.org.cgi-bin/display.pl?db=policies&id=361 (10 January 2003)

Clapham, D., Kemp, P. and Smith, S. J. (1990) *Housing and Social Policy*, London: McMillan Educational Ltd.

Cole, I. and Furbey, R. (1994). *The Eclipse of Council Housing.* London: Routledge.

Coleman, A. (1990) *Utopia on Trial. Vision and Reality in Planned Housing* (revised edition). London: Hilary Shipman Ltd.

Commission for Environmental Health. (1997) *Agendas for Change - Report of the Environmental Health Commission*, London: CIEH.

Commons Public Accounts Select Committee. (2002) *Tackling Obesity in England.* 9th Report. (Online - cited 2002 May 14). Available from URL: http://www.publications.parliament.uk/pa/cm200102/cmselect/cmpubacc/421/42103.htm

Commonwealth Department of Health and Aged Care. (2001) *Health Impact Assessment Guidelines.* National Public Health Partnership, Commonwealth of Australia. Online. Available HTTP: http://www.phel.gov.uk/hiadocs/hia_guidelines_australia.pdf.
Connelly, J. (1999) 'Housing conditions, diseases and injury', in W. H. Bassett (ed.) *Clay's Handbook of Environmental Health*, (18th Edition), London: E. & F. N. Spon.

Conway, J. (ed.) (1988) *Prescription for Poor Health. The crisis for homeless families*, London: London Food Commission, Maternity Alliance, SHAC and Shelter.

Cornell, S. J. (1996) Do Environmental Health Officers Practice Public Health? *Public Health* 110:73-75.

Council of European Municipalities and Regions. (1997) *Local Agenda 21. Basic Guide*. Online. Available HTTP: http://www.ccre.org/la21_an.html .

Cowan, D. (1999) *Housing Law and Policy*, London: Macmillan.

Crisis. (2000) *Health Action for Homeless People*. Online. Available HTTP: http://www.crisis.org.uk (28 August 2000).

Cumella, S., Grattan E. and Vostanis P. (1998) 'The mental health of children in homeless families and their contact with health, education and social services' in *Health and Social Care in the Community*, 6 (5) 331-342

Dahlgren, G. and Whitehead, M. (1991) *Policies and strategies to promote social equity in health*, Institute for Future Studies: Stockholm.

Davidson, M. and Leather, P. (2000) Choice or necessity? A review of the role of DIY in tackling housing repair and maintenance. *Construction Management and Economics*. (18): 747-756.

Davidson, M. Redshaw, J. and Mooney, M. (1997) *The role of DIY in maintaining owner occupied stock*. Bristol: The Policy Press Housing Repair and Maintenance Series.

De Soto, H. (2001) *The Mystery of Capital: Why capitalisms triumphs in the West and fails everywhere else*, London: Black Swan.

Department for Environment, Food and Rural Affairs. (1999) *A Better Quality of Life: a strategy for sustainable development for the UK. CM 4345*. The Stationery Office. Online. Available HTTP: http://www.sustainable-development.gov.uk/uk_strategy/content.htm.

Department for Environment, Food and Rural Affairs. (2000) *The Air Quality Strategy for England, Scotland, Wales and Northern Ireland: working together for clean air. CM 4548*. The Stationery Office. Online. Available HTTP: http://www.defra.gov.uk/environment/airquality/strategy/index.htm .

Department of Environment, Food and Rural Affairs and Department of Transport and Industry (November 2001) *UK Fuel Poverty Strategy* Available Online. HTTP: http://www.dti.gov.uk/energy/fuelpoverty/fuelpeng.html

Department for Environment, Food and Rural Affairs. (2002) *Achieving a Better Quality of Life. Review of progress towards sustainable development. Government Annual Report 2002*. Online. Available HTTP: http://www.sustainable-development.gov.uk/ar2002/03h6.htm

Department for Environment, Food and Rural Affairs (2003) *Sustainable Development - the UK Government's approach*, World Summit on Sustainable Development. Online. Available HTTP: http://www.sustainable-development.gov.uk/wssd2.htm

Department of Environment, Transport and the Regions. (1996) Housing Research Summary. Private Landlords in England (No. 54, 1996), London: DETR. Online. Available HTTP: http://www.housing.detr.gov.uk/hrs/hrs054.htm (3 August 2000).

Department of Environment, Transport and the Regions. (1997) Housing Research Summary. *Financing Temporary Accommodation in the Private Rented Sector: An Economic Analysis* (No. 56, 1997), London: DETR. Online. Available HTTP: http://www.housing.detr.gov.uk/hrs/hrs056.htm (2 February 2002).

Department of Environment, Transport and the Regions. (1998a) The English House Condition Survey 1996, London: HMSO. Online. Available HTTP: http://www.housing.detr.gov.uk/research/ehcs96/tables/index.htm (30 August 2000).

Department of Environment, Transport and the Regions. (1998b) Housing Research Summary: *Repairs and Improvements to Private Rented Dwellings in the 1990s* (no. 79, 1998). London: DETR. Online. Available HTTP: http://www.housing.dtlr.gov.uk/hrs/hrs079.htm (14 February 2002).

Department of Environment, Transport and the Regions. (1998c) Housing Research Summary: *Encouraging Home Owners to Repair and Maintain their Homes: A Review of Initiatives* (no. 92, 1998). London: DETR. Online. Available HTTP: http://www.housing.dtlr.gov.uk/hrs/hrs092.htm (12 April 2000).

Department of Environment, Transport and the Regions. (1998d). *Modern Local Government In Touch with the People.* Online. Available HTTP: http://www.local-regions.dtlr.gov.uk/lgwp (25 January 2002).

Department of the Environment, Transport and the Regions (1998e) Housing Research Summary: How local authorities used the private rented sector prior to the Housing Act 1996 (no. 86, 1998), London: DETR.

Department of Environment, Transport and the Regions. (1999a) *Fuel Poverty: The New HEES.* A programme for warmer, healthier homes, London: DETR.

Department of Environment, Transport and the Regions. (1999b) *Licencing of Houses in Multiple Occupation:* England Consultation Paper, London: HMSO

Department of Environment, Transport and the Regions. (2000a) The Housing Green Paper. *Quality and choice: A decent home for all,* London: Joint publication from the Department of the Environment, Transport and the Regions and the Department of Social Security, Online. Available HTTP http://www.housing.detr.gov.uk/information/consult/homes/index.htm (20 August 2000).

Department of Environment, Transport and the Regions. (2000b). *A Decent Home: the revised definition and guidance from implementation. Section 1.* London, ODPM. Online. Available HTTP: http://www.housing.odpm.gov.uk/information/dhg/definition/01.htm (28 August 2002).

Department of Environment, Transport and the Regions. (2000c). *A Decent Home: the revised definition and guidance from implementation. Section 2.* London, ODPM. Online. Available HTTP: http://www.housing.odpm.gov.uk/information/dhg/definition/02.htm (28 August 2002).

Department of Environment, Transport and the Regions. (2000d). Housing Research Summary No. 122, 2000. *Development of the Housing Health and Safety Rating System,* London: DETR. Online. Available HTTP: http://www.housing.detr.gov.uk/hrs/hrs122/htm (6 October 2000).

Department of Environment, Transport and the Regions. (2000e). Housing Research Summary No. 123, 2000. *Housing Health and Safety Rating System Quick Guide* London: DETR. Online. Available HTTP: http://www.housing.detr.gov.uk/hrs/hrs123/htm (6 October 2000).

Department of Environment, Transport and the Regions. (2000f) Housing Research Summary: *Repair and Maintenance by Private Landlords* (no. 138, 1000). London: DETR. Online. Available HTTP: http://www.housing.dtlr.gov.uk/hrs/hrs138.htm (14 February 2002).

Department of Environment, Transport and the Regions. (2000g) *Regeneration Research Summary: Indices of Deprivation 2000* (Number 31, 2000), Online. Available HTTP: http://www.urban.odpm.gov.uk/research/summaries03100index.htm (8 November 2002).

Department of Environment, Transport and the Regions. (2000h) 1998 Index of Local Deprivation (Regeneration Research Summary No.15), Online. Available HTTP: http://www.urban.odpm.gov.uk/research/98IId/results.htm (8 November 2002).

Department of Environment, Transport and the Regions. (2000i). Preparing Community Strategies. Government Guidance to Local Authorities. Online. Available HTTP: http://www.local-regions.dtlr.gov.uk/pcs/guidance (25 January 2002).

Department of Environment, Transport and the Regions. (2000j). Mapping Partnerships in Eleven Local Authorities. Online. Available HTTP: http://www.local-regions.dtlr.gov.uk/b...partnerships/research/newchurch (25 January 2002).

Department of Environment, Transport and the Regions. (2001a). Local Strategic Partnerships – Government Guidance Summary. March 2001 Online. Available HTTP: http://www.local-regions.dtlr.gov.uk/wellbeing (25 January 2002).

Department of Environment, Transport and the Regions. (2001b). Power to Promote or Improve Economic, Social or Environmental Well-Being (Final Guidance). Online. Available HTTP: http://www.local-regions.dtlr.gov.uk/wellbeing (25 January 2002).

Department of Environment, Transport and the Regions. (2001c) Private Sector Housing Renewal: Reform of the Housing Grants, Construction and Regeneration Act 1996, Local Government and Housing Act 1989 and Housing Act 1985: A Consultation Paper. London: DETR. Online. Available HTTP: http://www.housing.dtlr.gov.uk/information/consult/pshr/pdf/consult.pdf (12 February 2002).

Department of Environment, Transport and the Regions. (2001d) Health and Safety in Housing: Replacement of the Housing Fitness Standards by the Housing Health and Safety Rating System: A Consultation Paper London: DETR. Online. Available: HTTP: http://www.housing.dtlr.gov.uk/information/consult/hhsrs/pdf/housinghealth.pdf (13 November 2001).

Department of Environment, Transport and the Regions. (2001e) Housing Research Summary. Voluntary Accreditation for Private Landlords (No. 144, 2001), London: DETR. Online. Available HTTP: http://www.housing.detr.gov.uk/hrs/hrs144.htm (2 February 2002).

Department of the Environment. (1994) Circular 18/94: Gypsy Sites Policy and Unauthorised Camping, London: HMSO.

Department of the Environment. (1996a) Circular 17/96. Private Sector Renewal: A Strategic Approach. London: HMSO.

Department of the Environment. (1996b) Housing Research Summary No. 62 (1996): English House Condition Survey 1991 Energy Report, London: HMSO.

Department for International Development. (2000a) White Paper on Eliminating World Poverty: A challenge for the 21st Century. Online. Available HTTP: http://www.globalisation.gov.uk/ (12 September 2001).

Department for International Development. (2000b) An Introduction to the UK Government's White Paper on International Development: 'Eliminating world poverty: making globalisation work for the poor' December 2002, London: DFID.

Department of Health. (1992) The Health of the Nation. A strategy for health in England. London. HMSO.

Department of Health. (1997) The New NHS: Modern, Dependable, London: Department of Health. Online. Available HTTP: http://www.archive.official-documents.co.uk/document/Department of Health/newnhs/forward.htm (7 November 2002).

Department of Health. (1998a) *Green Paper: Our Healthier Nation: A Contract for Health*, London: HMSO. Online. Available HTTP: http://www.archive.official-documents.co.uk/document/doh/ohnation/title.htm.

Department of Health. (1998b) HSC LAC 1998/167 *Health Improvement Programmes: Planning for Better Health and Better Health Care*, London: Department of Health NHS Executive.

Department of Health. (1999a) *Saving Lives: Our Healthier Nation*, London: Department of Health. Online. Available HTTP: http://www.ohn.gov.uk/ohn/ohn.htm.

Department of Health. (1999b) HSC 1999/192 *Leadership for Health: The Health Authority Role*, London: Department of Health NHS Executive.

Department of Health. (1999c) HSC 199/244 LAC (99)39 *Planning for Health and Health Care: Incorporating guidance for Health and Local Authorities on Health Improvement Programmes, Service and Financial Frameworks, Joint Investment Plans and Primary Care Investment Plans*, London: Department of Health.

Department of Health. (2000a). *The NHS Plan: A Plan for Investment, A Plan for Reform*. Online. Available HTTP: http://www.Department of Health.gov.uk/nhsplan/default.htm (25 January 2002).

Department of Health. (2000b) *The Implementation Programme for the NHS Plan*, memorandum from Department of Health.

Department of Health. (2000c) *Investigating the Health Impact of Emissions to Air from Local Industry*. London: DoH. Online. Available HTTP: http://www.doh.gov.uk/comeap/statementsreports/goodpracticeguide.pdf.

Department of Health. (2001a) *Health Improvement and Modernisation Plans (HIMPs): Requirements for 2002*. Letter from Department of Health.

Department of Health. (2001b) *Shifting the Balance of Power within the NHS*. Online. Available HTTP:// http://www.Department of Health.gov.uk/shiftingthebalance (8 March 2002).

Department of Health. (2001c) *Strengthening Public Health*. CMO's report. London:The Stationery Office.

Department of Health. (2002a) *Shifting the balance of power: the next steps*. Online. Available HTTP: http://www.doh.gov.uk/shiftingthebalance/nextsteps5.htm (8 March 2002).

Department of Health. (2002b) *Health Improvement and Modernisation Plans*, Online. Available HTTP: http://www.doh.gov.uk/himp/index.htm (4 November 2002).

Department of Health. (2002c) *Getting ahead of the curve – a strategy for infectious diseases*. CMO's report. London: The Stationery Office.

Department of Health/Welsh Office. (2002d) *Health Protection: A consultation document on creating a health protection agency*. London: The Stationery Office.

Department of Health. (2003a) *Improvement, Expansion and Reform: the Next 3 Years Priorities and Planning Framework 2003 – 2006*, London: HMSO.

Department of Health. (2003b) *Tackling Health Inequalities: A Programme for Action*. London: The Stationery Office.

Department of Health. (2004a) *Choosing Health? A consultation on action to improve people's health.* London: Department of Health Publications.

Department of Health. (2004b) *Choosing Health? Making healthier choices easier.* London: Department of Health Publications. Online. Available HTTP:// http://www.dh.gov.uk/ PublicationsAndStatistics/Publications/PublicationsPolicyAndGuidance/PublicationsPolicyA ndGuidanceArticle/fs/en?CONTENT_ID=4094550&chk=aN5Cor (17 November 2004).

Department of Health and Office of the Deputy Prime Minister. (2002) *Home Improvement Agencies:* Development and Reform: A Consultation Paper, London: ODPM. Online Available HTTP: http://www.housing.odpm.gov.uk/information/consult/hia/index.htm (14 January 2003)

Department of Health/Department of the Environment. (1996) The United Kingdom National Environmental Health Action Plan. London: HMSO.

Doyal, L. and Gough, I. (1994) in J. Payne (1999) *Researching Health Needs: A Community Based Approach,* London: SAGE Publications.

Department of Trade and Industry. (1995). Home Accident Surveillance System (HASS) and Housing Accident Death Database (HADD) 1994, *19th Annual Report,* London: DTI.

Department of Trade and Industry. (2000) *Home and Leisure Accident Report.* Summary of 1998 data, London: DTI.

Department of Transport, Local Government and the Regions (2001a) Housing Research Summary No. 142, 2001. *Worked examples to support the Housing Health and Safety Rating System,* London, DTLR. Online. Available HTTP: http://www.housing.dtlr.gov.uk/hrs/hrs142/pdf/ hous142.pdf (1 November 2001).

Department of Transport, Local Government and the Regions. (2001b) *Housing and Housing Policy: Home Improvement Agencies,* London: DTLR. Online. Available HTTP:// http://www.housing.dtlr.gov.uk/information/hia/index.htm (14 January 2002).

Department of Transport, Local Government and the Regions. (2002) Statutory Instrument 2002 No. 1860: *The Regulatory Reform (Housing Assistance) (England and Wales) Order* 2002, London: HMSO. Online. Available HTTP: http://www.hmso.gov.uk/si/si2002/20021860.htm (1 October 2002).

Dickerson, J.W.T. (1998) 'Food, nutrition, anti-social behaviour and criminality.' *Journal of the Royal Society for the Promotion of Health* 118(4):224-226.

Dickerson, J.W.T. (2001) 'Aspects of the history of nutrition since 1876.' *Journal of the Royal Society for the Promotion of Health* 121 (2):79-84.

Donaldson, L. J. (2001) '125 years of Public Health in the UK.' *Journal of the Royal Society for the Promotion of Health* 121 (3): 146-151.

East Sussex Brighton and Hove. (2001) *Health Improvement and Modernisation Programme* (HMIP 2002-05) draft submission to the NHS Executive: South East. Unpublished

Ellery, S. (2002) 'Rooting out rogues' *Inside Housing,* 29 November 2002: 18-19.

Emmanuel, S. (1993) 'Meeting the needs of HMO tenants' in *Environmental Health,* January 1993: 5-7

Environmental Health Commission. (1997) *Agendas for Change.* Chadwick House Group Ltd.

Environmental Health News. (2001) Editorial 20 July 2001: 5

Environmental Health News (2002a) 'Bristol's private landlords line up for three-star status' in *Environmental Health News*, 3 May 2002: 9.

Environmental Health News. (2002b) 'Private landlord regulators learn art of networking' in *Environmental Health News*, 18 October 2002: 9

Environmental Health News 'Tasty food that's good for Bradford' (editorial). (2001) *Environmental Health News* 16(36):9

Evans, D. (2004) Shifting the balance of power?: UK public health policy and capacity building, *Critical Public Health* 14 (1), pp. 63-75.

Evans, R. (2002) 'Decency target rapidly receding' *Inside Housing*, 30 August 2002:1.

Ewles, L. and Simnett, I.(1999) *Promoting Health: A Practical Guide. 4th Edition.* Harcourt: Edinburgh.

Fieldhouse, P. (1998) *Food and Nutrition: Customs and Culture.* 2nd Edition. London: Stanley Thornes.

Forrester, P. (1998) 'Environmental Health and Housing' in P. Balchin and M. Rhoden, *Housing. The Essential Foundations*, London: Routledge.

French, P. (2002) Response on EHJ Online in *Environmental Health Journal*, 110 (04) : 99

Gabe, J. and Williams, P. (1993) 'Women, crowding and mental health', in R. Burridge and D. Ormandy, *Unhealthy Housing; Research, remedies and reform*, London: E. & F. N. Spon.

Garrow, J.S., James, W.P.T., and Ralph, A. (2000) *Human Nutrition and Dietetics.* 10th Edition. Edinburgh: Churchill Livingstone.

Gaster, L. and Taylor, M. (1993) *Learning from Consumers and Citizens.* Bedfordshire: Local Government Management Board.

GLA. (2001) *Homelessness in London 27.* Electronic sources available online at: http://www.london.gov.uk/approot/mayor/housing/homelessness_bull/docs/bull_27a_2001.rtf [30 December 2003].

GLA. (2002) *Homelessness in London 37.* April 2002. London: GLA.

GLA. (2002) *Homelessness in London 38.* Electronic sources available online at: http://www.london.gov.uk/approot/mayor/housing/homelessness_bull/docs/2002/bull_38_2002.rtf 30 December 2003).

Goodwin, M and Painter, J. (1996) *Local Governance, The Crisis of Fordism and The Changing Geography of Regulation. Transactions of the Institute of British Geographers.* 121 (4) :635-648.

Gordon, D. (University of Bristol and Director of Townsend Centre for International Poverty Research) (2002) 'The Scientific Measurement of Poverty and Social Exclusion: Findings of the Poverty and Exclusion Survey of Britain', from *Royal Statistical Society and Social Research Association's Cathie Marsh Memorial Lecture*, Royal Statistical Society, London, 26th November 2002.

Gordon, D., Townsend, P., Levitas, R., Pantaziz, C., Payne, S., and Patsios, D. (2000) *Poverty and Social Exclusion in Britain.* York: Joseph Rowntree Foundation.

Goss, S. and Blackaby, B. (1998) *Developing Local Housing Strategies. A Good Practice Guide.* Coventry: Chartered Institute of Housing and Local Government Association.

Gray, I. (2002) 'Environmental Health 2012: A key partner in delivering the public health agenda', in *Empowering Public Health: Environmental Health Conference and Exhibition:* Harrogate International Centre, 10-13 September 2002. Conference Papers, London: CIEH.

Greenwich Poverty Profile. (1994) *London Borough of Greenwich Department of Planning and Regeneration.* Directorate of Development.

Grey, M. and Sarangi, J. (2003) in Orme, J.,Powell, J., Taylor, P.,Harrison, T. and Grey, M. (eds) *Public Health for the 21st Century.* Basingstoke:Open University Press.

Hadjivassiliou *et al* (1996) in Dickerson, J.W.T. (1998) 'Food, nutrition, anti-social behaviour and criminality.' *Journal of the Royal Society for the Promotion of Health* 118(4): 224-226.

Ham, C. (1999) *Health Policy in Britain: The politics and organisation of the National Health Service (4th edition).* Hampshire: Macmillan Press Ltd.

Hamer, L. and Easton, N. (for HDA, I&DeA, DTLR and LGA) (2002) *Community Strategies and health improvement: A review of policy and practice,* London: HDA.

Hatchett, W. (2001) 'Modern farming methods increase risks', *Environmental Health News,* 16 (8):6.

Hatchett, W. (2002a) 'NASS clams up over asylum housing' in *Environmental Health News,* 29 November 2002: 3.

Hatchett W. (2002b) ''Backtrack' on HMO licencing' in *Environmental Health News,* 29 November 2002: 4.

Health Development Agency. (2001) *Coronary Heart Disease: Guidance for Implementing the Preventive Aspects of the National Service Framework.* London: Health Development Agency.

Health Development Agency. (2002a) *Evidence base: Putting public health evidence into practice.* London: NHS Health Development Agency, Online. Available HTTP: http://194.83.94.80/hda/docs/evidence/eb2000/corehtml/intro.htm (20 September 2002).

Health Development Agency. (2002b) *Community Strategies and Health Improvement: A review of policy and practice,* London HDA (with I&DeA, DTLR and LGA).

Health Development Agency. (2002c) *Cancer Prevention. A Resource to support local action in delivery.* The NHS Cancer Plan. Health Development Agency.

Health Development Agency. (2003) Draft Paper: *Evidence-based public health and local delivery plans: A briefing for the HDAs Regional Associate Directors,* London: Health Development Agency.

Hefferman, E. (2002) Reported in 'Asylum aid shambolic' in *Environmental Health News,* 29 November 2002: 4.

HIARU. (2002) *Health Impact Assessment in Practice.* Health Impact Assessment Research Unit, University of Birmingham. Online. Available HTTP: http://www.publichealth.bham.ac.uk/hiaru/practice.htm

HM Treasury and Department of Health (DoH). (2002) *Tackling Health Inequalities: Summary of the 2002 Cross Cutting Review* (London, Department of Health).

Holmes, S. (1985) 'Determinants of Food Intake.' *Nursing* 3(7): 260-264.

Holmes, S. (1999) 'Nutrition: A Necessary Adjunct to Hospital Care.' *Journal of the Royal Society for the Promotion of Health* 119 (3): 175-179.

Homeless International. (1998) *World Habitat Day – "Why Housing and Poverty?"* Open University Conference Centre, London 5 October 1998.

Home Office. (1989) *Fire Statistics*: United Kingdom, London: HMSO.

Homeless International. (1998) World Habitat Day – 'Why Housing and Poverty?' Open University Conference Centre, London. 5 October 1998.

Howarth, C., Kenway, P., Palmer, G. and Street, C. (1999) *Monitoring poverty and social exclusion*: Labour's inheritance, York: Joseph Rowntree Foundation.

HSE. (1999) *Gas Appliances: Get them checked, keep them safe.* Leaflet available from the Health and Safety Executive.

Hudson, B. (2002) Interprofessionality in health and social care: the Achilles heel of partnership? *Journal of Interprofessional Care.* 1 (1) : 7-17.

Hunter, D. J. and Sengupta, S. (2004) Editorial: Building multidisciplinary public health, *Critical Public Health* 14 (1) pp. 1-5.

Hutchinson, J. and Campbell, M. (Policy Research Institute, Leeds Metropolitan University) (1998) *Working in Partnership: Lessons from the Literature*, DfEE Research Brief Report No. 63, London: DfEE. Online. Available HTTP: http://www.dfee/gov.uk/research/report63.html (23 March 2000).

Ineichen, B. (1993) *Homes and Health: How housing and health interact*, London: E. & F. N. Spon.

Inside Housing. (1994). 'Facts and Figures on the Stonebridge Estate'. *Inside Housing;* 15 April 1994, 11.

IFST. (1999) 'Genetic modification and food', *Food Science and Technology Today*, 13 (4) : 213-219.

IFST. (2000) 'Foresight – Food's contribution to health in the future: A brave new world?' in *Food Science and Technology Today*, 14 (3): 147-149.

International Obesity Taskforce. (2002) Nutrition: *Controlling the global obesity epidemic.* (Online - cited 2002 July 29). Available from URL:http:// www.iotf.org

Jackson, P. (2002) Reported in 'Tougher line on bed and breakfast' in *Environmental Health News*, 29 November 2002: 4.

James, P. (Ed)(2000) *Ending malnutrition by 2020: An agenda for change in the millennium.* Final report to the ACC/SCN by the Commission on the Nutritional Challenges of the 21st Century (United Nations) http://www.iotf.org/php/execsum.htm

James, P. (2002) '*Ending malnutrition by 2010: An agenda for change in the millennium'* Final report of the ACC/SCN by the Commission in the Nutritional Challenges of the 21st Century. Online. Available HTTP: www.iotf.org/php/execsum.htm

Joffe, M. and Mindell, J. (2002) 'A framework for the evidence base to support health impact assessment', *Journal of Epidemiology and Community Health.* 56: 132-138. Online. Available HTTP: http://jech.bmjjournals.com/cgi/content/full/56/2/132.

Jones, A. (2002) 'Housing and health: Working in partnership. The Rhymney Neighbourhood Renewal Area Health Study'. Conference Paper given to 'Empowering Public Health', Environmental Health Conference, Harrogate International Centre, 10-13 September 2002.

Jung, R.T. (1997) 'Obesity as a disease.' British Medical Bulletin 53:307-321.

Joseph Rowntree Foundation. (1999) 'Housing and Social Exclusion' in JRF: Foundations for Housing, March/April 1999, York: JRF.

Kemmner, M. (2002) 'The art of maintenance', Inside Housing, 18 January 2002. 16-17.

Kitcher, C. and Jathanna, S. (2003) Health Impact Assessment of Harwich Container Port Development, Conference Abstract Book: 5th Annual UK and Ireland Health Impact Conference (2003) 'Informing Decisions for Health and Wellbeing'. Health Impact Assessment Research Unit, University of Birmingham. Online. Available HTTP: http://www.publichealth.bham.ac.uk/hiaru/practice.htm.

LACORS/LGA/FSA. (2004) Food Vision. (Online - cited 2004 October 30) Available from URL: http://www.foodvision.gov.uk

LACORS/LGA/FSA. (2002) Food:The Local Vision. LACORS/LGA/FSA.

Lalonde, M.(1974) A New Perspective on the Health of Canadians. Minister of Supply and Services.

Lang, T. (1996) Diet, Nutrition and Chronic Disease: Lessons from Contrasting Worlds. 6th Annual Public Health Forum. London School of Hygiene and Tropical Medicine. London, 31 March - 3 April Unpublished.

Leather, P. (2000) Grants to Home Owners: A Policy in Search of Objectives, Housing Studies 15(2):p149-168.

Leather, P. and Reid, M. (1989) Investing in Older Housing: A study of housing improvement in Bristol. Bristol, SAUS.

Lines, S. (2003) Personal Communications with Public Health Specialist, Dacorum PCT, Hertfordshire, January to May 2003.

Lock, K. (1999) 'Meeting the Need', Community Practitioner. 72 (6) : 157-8.

London Health Commission. (2001) Health Impact Assessment – Draft Air Quality Strategy.

London Health Commission and the Environment Committee of the Assembly. Online. Available HTTP: http://www.londonshealth.gov.uk/pdf/air.pdf

London Health Commission (2003) Health Impact Assessment. Online. Available HTTP: http://www.londonshealth.gov.uk/hia.htm#Top

London Voluntary Service Council. (1998) Barriers: Social and economic exclusion in London, London: LVRC.

Longfield, J., Hird V. (2001) ' Food Quality Lacks Taste' Health Matters 46: 10-11.

Lowry, S. (1991) 'Housing and Health', London: British Medical Journal.

LRC. (2000) *BABIE – the Bed and Breakfast Information Exchange,* Online. Available HTTP: http://www.london-research.gov.uk/hs/hsbabie.htm (30 August 2000).

MacArthur, A. D. (1999) 'Introduction to Environmental Health' pp. 1-22 in W. H. Bassett (ed.) *Clay's Handbook of Environmental Health (18th edition),* London: E and FN Spon.

MacArthur, I. (2001). The Agenda has Changed. *Environmental Health Journal.* 109 (10) : 306-9.

MacArthur, I. (1998) On the threshold of change. *For the Common Good. 150 years of Public Health.* An EHJ commemorative issue. CIEH.

MacArthur, I. (1995) Seminar for University of Greenwich Students.

Mackintosh, S. and Leather, P. (1993) *Renovation File: A profile of housing conditions and housing renewal policies in the United Kingdom.* Oxford: Anchor Housing Trust.

Mackintosh, S. and Leather, P. (eds.) (1992) *Home Improvement under the New Regime.* Occasional Paper 38. Bristol: SAUS.

Markus, T. A. (1993) 'Cold, condensation and housing poverty', in R. Burridge and D. Ormandy (eds) *Unhealthy Housing; Research, remedies and reform,* London: E. & F. N. Spon.

Marr, C. (2000) 'Asylum seekers 'go missing' in the south', *Inside Housing,* 11 February 2000:3.

Martin, D. (2002) 'Ratings plan heralds unfit homes drive', *Inside Housing,* 15 November 2002: 1.

Maslow, A. H. (1954) *Motivation and Personality,* New York: Harper and Row.

McKeown, T. (1976) The Role of Medicine – Dream, Mirage or Nemesis. London: Nuffield Provincial Hospitals Trust.

Melikian, G., Mmiro, F., Ndugwa, C., Perry R., Jackson, B., Garrett, E. *et al.* (2001) 'Relation of Vitamin A and Carotenoid Status to Growth Failure and Mortality Among Ugandan Infants with Human Immunodeficiency Virus,' *Nutrition* 17:567-572.

MORI Social Research. (2000) *Health Inequalities: Research study conducted for the Health Development Agency and Department of Health,* London HDA.

Morrow, V. (2002) 'Children's experience in 'community': implications of social capital discourses', in Swann, C. and Morgan, M. (eds.) (2002) *Social Capital: Insights from qualitative research,* London: Health Development Agency.

Naidoo, J. and Wills, J. (2000) *Health Promotion: Foundations for Practice (2nd edition),* London: Balliere Tindall in association with the Royal College of Nursing

National Assembly for Wales. (1999) *Developing Health Impact Assessment in Wales.* Health Promotion Division, National Assembly for Wales. Online. Available HTTP: http://www.wales.gov.uk/polinfo/health/healthimpact/pdf/healthimp_e.pdf

National Audit Office. (2001) *Tackling Obesity in England.* HC 220 Parliamentary Session 2000-2001. London: The Stationery Office

National Federation of Housing Associations. (1985) *Inquiry into British Housing Report,* London: NFHA.

O'Kane, P. (2002) 'Unlocking the puzzle', *Inside Housing,* 27 September 2002: 23.

Office of the Deputy Prime Minister. (2000) *Our Towns and Cities: the future – delivering an urban renaissance.* The Stationery Office. Online. Available HTTP: http://www.urban.odpm.gov.uk/whitepaper/ourtowns/fulltext/index.htm.

Office of the Deputy Prime Minister. (2002a) *Housing Renewal Guidance:* London; ODPM. Online. Available HTTP:// http//www.housing.odpm.gov.uk/information/consult/renewal/01.htm (20 February 2003).

Office of the Deputy Prime Minister. (2002b) Housing and Housing Policy: *Housing Renewal in the Private Sector,* Online. Available HTTP: http://www.housing.odpm.gov.uk/information//index07.htm (28 August 2002).

Office of the Deputy Prime Minister. (2002c). *Housing Renewal Guidance* (Consultative Document) Housing Research Summary 163, 2002. London, ODPM. Online. Available HTTP: http://www.housing.odpm.gov.uk/hrs/hrs163/index.htm (28 August 2002).

Office of the Deputy Prime Minister. (2002d) *More than a Roof: A Report into Tackling Homelessness,* London: ODPM. Online. Available HTTP: http://www.housing.odpm.gov.uk/information/homelessness/morethanaroof/04.htm (18 March 2003).

Office of the Deputy Prime Minister. (2002e) *Housing and housing policy: Gypsy sites policy,* London: ODPM. Online, Available HTTP: http://www.housing.odpm.gov.uk/information/index14.htm (28 October 2002).

Office of the Deputy Prime Minister. (2002f) 'Local authority gypsy/traveller sites in England: There is a need for more local authority residential and transit sites for gypsies and other travellers', in *Housing Signpost: A guide to research and statistics,* issue 14: 4.

Office of the Deputy Prime Minister. (2002g) Housing Research Summary 150: *Monitoring the Good Practice Guidance on Managing Unauthorised Camping,* London: ODPM. Online. Available, HTTP: http://www.housing.odpm.gov.uk/hrs/hrs150/index.htm (28 October 2002).

Office of the Deputy Prime Minister. (2002h) 'Home Improvement Agencies: Development and Reform', *Housing Signpost: A guide to research and statistics,* Issue 14, pp. 3.

Office of the Deputy Prime Minister. (2003a) *Sustainable Communities: Building for the future,* London: ODPM. Online. Available HTTP: http://www.communities.odpm.gov.uk/plan/main/overview.htm

Office of the Deputy Prime Minister. (2003b) *Housing Bill – Consultation on draft legislation,* ODPM, London. Online. Available HTTP: http://www.odpm.gov.uk/information/consult/housingbill/01.htm (April 2003).

Office of the Deputy Prime Minister. (2003c) *English House Condition Survey 2001.* London: HMSO. Online. Available HTTP: http://www.housing.odpm.gov.uk/research/ehcs/continuous/index.htm

Office of the Deputy Prime Minister. (2004) Housing Health and Safety Rating System Guidance (version 2) Safe and Healthy Hosuing Research Unit, Warwick Law School and ODPM, London. Outline available at: www.odpm.gov.uk/stellent/groups/odpm-housing/documents/page/odpm_house_032782.pdf

Ormandy, D. (1999) 'No fixed abode', *Environmental Health Journal,* April 102.

Ormandy. D, Moore, R. and Battersby, S. (2000) 'If it's broke, fix it fully', *Environmental Health Journal:* 108:12, 386-389.

Ormandy, D. and Burridge, R. (1988) *Environmental Health Standards in Housing*, London: Sweet and Maxwell.

Ormandy, D. and Burridge, R. (1993) 'The legal environment of housing conditions', in R. Burridge and D. Ormandy (eds) *Unhealthy Housing: Research, remedies and reform*, London: E. & F. N. Spon.

Ounsted, D., Wain J., Randall, B. and Williamson A. (2002a) *Foundations for the Future: Social, economic and environmental priorities for housing associations*. A guide for boards and staff on Sustainable Development. Part 1: The case for sustainability. Teddington: Sustainable Homes, Hastoe Housing Association.

Ounsted, D., Wain, J., Randall, B. and Williamson, A. (2002b) *Foundations for the Future: Social, economic and environmental priorities for housing associations*. A guide for boards and staff on Sustainable Development. Part 2: Checklists for sustainability. Teddington: Sustainable Homes, Hastoe Housing Association.

Page, A. (2002) 'Poor Housing and Mental Health in the UK: Changing the focus for intervention' in *Journal of Environmental Health Research*, vol. 1, issue 1, February 2002. Online. Available HTTP: http://www.jehr-online.org/volume1/issue1/5/1.asp

Parry, J. and Stevens, A. (2001) Prospective Health Impact Assessment: pitfalls, problems and possible ways forward. *British Medical Journal*, 323:1177-1182. Online. Available HTTP: http://bmj.com.cgi/content/full/323/7322/1177.

Payne, G., Payne, J. and Hyde, M. (1996) *'Refuse of All Classes'? Social Indicators and Social Deprivation*. University of Plymouth: Faculty of Human Sciences. Online. Available HPPT: http://www.socresonline.org.uk/socresonline/1/1/3html (24 September 2002).

Payne, J. (1999) *Researching Health Needs: A Community Based Approach*, London: SAGE Publications.

Power, A. (1993) *Hovels to High Rise. State Housing in Europe since 1850*. London: Routledge.

Power, A. (1999). *Estates on the Edge. The Social Consequences of Mass Housing in Europe*. London: Macmillan Press Ltd.

Putnam, R. (1993) *Making democracy work: Civic traditions in modern Italy*, Princeton, New Jersey: Princeton University Press.

Putnam, R. (2000) *Bowling alone: the collapse and revival of American community*, New York: Simon and Schuster.

Randall, B. (2002) 'Sustaining the Future', in *Housing*, September 2002: 23.

Ranson, R. (1991) *Healthy Housing*, London: E. & F. N. Spon.

Ranson, R. (1999) 'Health and housing', in W. H. Bassett (ed.) *Clay's Handbook of Environmental Health*, (18th Edition), London: E. & F. N. Spon.

Revell, K. and Leather, P. (2000) *The State of UK Housing: A factfile of housing conditions and housing renewal policies in the UK* (2nd edition). Bristol: The Policy Press.

RoSPA. (2000). *Home Safety*. Online. Available HTTP. http://www.rospa.co.uk/homesafe.htm (26 October 2000).

Rugg, J. and Rhodes, D. (2001) Chains or Challenges: The prospects for better regulation of the private rented sector. London: British Property Federation and Coventry: The Chartered Institute of Housing.

Rugg, J., Rhodes, D. and Jones A. (2000) Students and the Private Rented Market, York: Joseph Rowntree. Online. Available HTTP: http://www.jrf.org.uk/knowledge/findings/housing/d60.asp (11 November 2002).

Schafer Elinder, L. (2003) Public Health Aspects of the EU Common Agricultural Policy. National Institute of Public Health.Available from URL:http://www.fhi.se./english/eng_reports.asp

Scott-Samuel, A., Birley, M., and Ardern, K. (2001) The Merseyside Guidelines for Health Impact Assessment. 2nd Edition. International Health Impact Assessment Consortium. Online. Available HTTP: http://www.ihia.org.uk/document/merseyside3.pdf.

Seedhouse, D. (1986) Health: Foundations for Achievement, Chichester: John Wiley.

Shaw, A. (1999) 'Poverty a considerable barrier to dietary improvement.' Journal of the Royal Society for the Promotion of Health 119 (1): 5.

Shaw, M. (2001) 'Try our alternative slant on the top 10 tips for better health.' Health Service Journal 27 September: 20.

Shenton, J. (2002) 'Affordable Warmth: reality or fantasy? Environmental Health Journal, September 2002, vol. 110/09, pp. 272-275.

Simpson, M (2002) 'Hope for housing regeneration', Environmental Health News, 13 September 2002: 7.

Sirianni, C. and Friedland, L. (undated) 'Social Capital', Civic Practices Network Online. Available HTTP: http://www.cpn.org.sections/tools/models/social_capital.html (6 September 2002).

Sixsmith, J. and Boneham, M. (2002) 'Men and masculinities: accounts of health and social capital', in Swann, C. and Morgan, M. (eds.) (2002) Social Capital: Insights from qualitative research, London: Health Development Agency.

Social Capital Formation. (2001) 'What is social capital?', Online. Available HPPT: http://www.lks.net/~cdc/scapital/WhatIsIt.html (6 September 2002).

Spear, S. (2002). 'Health equality is a council issue', Environmental Health News, 15 March 2002,: 6.

Spear, S. (2002a) 'Fuel poverty targets will be missed', Environmental Health News, 12 July 2002,: 6

Spear, S. (2002b) 'Tough but tender approach to traveller encampments' in Environmental Health News, 12 July 2002: 3

Spear, S. (2004) 'Playing Catch Up.' Environmental Health Journal 112 (9): 268-271.

Spicker, P. (2002) 'Continental shifts on exclusion', Inside Housing, 11 October 2002: 29.
Stephens, C. (2001) Globalisation is killing us. Online. Available HTTP: http://www.healthmatters.org.uk/topics/globalisation.html (12 September 2001).

Steptoe, A., Pollard J.M., Wardle J. (1995) 'Development of a measure of the motives underlying the selection of food; the food choice questionnaire.' *Appetite* 25(3): 267-283

Stewart, J. (2001) *Environmental Health and Housing.* London: E. & F. N. Spon.

Stewart, J. (2002) 'A Step in the Right Direction' in *Environmental Health Journal,* April 2002, Vol. 110, No.04 (104-207) ISSN No. 1464-6862.
Online. Available HTTP: http://www.ehj-online.com/archive/2000/april2002.april2.html

Stewart, J. and Rhoden, M. (2003) 'A review of social housing regeneration in the London Borough of Brent' in *Journal of the Royal Society for the Promotion of Health,* March 2003, 123 (1) pp. 23-32.

Stewart, J. (2002) 'Housing Health and Safety Rating: a new method of assessing housing standards reviewed', *Journal of Environmental Health Research,* 1 (2) pp. 35-41. Online. Available HTTP: http://www.jehr-online.org.volume1/issue2/5/index.asp

Stewart, J. (2003) Home maintenance: Initiatives in the Bellenden Renewal Area, Peckham, *Journal of Environmental Health Research,* 2 (1) pp. 10-21. Online. Available HTTP: http://www.jehr-online.org.volume1/issue2/5/index.asp

Stewart, J. Clayton, J. and Ruston, A. (2004) Maintenance and repairs: an exploratory study into home-owners views on alternatives to grants, *Journal of Environmental Health Research,* 3 (2) pp. 58-65. http://www.jehr-online.org/volume3/issue2/3/index.asp

Styron, T.H., Janoff-Bulman R and Davidson L. (2000) ' "Please ask me how I am": Experiences of family homelessness in the context of single mothers' lives', in *Journal of Social Distress and the Homeless,* vol. 9, no. 2, 143-165.

Swann, C. and Morgan, M. (eds.) (2002) *Social Capital: Insights from qualitative research,* London: Health Development Agency.

Taylor, L. and Blair-Stevens, C. (Eds) (2002) *Introducing Health Impact Assessment (HIA): informing the decision-making process.* London: Health Development Agency. Online. Available HTTP: http://www.hda-online.org.uk/downloads/pdfs/hia.pdf.

Taylor, M. (1995). *Unleashing the Potential: Bringing residents to the centre of regeneration.* York: Joseph Rowntree Foundation.

Taylor, M. Hoyes, L. Lart, R. and Means, R. (1992). *User Empowerment in Community Care: Unravelling the Issues.* Bristol: SAUS Publications.

Thomas, M. (2002) 'TB returning with a vengeance', *Environmental Health News,* 13 December 2002: 4.

Thomas, S. and Stewart J. (2005) 'Optimising health promotion activities.' *Journal of Community Nursing,* 19(1) 9-12.

Townsend, P. Davidson, N. and Whitehead, N. (1988) *Inequalities in Health; the Black Report and the Health Divide.* Penguin Harmondsworth.

UK Bush Meat Campaign. (2002) *All About Bush meat.* Online. Available HTTP: http://www.bushmeatcampaign.org.uk (24 January 2003).

United Nations. (1992a) *Report of the United Nations Conference on Environment and Development.* A/CONF.151/26 (Vol.1). Online. Available HTTP: http://www.un.org/documents/ga/conf151/aconf15126-1annex.htm

United Nations. (1992b) *Agenda 21*. Online. Available HTTP: http://whs.un.org/esa/sustdev/documents/agenda21/english/agenda21toc.htm

University of the West of England, Bristol and the Office for Public Management. (1999) *Cross-cutting Issues Affecting Local Government*, London: DETR Local Government Research Programme.

US Office of Disease Prevention and Health Promotion. (1996) *Healthy People 2000 Midcourse Review and 1995 Revisions*. US Office of Disease Prevention and Health Promotion.

Vostanis, P., Grattan, E. and Cumella, S. (1998) 'Mental health problems of homeless children and families: longitudinal study' in *British Medical Journal*, vol. 316, 21 March 1998, 988-902.

Wanless, D. (2001) *Securing Our Future Health Taking a Long Term View*. (Online – cited 2002 May 14). Available from URL: www.hm-treasury.gov.uk/Consultations_and_Legislation/wanless/consult_wanless_final.cfm

Wanless, D. (2004) *Securing Good Health for the Whole Population*. H.M.Treasury. The Stationery Office.

Warburton, N. (2004) 'You are what you eat.' *Environmental Health Journal*.112 (4): 106-108.

Ward Richardson, Sir Benjamin. (1892) Speech at the Joint Conference of the Sanitary Inspectors Association and the Sanitary Inspectors Association of Scotland.

Watkins, K. (2000) 'Behind Closed Doors: Why the poor will suffer if globalisation is not controlled' *The Guardian*, December 13, 2000.

Webb, G.P. (2002) *Nutrition: A Health Promotion Approach*. 2nd Edition.London: Arnold.

Ward, S. (2002) 'A Heartfelt Boost.' *Health Development Today* 8: 20-22.

West Midlands Directors of Public Health Group. (2002) *Using Health Impact Assessment to Make Better decisions. A Simple Guide*. Health Impact Assessment Research Unit: University of Birmingham. Online. Available HTTP: http://www.publichealth.bham.ac.uk/hiaru/news.htm .

WHO. (1984) *Health Promotion: a discussion document on the concept and principles*. WHO Regional Office for Europe.

WHO. (1985) *Health for All in Europe by the year 2000*. Copenhagen: WHO.

WHO. (1986) *Ottawa Charter for Health Promotion*. Geneva: WHO.

WHO. (1997) *Health and Environment in Sustainable Development: Five Years after the Earth Summit: Executive Summary*. WHO. Online. Available HTTP: http://www.who.int/environmental_information/Information_resources/htmdocs/execsum.htm

WHO. (1997) *Jakarta Declaration on Leading Health Promotion into the 21st Century*. Geneva: WHO.

WHO. (1998) *Health 21: an introduction to the health for all policy framework for the WHO European Region. European Health for All series No. 5*. Online. Available HTTP: http://www.euro.who.int/document/EHFA5-E.pdf.

WHO. (1999) *Health Impact Assessment. Main Concepts and suggested approach. Gothenburg Consensus Paper*. WHO European Centre for Health Policy. Online. Available HTTP: http://www.euro.int/document/PAE/Gothenburgpaper.pdf

WHO. (2001) *Health and Sustainable Development. E/CN.17/2001/PC/6. United Nations Economic and Social Council.* http://ods-dds-ny.un.org/doc/UNDOC/GEN/N01/274/21/PDF/N0127421.pdf

WHO. (2002) *Technical Briefing: Health Impact Assessment.* EUR/RC52/BD/3. WHO Regional Office for Europe. Online. Available HTTP: http://www.euro.who.int/document/rc52/ebd3.pdf

WHO. (2000) *About WHO*, Online. Available HTTP: http://www.who.int/aboutwho/en/ definition.html (30 August 2000).

Wilcox, S. (2001) *Housing Finance Review* 2001/2002. York: Joseph Rowntree Foundation.

Wilkinson, P., Landon, M., Armstrong, B., Stevenson, S., Pattenden, S., McKee, M. and Fletcher, T. (2001) *Cold Comfort: The social and environmental determinants of excess winter death in England, 1986-1996,* Bristol: The Policy Press.

Williamson, J.D. (1996) Environmental Health and Public Health: Are they compatible? *Public Health* 110: 3-4 .

Wills, J. and Woodhead, D. (2004) 'The glue that binds ...': articulating values in multidisciplinary public health, *Critical Public Health* 14 (1) pp. 7-15.

Wohl, A. S. (1984) *Endangered Lives. Public Health in Victorian Britain.* Methuen.

Working Party on Environmental Health Education. (1996) *Consultative Document.* IEHO.

World Bank. (1986) in Lang T. (1996) *Diet, Nutrition and Chronic Disease: Lessons from Contrasting Worlds.* 6th Annual Public Health Forum. London School of Hygiene and Tropical Medicine. London, 31 March - 3 April, Unpublished.

World Commission on Environment and Development. (1987) *Our Common Future.* OUP.

World Health Organisation Regional Office for Europe. (2001) *The First Action Plan for Food and Nutrition Policy.* WHO European Region 2000-2005. Copenhagen: WHO Regional Office for Europe.

Wright, P. (2001). 'Health service in for overhaul', *Environmental Health News.* 7 December 2001, 6.